The National C

Your Choices for
Pregnancy and Childbirth

Helen Lewison

IN ASSOCIATION WITH
GOOD HOUSEKEEPING

EBURY PRESS LONDON

The National Childbirth Trust
offers information and support
in pregnancy, childbirth and early parenthood
and aims to enable every parent
to make informed choices

Published in 1991 by Ebury Press
an imprint of the Random Century Group
Random Century House
20 Vauxhall Bridge Road
London SW1V 2SA

Editor: Helen Southall
Designer: Gwyn Lewis
Illustrator: Helen Chown, BA(Hons.) Fine Art

British Library Cataloguing in Publication Data
Lewison, Helen
  Your choices for childbirth.
  I.Great Britain. Women. Pregnancy. Childbirth. Pregnancy &
  childbirth
  I. Title II. National Childbirth Trust
  618.200941

ISBN 0-85223-962-9

Typeset in Linotron Palatino from disk by Saxon Printing Limited, Derby
Printed and bound in Great Britain by Clays Ltd, St Ives plc.

Contents

Acknowledgements

As with having a baby, writing a book is a better experience if one is well informed and well supported. Both Mary Newburn and Patricia Donnithorne have made an enormous number of comments and contributions, giving generously both of their time and their ideas. Invaluable comments and support were also given by Eileen Hutton, Janet Stephen, Mavis Bartlett, Linda Gray, Kim Lewison, Ros Meek, Anne Thompson, Heather Thorn and Frances Blunden. The many people I have worked with in the NCT over the last eight years have enabled me to build up an ever-growing, ever-changing, multi-faceted picture of parents' experiences and needs. Finally, as ever, my greatest debt is owed to my husband Kim and to my children Joshua and Lydia for their continuing support, tolerance and love.

Helen Lewison

A message for midwives

The quality of a woman's birth experience depends in part on the quality of care she receives. She is dependent on the individual midwives and doctors who care for her during pregnancy, birth and after. Maternity units grow larger all the time but it is very easy for the needs of the individual parents at a birth to be forgotten as the scale of operations and equipment used for birth becomes less homely and less friendly. The knowledge and skills of midwives, developed over years of clinical practice, are sometimes also undervalued and not given adequate scope for expression.

It is hoped that midwives, the guardians of normal birth, will welcome the questions that this book encourages women to ask and will use the opportunity to forge relationships which will foster in turn the respect and support that they deserve.

PREFACE

Women have more choices for childbirth than ever before and are more prepared than ever to exercise them. Having a baby is a special experience in a woman's life, one that she may not often repeat. It is a time when women want things to go well; they want to be well-informed, to be offered appropriate care and to feel confident in those who attend them. The National Childbirth Trust (NCT) believes that pregnant women are able to make decisions about their bodies and their babies, that women want to make these decisions themselves after adequate consultation, and that parents make very responsible decisions because they care for their babies as no one else does. Yet, if you are new to all this, how do you know where to begin?

Often women do not know the full range of options for antenatal and delivery care available to them until they have already booked their care and feel it is too late to ask for something different. The choices available are different in every area: you can read here about the possible choices, but you can only find out about the actual choices available to you by asking your own questions. Sometimes pregnant women are reluctant to ask questions, especially if they feel that health professionals are overworked. It may be easier if you keep remembering how important your baby and a good birth are to you and your partner and that, whether the care you want is NHS or private, you are paying for it. The question-and-answer format used throughout this book is intended to encourage and inspire you to ask your own questions. Often women are afraid to express their needs and even more afraid of changing their minds: this book aims to give you the confidence to do both.

Descriptions of pregnancy, labour and birth are not a part of this book; the focus instead is on the important issues of choice and choosing which are sometimes forgotten. The Glossary gives short explanations of the obstetric and some other special terms used. The Index enables you to look up specific subjects. The appendix of Birth Statistics gives some of the latest national figures available for you to compare with those of individual hospitals in your area. The Bibliography lists useful books and other publications for further reading. The appendix of Useful Organizations provides many

5

possibilities for further information and informal support. This book makes a useful companion to the Third Edition of the NCT's own *Pregnancy and Parenthood* being published in Autumn 1991.

Many of your friends, relatives and colleagues will be able to share useful information and experiences with you. Your local branch or group of the NCT can also help you with information. Look in your local telephone directory or ring or write to NCT Headquarters at Alexandra House, Oldham Terrace, London W3 6NH (081-992 8637).

In May 1990 *Good Housekeeping* conducted a survey to discover what is important to women having babies in Britain today and to assess the need for more of the balanced information the NCT has to offer. 1,013 women who had had a baby within the previous two years replied and the results of the survey showed the need was great. The *Good Housekeeping* Survey questionnaire did not feature the NCT prominently, yet many respondents talked about the NCT favourably in their comments, and 29 per cent of them had attended NCT antenatal classes.

If you are fortunate enough to attend NCT antenatal classes you will have the support of the group and your NCT teacher in exercising your choices. Sometimes NCT antenatal classes become fully booked very quickly and it is impossible for NCT antenatal teachers to fulfil the demand for classes. It is always worth going to antenatal classes elsewhere; many are good and offer benefits similar to those of NCT classes.

The NCT is also constantly working behind the scenes to improve the maternity services in all kinds of ways for all women. The NCT plays a unique role at the interface of health professionals and service users, listening to both, learning from both and being a catalyst for change as well as a valuable source of information and experience. Please let us know what you like in this book and what could be improved, so that future editions can enable women to make informed choices and achieve what they want from the maternity services.

1: Becoming pregnant and preconceptual care

What can I do to conceive a healthy baby?

The conception and growth of a healthy baby may be partially dependent on both you and your partner being nutritionally fit, as a result of eating a well-balanced diet, including the full range of vitamins and minerals necessary for physical well-being. Stress can be a factor in inhibiting pregnancy, so minimizing the stress in your life can also be helpful. At least three months before you hope to start trying for a baby, you can choose to look at the lives and nutrition of both yourself and your partner, and see what is good and what could be improved.

It is important that if you have become pregnant unexpectedly you do not worry about not having looked after yourself in a special way. It is never too late to start looking after yourself.

EAT WELL
A well-balanced diet, including whole grain cereals and plenty of fresh fruit and vegetables, is something most people can achieve with a little planning. Some people choose to take vitamin and mineral supplements but this has not so far been shown conclusively to improve the chances of conceiving a healthy baby unless the woman or her partner has a deficiency. Usually any deficiency can be made up by changing the diet. If a deficiency is due to a medical condition, or the effects of drugs prescribed for a medical condition, you can take medical advice about the dosage of the particular supplement needed to correct it.

There is some evidence that taking folates (folic acid) during the first six weeks of pregnancy may lower the risk of neural tube defects such as spina bifida; unless you have a deficiency, 'the pregnancy dose for folic acid supplements is 500-800 mcg [per] day' (*Drugs in Pregnancy and Childbirth*, page 55 – see Bibliography). However, every woman's ability to absorb minerals and vitamins varies, so folates, like every other vitamin or mineral supplement, should only be taken under medical supervision.

Excess minerals in the woman's or man's working environment may also adversely affect the ability to conceive or the health of the baby. Some women change their dental fillings in order to prevent too many metals entering their system, but it is important to go to a dentist skilled in this form of replacement. People concerned about this particular problem may contact Foresight (see Useful Organizations) which offers information on preconceptual care and a hair analysis service to measure the level of minerals in the body, although the value of the latter has been questioned.

SMOKING

Smoking by either partner can affect the ability to conceive and can increase the risks of abnormality and miscarriage. If a pregnant woman smokes she increases the risks of bleeding during pregnancy, going into labour prematurely and stunting the growth of the baby. If a pregnant woman lives or works with people who smoke, 'passive' smoking can also affect the growth of the baby. Therefore, if you and/or your partner smoke, giving up or cutting down now can improve the health of your baby.

ALCOHOL

The Health Education Authority recommends women to refrain from drinking alcohol altogether while trying for a baby and until the end of the first three months of pregnancy, and thereafter to drink as little as possible. Since it is impossible to prove that even a little alcohol can do no harm, this is the counsel of perfection. For women who cannot or choose not to give up alcohol completely, slightly less strict limits may be easier to live with. However, it should also be borne in mind that any woman drinking more than 14 units of alcohol per week could be damaging her general health.

Excessive drinking by either partner may prevent conception. Binge-drinking by either partner may contribute to handicap and miscarriage. Drinking more than two measures of spirits, two glasses of wine, or one pint of beer or cider per day may stunt the growth of the baby.

YOUR WEIGHT

If you are overweight, you can do something about it simply by increasing your daily exercise and by eating nothing between meals, rather than going on a faddy crash-diet. Try to make all the food you eat healthy.

RUBELLA (GERMAN MEASLES)

You should have your immunity against rubella checked well in advance of trying for a baby: ask your GP for the simple blood test.

If you are not immune, you have time to be vaccinated and to wait three months for the vaccine to clear from your system before conception. It is commonly thought that women who had rubella or the vaccination while young are immune for life. *This is not always so*: your immune status can change or the disease may have been incorrectly diagnosed. (See also page 38)

EXISTING MEDICAL CONDITIONS

If you have a medical condition or if you are on long-term medication, it is wise to seek advice from your GP or specialist. Some drugs prescribed for chronic illness have an effect both on the ability to conceive and on the development of the baby, so you may find you have to make some difficult decisions. Judy Priest gives a thorough discussion of such decision-making and risk-taking in her book, *Drugs in Pregnancy and Childbirth* (see Bibliography).

BACKACHE

If you have chronic backache, you should see a physiotherapist, back specialist, osteopath, chiropractor or Alexander Technique teacher before you become pregnant, since many practitioners are reluctant to take on new clients who are pregnant. If you become pregnant during treatment, you may be able to continue it. (See Useful Organizations)

THE PILL

Women who are planning to become pregnant are usually advised to stop taking the contraceptive pill at least three months, preferably six months, before conception, since it depletes the woman's store of vitamins and minerals. Some women use natural family planning methods during this time, observing their cervical mucus, the height of the cervix and variations in daily temperature to build up fertility awareness (more information from the Natural Family Planning Service).

BE REALISTIC

It is important to remember that the above measures, wise though they may be, do not guarantee either conception exactly when you want it, nor a perfect, healthy baby, so it is wise to keep your expectations realistic. However, some people when planning to have a baby, choose to do all they can to promote healthy conception and growth. Whilst this is not a guarantee against things going wrong, the advantage of this approach is that couples can feel they did the best they could and that they and their baby are in the best possible state of health should any problems arise.

When is the best age to have a baby?

It is possible to have a baby at any age from the onset of regular periods to the menopause. Traditionally, doctors have recommended women to start their families in their early twenties or at any rate to have their first baby before the age of thirty. The current trend is for women to have their babies later, and many women may not be able to have babies at what is regarded as the optimum time physiologically. Factors women take into account when choosing to have their first baby include whether or not they are in a stable relationship; whether they and their partner are ready to become parents; whether their accommodation is large enough; whether they can afford to give up work, or to work part-time, or to pay for full-time childcare if they choose to stay in full-time work. Many are concerned about the best time for a career-break or for 'soft-pedalling'. For women who are older or who have older partners, a further consideration may be the age they will be when their children are financially independent. Many women who perhaps have married late or who have been given a jolt by their biological clock, have given birth joyfully to perfectly normal babies.

However, older parents often have additional difficulties to overcome. Older couples may be less fertile and some women undergo extensive antenatal screening accompanied by anxiety when awaiting the results, as the risk of fetal handicap increases with age. Although there is more help available for women having first babies late ('elderly primigravidae') than ever before, the following problems may also increase with age: miscarriage; handicap; difficult labours requiring medical intervention; and being tired when coping with a new baby.

It may be worth bearing these things in mind when considering when to have a baby, and also remembering that pregnancy does not happen on cue. 76 per cent of the respondents in the *Good Housekeeping* Survey who gave birth in the last three years were aged between 25 and 34 when they had their babies.

When am I at my most fertile?

You are most likely to conceive if you make love during the few days before ovulation. Conception is possible during a period of only 12 hours in a woman's menstrual cycle, when the ovum has entered the fallopian tube. For usually two to five days before ovulation, the cervix opens to admit sperm and produces a slippery 'fertile-type' mucus to nourish the healthy sperm, weed out defective ones and assist the survivors on their journey. This ensures that by the time ovulation occurs, 14 to 21 days after the onset of the last menstrual period, sperm await the newly-ripened ovum in the fallopian tube. The mucus can be used as an indicator of the fertile period as can the position and feel of the cervix and the woman's temperature on waking in the morning (there is a slight rise in temperature at ovulation which can be measured only by using a specially calibrated thermometer). Ovulation predictor kits are now on the market but these are an expensive way of replacing fertility awareness.

Some obstetricians working with infertile couples say that if a couple make love about three times a week, preferably on alternate days (it takes 36 to 48 hours for a man's supply of sperm to build up), they need not worry too much about pinpointing ovulation, since it is likely there will be sperm in the fallopian tube at the time of ovulation. This attitude also allows a couple to remain relaxed and retain spontaneity in their sexual relationship.

Can I choose the sex of my baby?

Some couples claim to have chosen the sex of their baby using diets and douches, but there is no evidence that these are effective and, at a time when you are trying to enhance your nutritional status, it is probably unwise to limit your intake of any healthy foods. Another method, no better evidenced but with some basis in known physiology, uses timing of sexual intercourse within the menstrual cycle. Female sperm move more slowly and live longer than male sperm. If you make love at the beginning of your fertile time and then abstain until after ovulation, you are more likely to conceive a girl; if you make love shortly before ovulation, you are more likely to conceive a boy.

I have had a previous late termination for fetal abnormality. Can I do anything to prevent it happening again?

First of all, it is important, if you haven't done so already, to ask the consultant responsible for your care about the nature of and reasons for the abnormality. It is often a chance occurrence, but you can also ask whether there is anything you can do to prevent it happening again.

A number of studies have been carried out on the effects on outcome of giving multi-vitamin and mineral supplements to women who had previously conceived babies with spina bifida. At present, there is no clear evidence that the giving of supplements reduces the chance of a recurrence, but there is a school of thought that good levels of folic acid and the B vitamins may help. As a way of wanting to do all you can to conceive a healthy child, you may choose to take supplements to enhance your general health, in addition to eating a healthy, balanced diet, but see page 7. Foresight (see Useful Organizations) gives couples advice and support for preconceptual care. However, it is important not to feel guilty: there is no way of guaranteeing perfection.

Years ago I had a termination. Could this affect my fertility?

Fertility is normally only affected if, as a result of the termination, you had an infection which damaged your ovaries or fallopian tubes. Very occasionally, if abortion is performed very late or unskilfully, an incompetent cervix (see Glossary) may be a problem. This can be treated successfully with a special stitch. Many women have had one or more terminations and then conceived normally.

From time to time I have genital herpes. Is it safe to have a baby?

Though rare, it is possible for babies to contract the *herpes simplex* virus from their mothers at birth, and it is a serious illness in the newborn. Women with the primary form of the disease are recommended to give birth by Caesarean section, thus preventing the baby from contracting the disease by contact with the genital tract, that is the vagina and its secretions. However, the advice for women with recurrent genital herpes (for whom there is an 8 per cent chance of passing on the disease) is less clear-cut. This is because it is impossible, with current techniques, to be 100 per cent sure at the time of delivery whether or not the woman is infectious.

Obstetricians prefer, where possible, to avoid performing Caesarean section. They have to give advice in each individual case on the basis of experience and the best knowledge available. Women who are known to have the disease at the time of delivery and those who show no symptoms when infectious, will be told a Caesarean section is advisable; for other women, vaginal delivery is probably safe. It is therefore safe for you to become pregnant, but you will need to ask for specialist advice so you may choose whether to give birth vaginally or by Caesarean section.

How long should we try before going for infertility treatment?

On the NHS, most doctors prefer you to have been trying for at least a year before coming to them and you may then have to wait several months for an appointment with a specialist. It may be possible to be seen earlier if you are older. Some couples choose private care to obtain infertility treatment more quickly, but this is becoming more expensive as many private health insurance companies exclude it and many couples also have to pay for the necessary drugs which are very expensive. Communications between NHS and private hospitals are not always good – lack of continuity and mistaken assumptions sometimes lead to basic tests being overlooked, so it is important to be vigilant if you move from one type of care to another.

In the meantime, it is worth building up fertility awareness so you know you are making love at the right time of the month and often enough. Looking after yourselves, minimizing stress and not trying too hard may help. If you do have a fertility problem, you may choose to contact the National Association for the Childless or Child (see Useful Organizations) who give information on treatment and informal support, including to couples choosing to try Artificial Insemination by Donor (AID), to adopt a child or to remain childless.

I recently miscarried and have been told the causes of miscarriage are usually only investigated after a woman has had three miscarriages. Why is this, and how can I find out why I lost my baby?

For a woman to be described as having 'recurrent miscarriage', she must have miscarried at least three times; some clinics that offer treatment for recurrent miscarriage treat only women who have lost at least three babies. However, if you have had two miscarriages, provided the policy of the particular hospital allows, an obstetrician or gynaecologist might be able to look into your case; sometimes it is possible to send samples from the placenta and baby to a laboratory for analysis. It may be of no comfort, but a large proportion of pregnancies miscarry – perhaps one in five – so after this miscarriage you have a good chance of carrying a baby to term (more information from the Miscarriage Association – see Useful Organizations).

Can any natural therapies help with infertility?

A state of well-being can be an important factor in fertility. Therefore any therapy which treats a woman holistically and promotes her general health may help with infertility. Many women have been helped by qualified homoeopaths, acupuncturists, osteopaths and other natural therapists (see Useful Organizations). Where psychological problems may be a barrier to conception, counselling, psychotherapy, hypnotherapy or psychoanalysis could also be considered; some gynaecologists treating women for infertility include counselling or psychotherapy as part of their programme.

Some members of my family are carriers of a rare blood disease: how likely am I to pass this on to my children?

If there is any genetically carried disease in your family, while contemplating pregnancy, you can ask your GP to refer you and your partner to a geneticist at a hospital near to you. The geneticist will investigate both your families, will advise you on the chances of your passing on the disease, or the status of carrier, to your children and tell you whether screening for the particular condition is possible during pregnancy and, if so, at what stage. Some hospitals have genetic counsellors who are experienced in helping couples come to terms with the implications of the genetic advice they receive. Whilst such investigations are carried out confidentially, you may choose to share the information you are given with other members of your family who may be similarly affected.

I am disabled, am in a steady relationship and would love to have a baby, but my GP was rather discouraging when we discussed my becoming pregnant. Where can I go for more information?

Many disabled women and men are able to have children and gain enormous satisfaction from doing so. Depending on the nature of your disability, it might be worth asking your GP for a referral to a specialist in your disability to discuss the possibility of pregnancy and birth, and to ask whether becoming pregnant would affect your disability, whether the disability could be passed to children, and all the other questions you might have. Another avenue for information and support of a more informal kind is the NCT's Parents with Disabilities Group (see Useful Organizations).

I have just become pregnant and a lump in my breast is being investigated. If it is cancer, how would this affect the baby?

If it is cancer, your case must be looked at individually, taking into account factors such as the nature of the cancer, how widespread it is and whether or not it is hormonally dependent (not all breast cancers are); the nature and urgency of treatment required and how this would affect the developing baby (who is most vulnerable in the first trimester); your age, fertility, whether or not you already have other children and whether or not you are likely to want or to be able to have children in the future. Of the treatments available for cancer, surgery is least likely to affect the developing baby; sometimes radiotherapy can be used early on in pregnancy while the baby is protected by the bones of the woman's pelvis and/or used after delivery; chemotherapy may be delayed until late on in pregnancy or after, or particular drugs and dosages chosen that will have as little effect as possible on the baby.

It is very rare for cancer to be passed from mother to baby and these days, in the case of many kinds of cancer, there is a good chance that a woman will be cured. In the case of breast cancer, women are sometimes advised not to breastfeed. If this applies to you and you would like a second opinion, ask to see someone else.

If you do have cancer and choose to continue the pregnancy (evidence to date indicates that terminating a pregnancy does not improve the chances of cure, even in the case of breast cancer, but this is a choice to be discussed with specialist doctors), you must obtain as much information as possible about the illness, the treatment and the effects on the baby and on yourself so that you are able to make informed choices at every step of the way. You may find it helpful to talk to other women who have gone through a similar experience (ask at your hospital or the NCT).

When we decided to get married over two years ago, we both talked about how we had always wanted to have children. Now that the house is sorted out and we are settled, it seems the right time to try, but I find myself terrified about birth because of the terrible experience my sister had. Will it get better if we wait a bit longer?

It is possible, but unlikely. It is quite common for a pregnant woman to become anxious and depressed apparently for no reason

15

until she realizes that the anxiety is based on fear caused by a previous birth experience of her own or someone close to her. The fact that you have become aware of this now means that you can try to resolve the effects of this experience before starting a family and hopefully enjoy your pregnancy and birth. You may find it helpful, with or without your partner, to talk to your doctor, midwife, health visitor or NCT antenatal teacher about it. They may be able to give you counselling themselves or refer you to a counsellor or psychotherapist, depending on your needs and preferences. These services are often free or subsidised so you pay what you can afford, or you might choose to go privately. Your sister may or may not be willing to talk to you about how she feels now: she may have resolved the experience or she too might welcome the chance to sort out her feelings. When you do become pregnant, choose your antenatal care and place of birth carefully and go to good antenatal classes so that your own pregnancy and birth can be a satisfying experience.

2: The pregnancy test

How early can I find out?

A pregnancy test measures the hormone human chorionic gonadotrophin (HCG) in your urine. The earliest it can give a positive result is one day after a missed period, that is at four weeks of pregnancy (pregnancy is counted from the first day of your last period, even if your menstrual cycle is longer than 28 days and even if you know exactly when you ovulated and/or made love in the month of conception). Since the test measures the concentration of HCG in your urine, if you want to obtain a positive result as early as possible, carry out the test first thing in the morning and try not to drink too much liquid the night before.

Some women know they are pregnant soon after conception. They may have a strange taste in their mouths, their breasts may increase in size more than in their usual menstrual cycle, or they may just 'know'.

For some women (often those who are receiving infertility treatment), it is necessary to diagnose pregnancy before the period is missed and it is possible to have a special blood test in hospital. A pregnancy test is not always necessary; some GPs are satisfied with a physical examination (from eight weeks onwards) or information from the woman. Of the respondents to the *Good Housekeeping* Survey, 67 per cent had their pregnancies confirmed by eight weeks; 29 per cent between eight and 12 weeks.

Is it better to go to the doctor or to do a test at home?

Either test can be equally reliable, but testing kits bought from a chemist are expensive to buy and your GP may be able to arrange for tests to be done free under the NHS: you can ask your GP for a sterile sample bottle for your early morning urine. Some women prefer to do a test in the privacy of their own home and to be the first to know the result; others prefer to use a laboratory, either through their GP or privately. It is also possible to have a test done at family planning clinics or at other agencies such as the Pregnancy Advisory Service (look in your local telephone directory for the number).

What if the test is negative?

You may not be pregnant or there may not yet be a strong enough concentration of HCG in your urine to yield a positive result: try drinking less the night before you next do the test. Positive tests are very rarely wrong but negative tests may be.

Should we wait before telling our friends?

This is a very personal choice. Some people want to share the glad news with their friends and relatives and celebrate straight away. Others prefer to wait until 12 weeks so as not to risk having to tell everyone about a subsequent miscarriage, since miscarriage during the first 12 weeks is relatively common. Many couples regard a publicly known miscarriage as an admission of failure or an advertisement of the fact that they want children. This may give rise to unwelcome family pressures. However, people who do 'go public' about a miscarriage are often amazed by the degree of sympathy and support they receive and the large number of women and men who are able to say, 'It happened to me too.' The other benefits of telling people are that they know the reason for your feeling low or under the weather: this is particularly helpful for older children who may be puzzled by an unexplained change in your behaviour or a sudden visit to hospital.

The test was positive, but by the time I got an appointment I stopped feeling sick and my period came. Was the test wrong?

What probably happened is that you miscarried by the time of your appointment, having been pregnant at the time of the test. A late period preceded by symptoms of pregnancy may actually be a very early miscarriage. Some women have a late, heavy period (also an early miscarriage) after experiencing no such symptoms.

I'm pregnant, so what do I do now?

Congratulate yourself! Then start thinking about the sort of antenatal care and delivery you want and read the next chapter. You can also start thinking about how this baby is going to affect your life and about any changes you wish to make.

3: Choosing antenatal care and the place of birth

The place where you choose to give birth to your baby will determine to some extent where and from whom you receive your antenatal care. Wherever your baby is to be born, ultrasound scans and other screening tests are available at the hospital and you and your baby can be visited at home by community midwives until up to 28 days after delivery.

SUMMARY OF PLACE OF BIRTH AND ANTENATAL CARE – NHS

BIRTH	BOOKED WITH	ANTENATAL CARE	DELIVERED BY
NHS consultant unit	Hospital midwives and doctors	Hospital midwives and doctors in hospital and, if 'shared care' booked, GP at surgery/practice midwife who may be community midwife	Hospital midwives or, if complications, hospital doctors. Student doctors/midwives may be present/assist in teaching hospital
Domino scheme	Community midwives	Community midwives at home and/or in hospital (+ option of shared care with GP)	Community midwife in consultant or GP unit with medical back-up
Team midwifery scheme	Team of community midwives	Team midwives at home and/or in local clinic	Team midwives at home/in hospital with usual back-up
In GP unit (separate unit or part of consultant unit)	GP	GP and community midwives at GP's surgery/at home	GP and community/hospital midwife with specialist back-up from hospital
At home	Community midwives or (rarely) GP	Community midwives at home (+ option of shared care with GP) or GP	Community midwife at home with support from GP and/or emergency obstetric flying squad, or GP

SUMMARY OF PLACE OF BIRTH AND ANTENATAL CARE – PRIVATE

BIRTH	BOOKED WITH	ANTENATAL CARE	DELIVERED BY
Private hospital	Private consultant obstetrician	Obstetrician in office/hospital	Obstetrician attended by midwives or sometimes midwives or junior doctor with back-up of consultant
Private at home	Independent midwife	Independent midwife at home (+ option of shared care with GP)	Independent midwife at home with support arranged by her

DELIVERY CHOICES OF RESPONDENTS TO GOOD HOUSEKEEPING SURVEY

	PREFERRED	ACTUAL
NHS consultant unit	37 per cent	68 per cent
NHS GP unit	15 per cent	12 per cent
Domino scheme	17 per cent	6 per cent
Home birth	10 per cent	6 per cent
Private hospital	4 per cent	2 per cent
No preference	17 per cent	
'Missing'		6 per cent

WHO DELIVERED THE GOOD HOUSEKEEPING SURVEY BABIES?

Hospital midwife	55 per cent
Community midwife	12 per cent
Consultant	12 per cent
Other hospital doctor	22 per cent
GP	2 per cent

(Note: Some respondents reported that their baby was delivered by more than one person.)

In recent years there has been a considerable move towards centralization of services in specialized maternity units where care is provided by, or in the name of, medical specialists, in particular obstetricians, anaesthetists and paediatricians. For a variety of reasons, many women wish to have their baby under the care of a midwife or their GP, or to give birth at home or in a local GP unit rather than under the care of an obstetrician in a large, relatively distant unit. However, in practice, women find the choices available to them limited. Of those who responded to the *Good Housekeeping* Survey, 30 per cent knew of a local GP unit, 32 per cent knew there was a local Domino scheme and 35 per cent knew they could give birth at home if they should wish. Similarly, 30 per cent were aware that private maternity care was available.

Although only 35 per cent of respondents said that home birth was available to them (regardless of whether it was medically advisable), it is in fact available to every woman in the UK. It is significant that although 68 per cent of respondents had their baby in an NHS consultant unit, that was in fact the preferred choice of only 37 per cent of respondents. It is surprising that the Domino scheme was the preferred choice of only 17 per cent of respondents, whereas care and advice from community midwives was rated very highly throughout the *Good Housekeeping* Survey. Since the Domino scheme is not available everywhere and often not publicized widely enough, perhaps many women who would be interested do not know what it is. Where it is known about, it is possible that the idea of six-hour discharge (usually part of the package but not compulsory) is unattractive.

77 per cent of respondents chose to have their antenatal care shared between a hospital and GP and 23 per cent chose to have antenatal care from community midwives. 61 per cent received most of their care from GPs and 35 per cent received most of their care from community midwives. 78 per cent said that their antenatal care provided sufficient information. 47 per cent of women receiving most of their antenatal care from community midwives rated it as excellent – a higher percentage than of those who chose shared care or hospital care. This rose to 84 per cent for those women who booked a home birth.

How do I get the birth I want?

Find out what is available in your area by asking your GP, your local NCT branch/group, and/or ringing up the community midwives at your local maternity unit. Then ask your friends and relatives who have had babies recently how they found their antenatal care and birth. Then think and talk carefully with your partner or someone else close to you about what you feel might be right for you. Do not rush this process. Sometimes, GPs are anxious to get you booked at your first appointment, but do not be afraid of taking your time. Asking him/her to act on a considered choice will involve less work than going back and asking him/her to change the booking. However, if you do change your mind, that is your choice too – it is your baby and your birth!

If you choose a hospital birth in an NHS consultant unit, your GP will write to the hospital asking them to book you and may offer you the option of shared care. If you want a particular consultant, the GP will address the letter to him/her at the hospital antenatal clinic. If you choose a home birth or a Domino, ring up the community midwives at your local maternity unit who will then book you, often at home. If you want private care at a hospital or with an independent midwife, you will have to book this yourself direct. You can find the telephone numbers of local hospitals in your local directory or Yellow Pages.

Where is the safest place to have my baby?

It is often thought that birth in a consultant unit is the safest place to have a baby, but statistics show that a planned birth at home is a very safe option in terms of both perinatal mortality and illness for both mother and baby. (This is the case even when the figures are adjusted to take account of the fact that women who plan to have their babies at home are those who are not at 'high risk' – see Glossary). Factors women often consider are how far they have to travel in labour to have their baby (many women outside large cities have to travel many miles in labour); whether a particular hospital has a special care baby unit; how long it would take the obstetric flying squad to get to them if there were an emergency at home; and what sort of support they have at home during labour and after. When a woman is considered to be 'high risk' or complications suddenly arise during her pregnancy or birth, hospital is generally considered to be the safest place. It is worth remembering that problems in pregnancy may resolve themselves and that if a woman's situation changes, she can always consider changing her place of birth.

Where is the best place to have my baby?

The best place for you to have your baby is where you feel most secure and comfortable. For some women this is a consultant unit; for others it is their bedroom at home. Some women choose to have their babies in hospital but welcome the opportunity the Domino scheme gives them to build up a relationship with a midwife or team of midwives and to know the person who will deliver their baby. Other women are fortunate in having a GP who delivers babies at home or in a GP unit, so they are able to have their antenatal care and birth with someone they already know and feel comfortable with.

What is the Domino scheme?

'Domino' is short for 'domiciliary in and out', meaning that women are looked after by the domiciliary services, that is the community midwives, and go into hospital to have their babies and come out soon after. It is a popular scheme for maternity care, but one which is not yet available in all areas or for all the women who want it. A woman usually books her birth directly with community midwives. After that they may visit her at home for her antenatal checks; or see her at a local clinic; or hold their own clinic within the main consultant antenatal clinic at the hospital or within a GP unit. Depending on their number, the community midwives may work in one team or in several, and each woman is encouraged to meet as many as possible of the team, one of whom will deliver her baby. Sometimes a single midwife is assigned to a woman as the one to deliver her baby, but a reserve midwife will be assigned in case of time off or illness. Teams often hold meetings for pregnant women to meet them and answer questions about the way in which they work.

When the woman goes into labour, she rings her midwife who will either come to see her at home straight away, or keep in touch over the telephone if the labour is progressing more slowly. The woman and midwife choose together when to go into hospital and they make their separate ways there (unless an ambulance is called), where the midwife delivers the baby. Six hours after delivery, provided all is well, the woman can go home where the same community midwife will visit her and her baby for up to 28 days if necessary.

There are variations in detail, but the essential elements of the Domino scheme are that it is community midwife-based. A woman does not usually obtain antenatal care from her GP. However, if she prefers, and if her GP agrees, there is no reason why her antenatal care cannot be shared between the community midwives and her GP. The main advantage of the Domino scheme is that women are given continuity of care. This means that they receive care from the same midwife or midwives antenatally, during labour and postnatally. Studies have shown that women receiving continuity of care use less artificial pain relief during labour which, in itself, indicates increased satisfaction with the experience of labour. In some places, there are so-called Domino schemes which only differ from standard consultant unit births in that women go home six hours after delivery. These are not true Domino schemes, because women do not have the opportunity to build up a relationship with the midwives who deliver their babies.

What is 'shared' care?

Shared care is an arrangement by which antenatal care is shared between the hospital and a woman's GP, often assisted by one or more midwives. The usual pattern of antenatal care is that a woman is seen every four weeks until she is 28 weeks pregnant; every two weeks until she is 36 weeks pregnant; then every week until the baby is born. A woman having shared care will go to the hospital early on in her pregnancy for a 'booking-in appointment' when a full history is taken, a blood sample is taken and possibly an ultrasound scan given; she may return at 16 to 18 weeks for an alphafetoprotein blood test and possibly an ultrasound scan; then at 36 and 38 weeks for routine check-ups. All the other antenatal appointments are with the GP (or midwife), usually in his/her surgery. A woman may book especially for maternity care with any GP offering this service. A few GPs do not provide maternity care, while others enjoy and specialize in the work.

I definitely want to have my baby in hospital, but how do I find out which is the best one?

Ask your GP and other women about the various maternity units. The local NCT can also help. Assuming there is a choice of maternity unit, you have to decide which is best for you on the factors that are most important to you. You may prefer a smaller unit to a larger one; one which has a Caesarean rate lower than the national average (see Birth Statistics); one where women seem to have the most satisfactory experiences; one where the Domino scheme is available for you; one where you can stay in for five days after the birth; one where you have already received gynaecological treatment; or simply the one which is nearest.

Can I choose my consultant? Will my choice of consultant make any difference to my birth?

You can ask your GP or midwife to request a particular consultant when booking your antenatal and delivery care. The preferences and usual practices of a woman's consultant are likely to affect decisions made during pregnancy and birth. The extent of the consultant's influence will vary, depending on whether there are any complications. On the NHS, if your pregnancy and labour are normal, you may never meet your consultant unless he/she makes a point of introducing him/herself at the antenatal clinic or in the labour ward. Due to limited time, NHS consultants tend to keep most of their time for women with problems who will most benefit from their specialist knowledge and experience.

However, even if they do not attend you personally, the consultant's views on the management of pregnancy, labour and birth may be reflected in the care you are given by the midwives and junior doctors. In some hospitals, the care of women is governed by protocols, policies and guidelines, irrespective of which consultant's list they are on (the consultants will of course have influenced to a greater or lesser degree the contents of those protocols, etc). In other hospitals, each consultant will have his/her own (unwritten) policy for care to be followed by the midwives and junior doctors: a midwife looking after two women in labour simultaneously may treat them differently if they are 'under' different consultants.

If you need specialist care, or if there are certain aspects of care you are concerned about, you may want to choose your consultant. You may have heard reports about individual consultants from other women and you may choose to ask specific questions of the consultant him/herself, the antenatal clinic sister or another senior midwife before you are booked in. If, for some reason, you wish to change consultant during your pregnancy, this can usually be arranged through the antenatal clinic sister unless a particularly popular consultant is oversubscribed.

Can I have my first baby at home?

All women are legally entitled to have a home birth if they so wish, and the local health authority is obliged to provide a midwife to look after the mother and baby. Women who are considered to be 'at risk' are discouraged from having their babies at home, and the 'at risk' category is usually taken to include women having their first babies on the grounds that their ability to give birth normally is untested. Some people believe that this approach treats birth as normal only in retrospect and is unduly pessimistic.

If you choose to have your baby at home, you may be invited to the maternity unit to discuss the matter with a consultant obstetrician who may or may not recommend you to have your baby in hospital once your case has been assessed. You may choose whether or not to see the consultant and whether or not to accept his/her advice. If you choose to book a home birth, even if the consultant has advised against it, the community midwives are legally obliged to attend you at home. They may also be very supportive of your choice, but this may depend on the consultant's reasons for refusal.

Should I have my baby at the private hospital where I received infertility treatment two years ago, or could I go to the local hospital where all my friends have had their babies?

It is your choice. Some women feel more secure returning to the obstetric team with whom they have built up a relationship and some couples feel that having spent a lot of money on private treatment (unless they are covered by private health insurance) they would rather not risk something going wrong despite the continuing costs involved. Other women feel that having gone through the ultra-high-tech of infertility treatment, they want to give themselves the satisfaction of having as natural a birth as possible; once a woman's fertility has been restored, there is often no reason why birth should not be straightforward. (One exception to this is that where there has been 'in vitro fertilisation' – see Glossary – there is some evidence that labour may begin before 40 weeks, but there is no reason why an 'early' labour should not proceed normally.)

If you pay for private care, you can of course still ask for as natural a birth as possible, but in high-tech settings professionals have often lost their confidence in a woman's ability to give birth normally (and her partner's ability to support her through a natural labour) so use obstetric interventions such as induction, acceleration or Caesarean section earlier and more readily in the case of a 'precious' baby, especially where the mother is older.

Another important factor is the availability of a special care baby unit (SCBU), particularly where infertility treatment results in multiple births. Some private hospitals do not have SCBUs so babies needing intensive care have to be transferred by ambulance to the nearest SCBU. Because of the increasing pressure on SCBUs arising from infertility treatment, some NHS hospitals offering infertility treatment privately are unable to take bookings for delivery from patients who are successful if they live out of the health district's catchment area. Even if your infertility treatment and antenatal and delivery care are covered by health insurance, this may not be the case with care for your baby in a SCBU which is extremely expensive: check with your insurer.

My GP said that a Domino birth was not available for me, but my friend who lives in the same road had one. What should I do?

Domino schemes are run by community midwives based at particular hospitals within district health authorities (see Glossary), both of which have boundaries, so that there are no overlaps and no gaps in the cover given by community midwives. This means that you are served by only one set of community midwives. Whether or not the Domino scheme is available can depend on the policy of the particular hospital or district health authority which employs your community midwives. District health authority boundaries have to be somewhere and sometimes run down the middle of a road: perhaps you are just outside the boundary.

Sometimes GPs do not know all the options for delivery available and occasionally they may prefer to look after their pregnant patients themselves through the 'shared care' scheme. However, shared care is usually available within the Domino scheme if you choose to have it. You could either double-check with your GP or ring up the community midwives at your local maternity unit. If you are within their boundaries you can book your delivery and antenatal care with them direct; if you are not, they will be able to tell you whether the Domino scheme is available with the community midwives who do cover your area, based at another local unit. It is important to remember, though, that since Domino schemes can often only take a certain number of women due each month, demand sometimes exceeds supply.

Why is it that you have to wait so long at the hospital antenatal clinic?

The closure of more and more small maternity units means the remaining, specialist maternity units grow larger all the time. Particularly in teaching hospitals, it is considered important to have as many women as possible booked for care so as to keep costs per patient down and have enough 'interesting' cases for medical students to learn from. There are only five days in a working week and it is considered necessary to see women a certain number of times during their pregnancies: this makes for heavy traffic. Doctors also have a dread of being kept waiting, so they prefer women to be booked in 'batches' (for example, 10 women at 9am, 10 at 9.15, etc).

Although most antenatal checks can be carried out by midwives, it is usually thought that some should be done by doctors, and sometimes a midwife refers a woman to a doctor for a second opinion if she feels there may be a complication in a hitherto normal pregnancy. Now that increasing numbers of women choose GP shared care, many women have fewer hospital antenatal checks. They often save up their questions for their hospital appointments and, of course, will want to discuss their choices for birth with the hospital staff, so appointments often take longer than the time allotted. Doctors and midwives may also be called away to the labour ward and this can lead to delays.

Many women are put to considerable inconvenience (and sometimes expense) by long delays at hospital antenatal clinics where often no explanations or apologies for the delays are given. It may be even worse for women accompanied by one or more children, even if a crèche is available in the antenatal clinic. It is not surprising that many women's blood pressure is found to be higher at antenatal appointments than at other times! This is an area of maternity care in need of improvement; meanwhile, there are practical ways in which you can deal with the existing system.

Sometimes asking for an appointment first thing in the morning means less time to wait. If long waits at the clinic are inevitable, warn your place of work (if appropriate), assume you will have a two- or three-hour wait and go equipped with food, drink and a book or magazine, or some work papers. If you have a friend booked at the same hospital, try to book appointments for the same time so you can travel together or meet there and have a chat. You could get to know some of the other women waiting. Practise your labour relaxation techniques: these can work wonders for your blood pressure!

Can my partner come with me to antenatal appointments?

You can be accompanied by your partner or anyone you like, but they may be asked to leave during certain procedures such as vaginal examinations or ultrasound scans. Many women whose first language is not English take their partner, a friend or relative to be with them. Fathers (and older children) often accompany women to ultrasound scans. This may be found to be an exciting experience, but it is as well to remember that ultrasound scans are a serious diagnostic tool which may reveal an abnormality, and are therefore not to be taken lightly. Many women find the support of their partner or a close friend or relative helpful when they have an appointment at which a special decision is to be made regarding their care, or when they want to discuss their birth plan.

Can I ask to be examined by a woman doctor?

Yes, you can. All hospitals are used to such a request and many women can only be examined by a woman doctor for religious reasons.

My friend carried her own notes; can I do that?

This scheme, popular with many women and midwives, is an extension of the use of the cooperation card which is carried by a woman between her GP and the hospital and which contains minimal information about the pregnancy, such as dates, growth of the baby, urine and blood test results, blood pressure and weight gain. Women carry a small file containing all their pregnancy notes between the hospital, GP and/or community midwives, depending on the care they have chosen, and the hospital keeps only the barest essential information. Between ten and 28 days after delivery – when the woman has been discharged by her community midwife – the file is returned to the hospital and will be used again during a subsequent pregnancy. It may be that the scheme is not available at your hospital or that when your friend attended your hospital she took part in a pilot scheme. If it is a scheme which appeals to you, tell the antenatal clinic sister: such feedback may benefit other women or yourself later on.

What is the difference between community midwives and hospital midwives?

Hospital midwives staff the antenatal clinic, and antenatal, labour and postnatal wards of a maternity unit. Depending on the way the unit is organized, they may work permanently in one part of the unit or circulate on a regular basis.

Community midwives do most, if not all, of their work away from the hospital, although they usually have an office or other base either in the maternity unit or in a clinic serving the unit. They can be contacted directly at this office: first thing in the morning is often a good time. They visit women at home after they have had their babies, normally up to 10 days after the birth, when, unless there are any problems, they hand over women to the care of the health visitor. Women who have had a late miscarriage, late termination for fetal abnormality or a stillbirth also receive postnatal care from a community midwife. When women book Dominos and home births, community midwives usually give women most of their antenatal care. This antenatal care is given at home, in local clinics or sometimes at a special community midwives' clinic within a hospital antenatal clinic.

All midwives are highly skilled, but community midwives are often more used to relying upon their own skills because they are used to working as independent practitioners outside the hospital rather than within its often hierarchical setting. They are usually very supportive of women who wish to have a home birth and are available to answer any queries concerning pregnancy, labour, birth and the care of women. (Ring your local maternity unit and ask for the community midwives.)

Some district health authorities operate an integrated midwifery service whereby midwives rotate from hospital to community and back again. The effect of this is to give midwives a wider perspective and to utilize all their skills.

QUESTIONS TO ASK YOUR GP
Would you be willing to attend me if I have my baby at home?
Is the Domino scheme available?
At which hospitals can I have my baby?
How have other women found their care at the(se) hospital(s)?
Is there a particular consultant you would recommend? What are your reasons for doing so?
Do you offer shared care?
If you do not offer shared care, would it be available from another doctor in the practice or elsewhere in the area?

QUESTIONS TO ASK A COMMUNITY MIDWIFE
How do you feel about attending a woman having her first baby at home?
If I have a Domino birth, where would I receive my antenatal care?
Can you see me at home?
Can I have antenatal care shared with my GP?
How is antenatal care under the Domino scheme organized?
How likely am I to be attended during labour by the midwife assigned to me?

Will I have an opportunity to meet the other midwives in the team?
What happens when I go into labour?
How do we get to hospital?

*QUESTIONS TO ASK THE HOSPITAL MIDWIVES/DOCTORS
WHEN CHOOSING A HOSPITAL OR AT THE BOOKING-IN
APPOINTMENT*
Can I carry my own notes?
It is possible for me to be introduced to my consultant?
When can I talk to someone about antenatal screening?
Do you give ultrasound scans to all women? When are they given
and what are they designed to look for?
How long is the usual wait in the antenatal clinic?
What are the hospital policies concerning a woman's choice of
position for labour, vaginal examinations and delivery; time-limits
for the different stages of labour; artificial rupture of the mem-
branes; routine episiotomy; monitoring of the baby?
Which obstetric procedures are carried out routinely? (Unless
already known) do these policies differ from consultant to
consultant?
Is there a birthing pool? Can I bring in a hired pool?
What are the delivery rooms like? Are there 'low-tech' rooms?
Is a woman ensured privacy for the entire time of her labour spent
in hospital?
Is there a Special Care Baby Unit?
What is the Caesarean section rate?
What proportion of women (having their first babies) have an
intact perineum after delivery?
What is the usual length of stay after a normal delivery?
Are there large postnatal wards or smaller rooms where only a few
women share each bathroom?

4: Looking after yourself during pregnancy

I don't have time for breakfast and have snacks to keep me going at work. How important is good food when you're pregnant?

Good food is even more important when you are pregnant than at other times since the baby needs vitamins and minerals to grow and develop healthily. Whilst there is a tendency for a pregnant woman's body to use her food more efficiently and to meet the baby's nutritional needs first, it is possible for a woman's system to become depleted and anaemia and other illnesses to follow. These in turn could adversely affect the baby.

Research has shown breakfast to be a very important meal for keeping up energy during the day, but there is no reason why you should not snack at work if that is what suits you better. The danger with snacking is that it is easy to choose foods which are tempting and easy to eat, such as crisps, cakes, biscuits, sweets and fizzy drinks, which are high in fat and sugar, but low in vitamins and minerals. It is possible to choose snacks which give the same nutrients as a more traditional breakfast and lunch. Wholemeal bread sandwiches filled with meat, cheese, eggs and salad, baked potatoes, fresh fruit, yogurts, juices and milk, are all good sources of vitamins and minerals yet can be low in fat and sugar. Raw vegetables and dips are fun to eat and you could nibble peanuts (high in iron and folates) or sunflower seeds.

If you are concerned about your diet, talk to a midwife or to a hospital dietitian who will help you choose foods which fit in with your way of life and provide all the nutrients you need.

I had a lot to drink at a party before I realized I was pregnant – will it have damaged the baby?

Whilst the first trimester of pregnancy is the most vulnerable time for the baby, it is unlikely that your baby will have been harmed by one bout of social drinking unless it was a 'binge'. 'What matters is whether or not you drink enough quickly enough to cause a surge of alcohol to flood your system. If this happens around the time of conception, in either the father or the mother, it could damage the egg or sperm. If it happens between about the fourth and tenth week of your baby's life (that's the sixth to the twelfth week after your last period started) it could alter the way the baby develops.' (*Drugs in Pregnancy and Childbirth*, page 111 – see Bibliography)

Heavy daily drinking can affect the baby's growth. Numerous studies have led to the general agreement that there is no safe limit for pregnant women drinking alcohol. For a non-pregnant woman a sensible limit is no more than 14 units of alcohol per week, with two or three drink-free days. One unit of alcohol is equivalent to a wine-glass of wine; a sherry-glass of sherry or other fortified wine; half a pint of normal-strength beer; or a single measure of spirits. If a pregnant woman drinks more than 10 units per week she runs the risk of a slightly premature baby who may also be 'small for dates' (see Glossary). Beer seems to be more strongly associated with adverse effects than other alcoholic drinks, but this may be due, at any rate in part, to under-reporting of consumption in studies by people who underestimate its alcoholic content. In this connection, it is particularly important to remember that some of the stronger beers contain as many as two and a half or four units of alcohol per can.

As a result of the general uncertainty about safe levels of drinking during pregnancy, many women choose not to drink any alcohol at all. You may choose to avoid alcohol completely to be on the safe side, or you may decide to keep your drinking below 10 units a week. As it is not possible to prove that drinking small amounts of alcohol is completely safe, many authorities advise women to avoid alcohol altogether if possible during the critical stages of development so as to err on the side of caution. 57 per cent of respondents to the *Good Housekeeping* Survey did not drink alcohol during pregnancy.

Is it normal to feel so tired in pregnancy? I am sleeping much more than usual.

Very many women feel very tired during the first trimester, but find their normal energy returning during the second trimester, when they are traditionally expected to 'bloom'. It is perfectly normal and there is nothing you can do about it but give in to it, have early nights and rest as much as possible. Excessive tiredness may be a side-effect of the high levels of progesterone being produced by a gland present in the ovary after ovulation before the placenta takes over production of the hormone, usually at a more tolerable level, at around 14 weeks of pregnancy.

I am sick two or three times a day – will it harm the baby?

This level of nausea and vomiting rarely affects the growth of the baby, and if it is of any comfort, women feeling very sick are less likely to miscarry than those who do not: it is a side-effect of the high levels of progesterone (see answer to previous question). (This is not to say that if you do not feel sick, you will miscarry.) Very occasionally, pregnancy sickness which continues into the third trimester may be associated with pre-eclampsia (see Glossary), but regular antenatal check-ups minimize any risks to the mother and baby.

The main problem with sickness is that your physical reserves can become very depleted and you may become very weak. It is therefore essential that your condition is monitored by either your GP or the hospital on a regular basis and that you rest as much as possible: ask for a doctor's certificate if you feel you need to take time off work. If the condition does become serious, particularly if the vomiting does not stop at around the end of the first three months, the hospital may admit you and feed you intravenously, which will make you feel better and ensure the baby grows.

Many individual women find their own ways of coping with nausea and vomiting. They eat as much as they can of whatever suits them and generally find that small, frequent snacks are easier to keep down than three large meals a day. Once the vomiting has stopped, it is essential that all the food you eat helps to replenish your stores of vitamins and minerals. Your body will generally see to the needs of your baby first, but it is essential that you build up your own strength so you can enjoy the rest of the pregnancy and be ready for the hard work of a new baby. Do not hesitate to consult a community midwife or a hospital dietitian about the best way of doing this.

I feel sick all the time, but my doctor won't give me anything - is there anything else I can do?

The probable reason for your GP not being willing to give you a drug for pregnancy nausea is that none of the anti-histamine drugs currently available have undergone the necessary trials to be proved safe for pregnant women and their babies.

There are a number of other things you could try yourself. Many women find that eating a large number of small snacks frequently during the day, with a high proportion of carbohydrate, can relieve the symptoms. Dr Barbara Pickard suggests a diet which some women have found to be helpful (see Bibliography). Getting up slowly in the morning (preceded by a cup of tea and a biscuit in bed) may make the start of the day easier. Some women find Sea Bands worn on the wrists helpful, but there is a risk that positioned on the wrong pressure point of the wrist, they might cause a miscarriage. A study of Sea Bands showed the placebo effect to be more effective than the genuine article. Other women find ginger in the form of biscuits, tea, capsules or fresh in food (as used in Chinese and other oriental cookery) makes them feel better. The same trial did demonstrate ginger to be effective. Natural therapies such as homoeopathy and acupuncture, given by trained practitioners, can be extremely effective (see Useful Organizations).

> *I have cut down smoking a lot since discovering*
> *I was pregnant - is there anyone who could help*
> *me give up?*

Many women smoke more than usual when they are pregnant so congratulations on cutting down. You can contact ASH or QUIT (see Useful Organizations) for a local self-help group and/or seek the support of your health visitor or community midwife, both of whom will support you in giving up. Perhaps they could introduce you to another pregnant woman also trying to give up, so that you could support each other? It is very helpful to have a supporter (pregnant or otherwise) who cares about your giving up and encourages your every success. If you live with a partner or other person who still smokes, ask them not to leave any cigarettes lying around and not to let you 'borrow' their cigarettes under any circumstances.

You can choose your own way of giving up. Some people prefer not to frighten themselves by giving up completely, but to think of themselves as just having (drastically) cut down to one a day, one a week, one a month or one a year. Unfortunately, nicotine chewing-gum is not an option from your GP when you are pregnant, but many people find chewing ordinary gum helpful or having a glass of water every time they feel like a cigarette. There is no doubt that stopping completely is best for you and your baby. You may consider it an incentive to know that if a woman gives up smoking immediately she knows she is pregnant, by 20 weeks her health status is that of a non-smoker and her baby is likely to grow at the normal rate.

92 per cent of the respondents to the *Good Housekeeping* Survey did not smoke during pregnancy. A larger proportion of the

smokers had babies born early or late; 38 per cent of the smokers' babies and 51 per cent of the non-smokers' babies were born at term.

Are over-the-counter drugs, such as cold cures and aspirin, safe for pregnant women to take?

You should always check with your pharmacist or GP if you are thinking of taking any drug while pregnant. They will be able to advise you on safe medicines and dosages. If you are feeling miserable with a cold or 'flu (from which, unfortunately, pregnant women are not immune!), it may be perfectly safe to take something to help, but ask your pharmacist or GP first.

If you find yourself becoming ill rather often, it is worth looking to see if there are any reasons for this. For example, if you are getting a lot of colds, are you getting enough vitamin C in your diet? If you are getting a lot of headaches, are they due to stress which could be reduced in some way? A chat with a midwife or your GP might be helpful.

I have been on medication for my epilepsy for years. They say drugs cross the placenta, but if I stop I may get fits again. What should I do?

Many chronic illnesses may have a bearing on the management of pregnancy and labour; and pregnancy and labour may affect the medication given for a chronic illness. Therefore, it is essential that as soon as possible you see a specialist who knows enough about both to give you the best possible medical advice. Your GP will be able to make the referral for you; or if you already see a specialist, ring and ask if he/she could advise you on any changes necessary in your treatment or any special care for pregnancy and labour. If they cannot, they should be able to put you in touch with another specialist who can.

I conceived through IVF (see Glossary). Should I take any special precautions during pregnancy?

You have as good a chance of your pregnancy proceeding normally as if you had conceived in the usual way. However, some women prefer to look after themselves extra carefully - it is important to use your commonsense and do what feels right for you. Some obstetricians give women who have conceived by artificial means synthetic progesterone during the first three months of pregnancy. Although this has not been shown by research to improve the chances of carrying the baby to term, and the drug tends to make women feel tired and nauseous, some women choose to put up with this because taking it makes them feel they are doing all they can.

Research has shown that artificial methods of conception can sometimes cause specific emotional problems. If you feel yourself becoming over-anxious or guilty as a result of the ambivalent feelings about parenthood which many prospective parents have, think about getting some good emotional support. If talking to your partner or family and friends is not enough, you may talk to a midwife, counsellor or psychotherapist – whichever feels right for you (see Useful Organizations).

I have been having acupuncture regularly for three years now - is it safe to continue during pregnancy?

Yes it is, because your practitioner will be familiar with your body and will be able to treat you for the so-called minor ailments of pregnancy as well as continue your ongoing treatment. (Acupuncturists can also sometimes turn breech babies.) However, most acupuncturists are reluctant to start treating pregnant women for the first time, because of the risks of treating an unfamiliar body at this special time. Some women ask their practitioners to attend them during labour for pain-relief, but this is rarely done, even in China, where acupuncture is a very widely used therapy. Acupuncturists often find that pregnant women they have treated go on to have straightforward labours, because their bodies are in an optimum state of balance and well-being.

Do I really have to give up soft cheese?

There is a risk of contracting listeria from soft cheeses such as Brie and Camembert, particularly if they are made from unpasteurized milk; soft blue cheeses; pâtés; salami; pork sausages; pre-cooked ready-to-eat poultry; shop-prepared salads and other prepared foods such as pizza. Pre-packed cottage cheese is not a carrier of listeria. If a pregnant woman catches the disease early on in her pregnancy, it can cause miscarriage; if caught later, it can cause a stillbirth or the baby may be born alive but affected by serious problems including meningitis and hydrocephalus. To minimize the risks, foods should be kept at a refrigerator temperature of no higher than 5° Celsius; they should be covered, and raw and cooked foods should be kept apart.

Many women feel the inconvenience of restricting their diet is outweighed by peace of mind about their baby. However, some people are beginning to complain that there are too many restrictions to consider. It could be said that taking responsibility for most things is not easy, particularly another life, but hopefully worthwhile in the long run. Anyone who has contracted listeria or who wants more information can contact the Listeria Support Group (see Useful Organizations).

Someone told me it is dangerous to change cat litter when you are pregnant. Is this true?

There is a risk of contracting toxoplasmosis from handling cat faeces. The disease can also be caught from eating raw vegetables from the garden or from eating and handling raw meat (and therefore tends to be more common in countries like France, where raw and under-cooked meat is widely enjoyed). The infection can be caught only once, since it confers immunity. Although it is more easily passed on to the baby in the last three months of pregnancy, it has more serious consequences for the baby in the first three months: these include hydrocephalus, recurrent seizures and brain damage. Therefore, when pregnant, always wear rubber gloves when changing cat litter or when gardening; avoid eating raw or under-cooked meat; cook vegetables from the garden after washing them thoroughly; and wash your hands thoroughly after preparing raw meat.

I spent the other day with my niece who came out in German measles the next day. What should I do?

Rubella (also known as German measles) can have serious consequences if contracted by a pregnant woman within the first 16 weeks of pregnancy, when the fetus is going through its most radical phase of development. Potentially, a baby whose mother had rubella could die *in utero* or be born deaf, or with cataracts, heart disease, or mental retardation. Women can be immune either from having had the disease as a child or from being vaccinated but they should always have their immune status checked when contemplating pregnancy even if they had the disease or were immunized as children. If you are more than 16 weeks pregnant and you contract German measles, there is a good chance the baby will not be harmed at all.

If your immune status was checked before you became pregnant and was positive, you have nothing to worry about. If not, and if the hospital has not yet done the standard early pregnancy blood test, ask them to do a blood test immediately to check whether or not you are immune. If you are not immune, you cannot be vaccinated while you are pregnant, so you will have to wait to see whether or not you develop the disease (the incubation period is 10 to 14 days). If you do, you may choose to have a termination: the hospital will advise you accordingly and should offer you counselling. If you are not immune, but do not contract rubella, all will probably be well (although sometimes women remain symptom-free during rubella), but it is essential that you are vaccinated as soon as possible after the birth. (Women should also be vaccinated after stillbirth or termination as a result of rubella.) You should then wait three months before becoming pregnant again.

I am expecting twins and my GP has recommended bed-rest. I feel perfectly well and had planned to work until 30 weeks. Is bed-rest necessary?

Recent research has shown that bed-rest for twins makes no difference to the outcome of the pregnancy and may in fact adversely affect the condition of the mother and her babies. You may find yourself becoming more tired than other women expecting singletons as the babies grow bigger, but resting and relaxing in accordance with your body's needs should be sufficient. The idea behind bed-rest for 'problems', such as twins, high blood pressure or babies who appear not to be growing well, is that the blood flow through the placenta is maximized rather than circulating so much round a woman's arms and legs. However, bed-rest carries its own risks – hence, for example, women are encouraged to be as mobile as they can after a Caesarean section.

I have read that women having their first babies whose mothers had pre-eclampsia (see Glossary) have a higher risk of getting pre-eclampsia themselves. Is there anything I can do to lessen the risk?

Research does seem to show a genetic factor in pre-eclampsia and it is far more common in first pregnancies. The condition is diagnosed by three symptoms occurring together: large increase in blood pressure during pregnancy; protein in the urine; and swelling. The only way of controlling the situation is with relaxation; bed-rest is prescribed, but its benefits remain uncertain. In severe cases, the baby is either induced or delivered by Caesarean section.

There is much interest in the effect of diet on pre-eclampsia and this is shared by the Pre-eclamptic Toxaemia Society (see Useful Organizations). A research study showed beneficial effects from a diet high in protein; low in fat; salt only to taste; whole grains for fibre; and with as many foods as possible being fresh and unprocessed. Since this is a healthy diet for most people, you could choose to try it, at the same time keeping your blood pressure low by resting and relaxing whenever necessary and minimizing stress. Research is also in progress to explore the benefits and risks of using low doses of aspirin during pregnancy to treat pre-eclampsia and intra-uterine growth retardation. However, aspirin should be taken in pregnancy only as part of a controlled clinical trial or under medical supervision.

> *I have terrible heartburn - is it true that I am*
> *more likely to have a girl?*

You may choose whether or not to believe folklore. None of the traditional means of knowing the sex of the baby before birth is reliable. To help cope with the heartburn you may ask your GP to prescribe antacids (after the first three months of pregnancy) or dilute hydrochloric acid to relieve the condition. Other ways of relieving the condition are to raise the head of your bed at night and to do stretching exercises for your digestive tract (*New Active Birth* – see Bibliography). You can also avoid eating large meals, especially in the evening, and have smaller, more frequent meals instead. Heartburn in pregnancy is caused by the hormones relaxing the sphincters of the stomach so that the contents leak into the oesophagus and cause discomfort.

> *We booked our skiing holiday before I got*
> *pregnant. Would it be all right to go?*

The choice is yours. The general rule about sport and exercise is that anything you were accustomed to doing before pregnancy is safe to continue during a normal pregnancy. In the past, women were discouraged from activities in which there was a high risk of falling, such as skiing or horse-riding, but it is now thought that these activities do not increase the risk of miscarriage. Many women continue with competitive sports until playing them becomes uncomfortable, though 'contact' sports are sometimes thought unsuitable. Some women prefer not to take any risks during pregnancy, particularly if they are elderly primigravidae or if they have had problems with fertility.

I travel a lot on business. At what stage of pregnancy do they stop you flying?

All airlines refuse to fly pregnant women after 28 weeks of pregnancy for insurance reasons. Some women prefer to stop flying earlier than that because they find any swelling of the legs or ankles is aggravated by flying, making them uncomfortable.

Is there anything I can do for these varicose veins? My GP recommended support tights, but they don't seem to help.

Varicose veins are a common minor ailment of pregnancy. The more you rest your legs during pregnancy, the less discomfort you will have and the less likely they are to remain once the baby is born. Therefore, avoid standing as much as possible and, whenever you sit down, put up your legs, on a sofa or on another chair. You can find ways of doing this at work, at home and in other people's houses: everyone will understand if you explain why this is necessary. Crossing your legs or ankles as you sit may exacerbate varicose veins by impeding circulation.

A good active birth exercise to stretch the leg muscles is to lie on the floor on your back forming a right-angle with your legs against the wall. Spend a few minutes with your legs straight, then apart and then with your knees bent. Ankle circling is also helpful. Think about the way you do things: is it necessary to stand to make a telephone call, prepare a meal or do the ironing? A little organization and forethought can take a lot of unnecessary strain off your legs. A homoeopath (see Useful Organizations) may be able to prescribe a remedy to alleviate the condition, even if you had varicose veins before becoming pregnant. If you wear tights or stockings, they may as well be support tights for extra comfort. Massaging with a few drops of essential oil of lemon mixed into a neutral oil may also afford relief.

Very rarely, varicose veins occur in the vulva and can be so painful that making love can be extremely uncomfortable, if not impossible. A sanitary pad worn during the day is said to support vulval veins and may relieve the discomfort.

Is it true that VDUs can harm the baby?

There have been concerns that VDUs may cause harm to pregnant women, either directly or indirectly. It has been suggested that there may be a risk from extra-low-frequency radiation, or that the sitting position at the work terminal and the work environment may cause pregnant women specific problems, or that the stress of VDU work may lead to greater consumption of cigarettes, alcohol, caffeine and tranquillizers. There have been some reports of higher than average rates of miscarriage and neonatal death among women who worked regularly on VDUs while pregnant, and other reports suggesting that VDU work is safe for pregnant women. The VDU Workers' Rights Campaign (see Useful Organizations) feels that, despite some favourable reports, safety is not completely proved and there is still cause for caution and concern.

Working on VDUs can be stressful whether you are pregnant or not. Regular breaks are suggested, which should include exercise, such as walking, to increase the blood circulation and avoid 'pooling'. Attention should be paid to seating, lighting and position of screen and keyboard. Protective screens are available, but some are more effective than others. Some British trade unions have negotiated technology agreements with employers which include provision for those pregnant or wishing to become pregnant to be moved from working on VDUs. If you have the opportunity, you may choose to reduce the work you do on a VDU or stop using it at all. Your Health and Safety Representative may be able to help you in minimizing the stress caused by using a VDU and advise you on the use of a protective screen.

My doctor says I am putting on too much weight, but the hospital says I am fine. How do I know who to believe?

Weight-gain in pregnancy is one of the many grey areas of obstetrics for which there are no clear-cut answers: this may account for the different reactions of your GP and the hospital. Many women find the change in their shape and weight the most difficult change to bear in pregnancy: this is not helped by the sylph-like image of women projected in the media, even if many models are accompanied by babies or young children, the 'designer accessory' of the 1990s. It is also not helped by health professionals being alarmist (albeit with the best of intentions) without asking each woman exactly how much she is eating.

The concern about excessive weight-gain in pregnancy is that it will lead to high blood pressure which in turn may affect the growth of the baby, especially in the last three months. Just like babies and children, many pregnant women tend to gain weight in leaps and bounds rather than at a steady rate. Basic weight-gain in pregnancy is accounted for by the baby; the enlarged uterus and amniotic sac (see Glossary); the placenta; the increased blood circulation of the mother to service the uterus and baby; breasts enlarged in readiness for breastfeeding; and fat stores, particularly on the hips and thighs, ready for breastfeeding. Research shows very little extra food is needed to achieve this weight-gain.

Women's physiological response to pregnancy varies enormously. Some find their appetite leaps into top gear while others are unaffected. Some seem to burn up the calories they eat while others put on weight very readily. Appetite and weight-gain are not always directly linked. Some women are prone to powerful cravings for certain foods.

There is not much you can do about your body's personal programme for weight-gain in pregnancy, but you can try not to eat to excess and to ensure that as much as possible of what you eat is rich in minerals and vitamins, and is a good quality, varied, well-balanced diet. If you need help with your diet, ask your community midwife or the hospital dietitian for support. It may be that you are eating more than you should because you are anxious or depressed about some aspect of your pregnancy or something else. If this is the case, enlist the support of your GP or midwife; ask for information and/or reassurance about any aspect of your pregnancy or birth which is troubling you, or ask to be referred to a counsellor or psychotherapist.

5: Testing for a healthy baby: antenatal screening

Routine antenatal screening is universal in hospital-based antenatal care. When women receive midwife-based care, screening is often tailored specifically to each woman's individual needs and choices. Whilst some women are reassured by the tests, others are made anxious by them, even when the results of the tests are favourable. Sometimes women are upset by the lack of time and sympathy given by health professionals when voicing their anxieties. This may be caused by the fact that women throughout pregnancy tend to seek reassurance that the pregnancy is progressing normally and that their babies are healthy; whereas obstetricians' attention is generally focussed on detecting and dealing with any abnormalities. If you feel anxious or you need someone to explain in more detail the significance of a test or a test result, you can usually find someone to talk to who will listen and help you: it may be a midwife or doctor at the hospital; a community midwife; your GP; a health visitor; or an NCT antenatal teacher.

51 per cent of the respondents to the *Good Housekeeping* Survey had their first antenatal appointment before 12 weeks and 45 per cent between 12 and 16 weeks. Respondents living in the North of England and Scotland were more likely to attend before 12 weeks, 80 per cent of respondents were offered an ultrasound scan; 58 per cent an alphafetoprotein blood test; 18 per cent an amniocentesis; 5 per cent chorionic villus sampling; and 4 per cent were offered none of these. Amniocentesis was offered less in London and the South-East than in the North, the Midlands and Scotland.

SUMMARY OF USUAL SCREENING PROCEDURES IN PREGNANCY

PROCEDURE	REASONS	TIMING
The following seven procedures are usually carried out on every pregnant woman as a matter of routine:		
Urine test	To check for sugar, protein and ketones, the presence of which may indicate diabetes or pre-eclampsia	Every appointment

44

PROCEDURE	REASONS	TIMING
Weighing the mother	To check growth of the baby and for pre-eclampsia	Every appointment
Taking blood pressure	To check for pre-eclampsia	Every appointment
Examining woman for swelling	To check for pre-eclampsia (symptoms are swelling + protein in urine + raised blood pressure)	Every appointment
Feeling the baby through your abdomen	To check growth and position of baby	Every appointment
Listening to the baby's heart using fetal stethoscope or monitor	To check the baby's heartbeat is normal	Every appointment after 18 weeks
Blood tests	To check haemoglobin and blood group; immunity to rubella; for syphilis and hepatitis B	Booking-in appointment

The following procedures are carried out only on some women. Which these are may be determined by a woman's age, country of origin and medical history. Other factors which may come into play are hospital policy and financial considerations.

Blood tests	a) To check for HIV (sometimes anonymously); sickle-cell anaemia (in Afro-Caribbean women); thalassaemia (in women from India, SE Asia and the Mediterranean); Tay-Sachs disease (in some Jewish women) and other genetically inherited diseases; for toxoplasmosis on request	Booking-in appointment
	b) To check for alphafetoprotein (AFP) which if high may indicate spina bifida or other neural tube defect; if low, may indicate increased possibility of Down's syndrome in older mothers	16-18 weeks

PROCEDURE	REASONS	TIMING
	c) Combined maternal serum test which measures AFP, human chorionic gonadotrophin (HCG) and oestriol levels in relation to mother's age and is more reliable indicator of need for amniocentesis than more common AFP test.	16-18 weeks
Ultrasound scan	To check age, size and development of baby; position of placenta and baby; for ectopic pregnancy, multiple births etc; after high AFP test; to assist CVS and amniocentesis	Usually 16 weeks; sometimes earlier/later routinely or for special reasons
Chorionic villus sampling (CVS) sometimes known as Chorionic villus biopsy (CVB)	To check for Down's syndrome and other genetic problems (not spina bifida)	8-11 weeks
Amniocentesis	To check for Down's syndrome, other genetic problems and spina bifida	16-18 weeks
Counting fetal movements	'Kick-chart' filled in by mother to monitor well-being of baby	Last month of pregnancy

How do they make sure the baby's all right?

The midwives and doctors giving you antenatal care will carry out some of the above screening procedures; which they are may be determined by your age, medical and family medical histories and the policies of the particular district health authority (see Glossary). The first seven forms of screening are carried out universally and their usefulness generally agreed upon. The other procedures are deemed more useful in some cases than in others, so may be the subject of local policy (determined on a combination of clinical and economic grounds) and your own personal choice.

It is important to remember that screening procedures in themselves do not ensure healthy babies – they can only point up particular problems at the time they are carried out. There is no cure for the conditions shown up by amniocentesis and chorionic villus sampling; when a serious abnormality is discovered the choice for the parents is either to continue with the pregnancy or to terminate it. Some couples are upset to discover that in some hospitals it is assumed that they will automatically choose termination in such a situation. Another thing to be aware of is that test results are occasionally inconclusive so that further tests are needed. It can be quite a long wait before the results are available.

Why do they test for diabetes and pre-eclampsia every time? Are they so common?

There are a certain number of women who become affected by these conditions, but these days the serious effects of them are preventable by careful management. Some people believe that the conditions can be prevented and even controlled by healthy diet, but this is controversial. If gestational diabetes is of concern to you, there is no harm in keeping refined sugars to the minimum and ensuring the carbohydrate you eat is as far as possible unrefined, as in wholemeal bread, potatoes, plenty of fresh fruit and vegetables, etc. The Pre-Eclamptic Toxaemia Society (see Useful Organizations) recommends a high-protein, low-fat diet to prevent pre-eclampsia.

My cousin had a baby with Down's syndrome, but is it worth having an amniocentesis if we would never consider a termination?

Amniocentesis carries an increased risk of miscarriage of about 0.5 per cent. Some couples, often those who are older and possibly with a history of infertility, consider this risk unacceptable and would rather risk having a handicapped child. For other couples, the unacceptability of a disabled child outweighs the increased risk of miscarriage. Some couples would not terminate a pregnancy for religious or ethical reasons, but even so would prefer to be prepared for the birth of a disabled child. Only you can choose what is right for you. If you need to, talk to your hospital consultant and/or a genetic or obstetric counsellor if there is one available.

Can they test your blood for AIDS without telling you?

Since January 1990, some hospitals have been allowing a little blood to be taken from samples given for testing for other purposes to be tested for the Human Immuno-deficiency Virus (HIV). This testing is being done to get a better idea of the true prevalence of HIV and is done anonymously, so that there are no implications for your care, treatment, job or insurance. In the hospitals where this anonymous testing is being carried out, you will be informed this is being done, but you will not be told the result. You may prefer not to allow any of your blood to be used for this purpose and refuse consent. If there is any chance of your being infected by HIV and you want to know, you can ask for a separate test to be done and counselling should be provided both before and after the test.

Some women who have been infected with HIV decide to terminate their pregnancy; others decide to keep their baby. HIV-positive mothers must choose whether to breastfeed, since it is possible that they might pass HIV on to their babies in this way (so far there is a possibility that one baby in the UK may have contracted HIV from breastmilk). The knowledge in this new area is growing all the time so ask for the latest information available to help you when making your choice. Not all babies born to women infected with HIV inherit the disease (only 35 to 60 per cent), but it is possible that pregnancy or more than one pregnancy may encourage the development of the Acquired Immune Deficiency Syndrome in women who are HIV-positive. There is still much to be learned about both HIV and AIDS.

Can I have my blood tested for toxoplasmosis and listeria?

If you believe you are at risk, you can ask at the hospital to be tested for these diseases, but it makes more sense to avoid contracting the diseases in the first place. Toxoplasmosis is a disease with mild flu-like symptoms which can be contracted from handling cat faeces and undercooked meat. If a pregnant woman catches the disease it can have serious consequences for her baby: early on in her pregnancy it can cause miscarriage or stillbirth; a baby born alive can be affected by serious problems including hydrocephalus, brain damage and blindness. The best course of all is to avoid handling cat faeces and handling or eating raw meat. Although toxoplasmosis is 20 times more common than rubella, routine testing is not carried out, partly because of the costs involved: some people believe it should be. In practice, your hospital will probably do the test if you ask. If not, you could arrange for the test to be done privately.

Listeria is a disease contracted from soft cheeses, among other foods, and can have similar effects on the fetus as toxoplasmosis. Again, avoidance is the best policy, but do not hesitate to ask for a blood test if you are in any doubt. If the test is positive you may then be offered a termination of pregnancy. (See also page 37)

I gave a large sample of blood at my booking-in appointment which made me feel very queasy. Why do I have to give blood again at 16 weeks?

Many hospitals routinely offer a blood test for alphafetoprotein (AFP) at 16 to 18 weeks, having earlier taken blood to check haemoglobin levels, blood group and so on. If the count of AFP cells is raised, it may indicate that the fetus has spina bifida or some other neural tube defect and the test may be repeated to confirm the result. The count may also be raised because of a multiple pregnancy or because the actual gestational age of the baby is more advanced than originally thought. A lower than normal AFP count could indicate an increased possibility of Down's Syndrome in older mothers. If the level is still above or below normal when the test is repeated, the woman is usually offered a detailed ultrasound scan: this is hoped to determine whether there is an abnormality, multiple pregnancy or gestational discrepancy. If none of these is found, she will be offered an amniocentesis to test for a chromosomal abnormality.

Some hospitals offer the AFP test routinely only to women over a certain specified age as the risk of abnormality increases with maternal age. The age varies from 35 to 38 in different hospitals. Younger women who would like the test may have their request turned down on grounds of cost. If you feel strongly, argue your case. Any woman may choose not to have the test.

What is the difference between amniocentesis and chorionic villus sampling (CVS)?

Both tests are used to detect chromosomal abnormalities such as Down's syndrome; genetic disorders such as thalassaemia and sickle cell anaemia; and the sex of the fetus where there is a history of a sex-linked disorder such as haemophilia. CVS cannot show up developmental defects such as spina bifida, it is not available in every maternity unit and obstetricians may be reluctant to perform it on women with a history of miscarriage in the first three months of pregnancy or with bleeding in the current pregnancy. However, as analysis of CVS becomes more sophisticated, it is hoped that many other inherited and metabolic disorders such as cystic fibrosis and Tay-Sachs disease will be detected.

After amniocentesis (a sample of amniotic fluid usually taken at 16 to 18 weeks) there is a waiting time of two to three weeks for the culture to develop (a spina bifida result can be obtained earlier) which is often an anxious time for both parents. Further anxiety can arise in the case of culture failure (which happens in 2 per cent of cases) when the woman has to choose whether to have another amniocentesis (waiting for the results of which will take her two or three weeks further into pregnancy) and take on the further increased risk of miscarriage. She may have to choose between two or three more weeks' anxiety waiting for the result or not having a second test and worrying for the rest of the pregnancy about the baby. It is at such times that counselling, either at the hospital or elsewhere, can be very helpful.

The result of chorionic villus sampling (taken at eight to 11weeks from what will become the placenta) is known within a few days since no culture is necessary. However, sometimes a doctor stops in the middle of the procedure if the woman suddenly starts to bleed and threatens to miscarry, in which case a woman will have risked miscarriage without getting the benefit of the result of the test.

What amniocentesis and CVS have in common is that they are both diagnostic tests, the results of which a woman may have to act on in choosing to have a termination. Nor does a negative result guarantee a perfect baby, since neither of the tests can detect such conditions as congenital heart defects.

CVS is currently undergoing trial in a number of hospitals in the UK. So far, it is shown to carry a higher increased risk of miscarriage than amniocentesis. This may be due to a combination of two factors: first, the fact that the sample is taken from the tissue that will become the placenta; and second, the fact that the test is usually performed between the eighth and eleventh weeks of pregnancy when the pregnancy is less stable than between the sixteenth and eighteenth weeks when amniocentesis is performed.

> *I had a normal alphafetoprotein result, but still*
> *feel anxious. I am only 32 but can I ask to have*
> *amniocentesis?*

With all such choices there are a large number and variety of factors to be weighed up and it is up to you (and your partner) to decide which are most important for you, because at the end of the day it is you, your partner and possibly your child, who will have to live with the consequences. At the age of 32 the increased risks of miscarriage after an amniocentesis are greater than the risks of producing a disabled baby. You may decide that the increased risk of miscarriage is less important to you. If it would be helpful, do not hesitate to see a consultant, your GP, a geneticist and/or an obstetric counsellor – whichever of these you feel could help you with information and who would listen and talk to you generally about the issues involved. Many hospitals put the result of the alphafetoprotein test together with the woman's age to obtain a combined factor which indicates more clearly the need for amniocentesis. Whether or not your hospital does this, you can still ask for an amniocentesis but it may be refused.

> *Why isn't chorionic villus sampling available at*
> *my hospital? I would much rather have that*
> *than risk a late termination for fetal*
> *abnormality after a positive amniocentesis.*

Chorionic villus sampling (CVS) is available only at some hospitals while still undergoing trial. Check with your hospital to see if CVS is in fact available: it may only be offered to certain groups of women. Because of the increased risk of miscarriage following CVS, some hospitals offer the test only to women over 40 for whom speed is of the essence or where there is a specific genetic problem. If it is available, you may be able to have CVS if the higher risk of miscarriage is less important to you than the risk of a late termination for fetal abnormality. If it is not available at all, you could choose another hospital for your care or pay to have the test done privately.

The major advantage of CVS is that if a termination is chosen after the result, it can be performed earlier, when it is less distressing. However, the risks of miscarriage are greater following CVS than following amniocentesis - between one and 4 per cent for CVS as opposed to 0.5 per cent for amniocentesis. This may be a result of the relative newness of the procedure and the fact that it is performed earlier than amniocentesis, when the pregnancy is less stable. A further factor to bear in mind is that the test does not detect neural tube defects such as spina bifida. If a woman's previous obstetric history indicates she is already at higher risk of miscarriage, an obstetrician would probably recommend amniocentesis in preference to CVS as a method of screening.

A recent study has shown that because of the higher rate of unprovoked miscarriage among older women, it is not, on balance, worth having CVS before 12 weeks since a high proportion of pregnancies may naturally terminate themselves in that time. It is therefore recommended that women over 40 have the test no earlier than 12 weeks, when there is still time for a straightforward termination after a negative result should women so choose.

What is the difference between a late termination and an early one?

Up to about 12 or 14 weeks, a pregnancy can be terminated by suction under general anaesthetic. After that time, it is safer for the woman for termination to take the form of an induced labour, using prostaglandins, artificial rupture of the membranes and syntocinon drip, as necessary. However good the reasons are for choosing a late termination, it is inevitably a distressing and painful experience, both physically and emotionally. Generally, hospital policies ensure that as little distress is caused to the woman (and her partner) as possible, that good pain relief is offered and that counselling is available.

Are there any tests other than chorionic villus sampling and amniocentesis?

There is a non-invasive test which estimates an individual woman's risk of carrying a handicapped child. It can help women decide whether to choose to have an amniocentesis. The test, known as the maternal serum screening test, extracts genetic information about the fetus from a sample of the woman's blood taken at 16 weeks. This combined blood test measures three factors in the woman's blood – alphafetoprotein, human chorionic gonadotrophin and oestriol – against maternal age and is a more reliable indication than the more usual alphafetoprotein test of whether a woman might benefit from amniocentesis. The test is becoming more widely available so you can ask your hospital if they will carry it out for you.

I am thinking of booking a home birth, but am I still entitled to all the tests?

Yes, you are, and your community midwife would ensure that appointments were made for you at the right times. However, if you are of an age (say over 37) when screening for chromosomal abnormalities and neural tube defects is offered routinely, you may find yourself under pressure from the hospital not to have a home birth anyway. Anxieties about the well-being of the baby (universal among pregnant parents, but with a little more justification in women over 37) may become translated into anxiety about normal labour and delivery, particularly if this baby is your first.

Some women having their babies at home are fortunate enough to have all their antenatal care at home also and, perhaps from a desire for their pregnancy and birth to be as 'low-tech' as possible, choose not to have ultrasound scans even if these are routinely on offer. So be clear about what you want to choose and go for it!

> **The hospital gave me iron tablets (Pregaday) to take, but they make me constipated. I am not anaemic – should I continue taking them?**

Many women dislike the effects of iron tablets and fail to take them during pregnancy even when they are prescribed. The routine giving of iron tablets to all women is not justified by improved outcome of the pregnancy for either mother or baby. *A Guide to Effective Care in Pregnancy and Childbirth* (see Bibliography) says that some research shows that giving women iron supplementation during pregnancy when they are not anaemic may adversely affect the growth of the baby, possibly because it slows down the flow of blood through the placenta (page 23). There is also a school of thought that unless a woman is already known to be genuinely anaemic, there is a disadvantage in giving her iron supplementation until 28 weeks' gestation, because it can mask true anaemia in pregnancy. The other problem with iron supplementation is that it can interfere with the absorption of zinc, another mineral needed in increased amounts during pregnancy.

True anaemia, as well as consisting of a low haemoglobin count, includes the symptoms of tiredness, a fast beating heart when you exert yourself, cracks at the corners of the mouth and difficulty with swallowing. If you are not anaemic, you may choose to stop taking the tablets and instead ensure your diet contains regular amounts of iron-rich foods such as heart, kidney and red meat, egg yolk, peas, beans, pulses, cocoa, cane molasses, shellfish, parsley, wheatgerm, lightly cooked green vegetables, watercress and dried fruit. The Department of Health has warned pregnant women not to eat liver because it contains abnormally high levels of vitamin A due to supplements used in animal feed. (Very high levels of vitamin A can occasionally cause defects in the developing baby.) Vitamin C may help the absorption of iron so it is important to eat plenty of raw fruit and vegetables. It is a well-established fact that the body absorbs minerals and vitamins more efficiently from food than from supplements.

If you are or become anaemic, in addition to improving your diet, you could ask your doctor to prescribe a different iron formula which may have fewer side-effects: Pregaday tends to be given on the NHS because it is the cheapest brand. If this is not possible and you could afford it, you might choose to buy from a chemist or health food shop a different brand of iron tablet. When taking any form of iron supplement, women are often recommended to have a glass of orange juice with it to aid absorption of the iron.

> *The hospital where I am booked have asked me*
> *to take part in some research - my husband is*
> *not keen, but I shall feel guilty if I don't.*

In recent years there has been much criticism that certain obstetric procedures have not been properly evaluated to show the possible risks and benefits to women and their babies. No screening test, treatment or protocol should be introduced unless there is reliable evidence that the benefits outweigh the risks. Some forms of treatment may be merely an unnecessary inconvenience and expense; others can have serious long-term consequences. The drug Thalidomide which was used as a sleeping pill in pregnancy is one example. Doctors prescribe drugs they believe to be safe, but their understanding can only be as good as the available evidence. 'Prospective randomized controlled trials' are used to test out the effects of a screening test, treatment or protocol in one or more study groups as compared with a control group of randomly assigned people who do not receive the treatment. Various combinations of treatment may be tested in a single study. The results enable women and the people caring for them to have sound information on which to base their decision making.

When choosing whether or not to take part in such a trial, you might like to ask the person requesting your participation a number of questions to elucidate two main areas of concern. First, is it a worthwhile, properly conducted trial, run by a reliable institution and likely to benefit women and/or their babies? Second, does the research entail any unacceptable risks, inconvenience or expense to yourself? There should be available some literature about the research for you to take home and discuss with your husband. You might find useful the NCT Information Sheet, *Clinical trials and medical research: helping you decide* (see Bibliography).

I feel very well: are all the antenatal appointments necessary?

Attending antenatal appointments does not in itself guarantee a healthy mother and a healthy baby, but regular antenatal care from midwives and/or doctors has a number of benefits. A woman may be encouraged to look after herself better than she would on her own, so she takes adequate rest and eats well. She has opportunities to seek reassurance about the growth of her baby and can ask for advice about measures to minimize the minor ailments of pregnancy. She can build up a relationship with the professionals who are going to deliver her baby and look after her postnatally. The small number of women who have pre-eclampsia or any other condition requiring treatment or special observation can be diagnosed as early as possible so as to minimize the risks of the condition. You can make your antenatal care work for you by asking the questions to which you need answers.

The current pattern of antenatal check-ups (once a month until 28 weeks, fortnightly until 36 weeks and weekly until delivery) has remained unchanged in this country since 1929. The efficacy of women's attending in this way has never been proved. It is well established that during this century it is the improved socio-economic conditions in which women live which have improved both maternal and child perinatal mortality to a much greater extent than antenatal care. Unfortunately it tends to be the women most in need of antenatal care who attend least frequently.

6: Pregnancy, work and benefits

Maternity pay and benefits are a complex subject. Your GP, midwife or hospital will give you some leaflets and forms, but it is essential that as soon as you become pregnant you spend time reading the DSS leaflets so you learn exactly what you are entitled to and when you should claim. Make a note in your diary or on your calendar of all the important dates for claiming, giving notice, etc. If you are at all unsure of what you are entitled to, talk to your employer and/or your local DSS office. The Maternity Alliance (see Useful Organizations) produces excellent explanatory leaflets and will answer particular queries. Always make a claim if you think you may be entitled to benefit.

SUMMARY OF STATUTORY MATERNITY RIGHTS AND BENEFITS

DESCRIPTION	DATES FOR ACTION
Maternity leave (if you have worked full-time for 2 years for the same employer by the end of the 15th week before your due date) From the 29th week of pregnancy until 29 weeks after the birth	a) From 26 weeks onwards give your employer 3 weeks' notice of leaving and of your intention to return b) If your employer writes to you after the birth asking if you intend to return, reply within 2 weeks c) Give your employer 3 weeks' written notice of your return to work, that is 26 weeks after the birth at the latest
Statutory Maternity Pay * (if you have worked for the same employer for at least 6 months by the end of the 15th week before your due date: £39.25 per week; if you have worked for the same employer full-time for 2 years by the end of the 15th week before your due date: 90 per cent of your average pay in the last 8 weeks for 6 weeks; then £39.25 per week)	a) Notice as in a) above b) Claim before you start maternity leave

DESCRIPTION	DATES FOR ACTION
For up to 18 weeks between the 11th week before the birth and the 11th week after the birth, losing a week's SMP for every week you work after the 7th week before your due date	
Maternity Allowance * (if you are self-employed or have recently changed or given up employment and have paid National Insurance Contributions for 26 out of the last 52 weeks ending with the 15th week before your due date) For up to 18 weeks between the 11th week before your due date and the 11th week after the birth £35.70 per week	a) Give notice to your employer 3 weeks before stopping work b) Claim before stopping work
Sickness Benefit * (if you have worked at all in the last 3 years it is worth claiming) From the 6th week before your due date until the end of the 2nd week after the birth £35.70 per week	Claim as soon as possible after 26 weeks
Social Fund Maternity Payment * (Lump sum for women on Income Support or Family Credit to buy things for the baby) £100	Claim from 11 weeks before your due date until 3 months after the birth
Free prescriptions, dental care and chiropody (for all women)	Obtain certificate of due date from midwife or GP to show pharmacist and dentist
Free milk and vitamins and help with fares to hospital (if you receive Income Support or Family Credit)	Tell DSS and claim
Child Benefit * £8.25 per week for the first child and £7.25 per week for other children	a) Register birth within 6 weeks b) Send form to DSS in Newcastle
One-Parent Benefit * £5.60 per week	a) Register birth within 6 weeks b) Send form to DSS in Newcastle
Other benefits	Check with your local DSS office

* Figures given are correct as at 1 November 1990

When is the best time to stop work?

Only you can choose the best time for yourself. Factors you consider may include whether or not you are entitled to statutory maternity benefits; whether you are going to take statutory maternity leave; whether or not you intend to return to work after the birth; your health; and how you want to spend the time of your pregnancy.

When is the earliest I can stop work without prejudicing my maternity rights?

Unless you are entitled to sick leave, the earliest date you can start maternity leave and receive Statutory Maternity Payments or Maternity Allowance is 11 weeks before your baby's due date, that is at 29 weeks. The latest date you can start maternity leave without losing any of your Statutory Maternity Payments or Maternity Allowance is six weeks before the baby is due, that is at 34 weeks.

I am self-employed: can I claim?

You are still entitled to statutory maternity leave. You claim Maternity Allowance rather than Statutory Maternity Payments and have no employer to whom you give notice. If you pay tax under Schedule D6 and are taxed on a preceding-year basis, you are in a more favourable position than a woman paying tax under Schedule E, because you will not pay tax on the year of your pregnancy until you are assessed after the end of that year; women on PAYE under Schedule E will have paid out too much tax for the weeks in the tax year preceding their maternity leave and this is adjusted in the form of a tax rebate once they return to work or give notice of their not returning to work.

I am unemployed: can I claim?

If you have become unemployed within the last year you are probably entitled to claim Maternity Allowance. If you have been unemployed for longer than that, you may be entitled to Sickness Benefit or to a Social Fund Maternity Payment if you receive Income Support or Family Credit. The system is so complicated that it is worth contacting your local Citizens' Advice Bureau and Department of Social Security office about your own case.

I work as a volunteer: do I have a right to return after the baby?

You do not have a statutory right to return, since you are not in paid employment. However, depending on the relationship and on any contract you have with your organization, you may be able to negotiate maternity leave and obtain an agreement in writing that your job will be kept for you.

I cannot decide whether or not to return to work after the baby; what can I do?

To protect your right to return, you have to give notice to your employer of your intention to return, but you may then change your mind after the baby is born without incurring any penalty. You may have until 26 weeks after the birth to make up your mind (which is the last date of giving notice to your employer of your actual return) unless your employer exercises his/her right to write and ask you whether you are returning to work seven weeks after the baby is born: you then have only two weeks in which to reply. However, if you still cannot decide, you could reply that you will return and still change your mind up to 26 weeks after the birth.

I'm not going back to work; should I say I am?

If you are absolutely positive that you will not want to return after the birth, the effect of giving notice of your intention to return is to inconvenience your employer and delay the payment of tax rebates for the tax year in which your baby is born. Inconveniencing your employer in this way may affect the possibility of returning to work for that employer at some time in the future, or the kind of reference you receive if you choose to seek employment elsewhere. Many women who give up work after a baby choose to stay on good terms with their previous employer with an eye to future employment and for social reasons: keeping in touch socially is a way of keeping in touch with the world of work in preparation for return at some future date.

Many women who feel fairly sure that they will not return to work, nevertheless give notice of their intention to return in case they change their minds, or they have to return to work earlier than expected for financial reasons or because they lose the baby and prefer to return to work in familiar surroundings until they are ready to try for another. They may also choose to allow for the possibility of changing their minds about returning to work; they may find actual life at home with a baby different from how they had imagined.

Some women know they do not want to return to their previous job, either because they want a change of employment or because they want to work part-time and part-time employment or job-sharing is not available with that particular employer. Nevertheless, they give notice of their intention to return and in fact do return, either because part-time work or a job-share becomes a possibility with that employer or because they believe it is easier to find new employment if one is employed rather than unemployed.

I am finding it so difficult to get time off for my
antenatal appointments that I dare not ask for
time off to go to the hospital antenatal classes
held during the day.

You are entitled to paid time off work for both antenatal check-ups and antenatal classes and you owe it to yourself and your baby to take that time off. It may help to show your employer the DSS leaflet setting out your rights or to ask another senior person such as a personnel supervisor to speak to your boss on your behalf. Another approach is to minimize the time you are away from work for antenatal appointments by choosing shared care with a GP and asking for appointments at the beginning of clinic sessions.

This may be a good time to practise or acquire assertiveness skills (see Bibliography). Many women find attitudes to them at work change once they are pregnant and that some people assume that the physical changes of pregnancy are accompanied by corresponding changes in their ability to perform well. This may lead employers to expect either more or less of a woman. Some women are furious at being expected to soft-pedal while others view with dismay the fact that work missed because of a long antenatal appointment has to be done in their own time later. Every woman is an individual and should feel able to communicate her individual needs at work to the people she is working with.

I want to have as much time as possible with
the baby before returning to work; working
until 40 weeks won't harm the baby, will it? I
am very fit.

The date you begin maternity leave does not affect the date by which you must return: the latest statutory date by which you must return is 29 weeks after the actual date of birth. Some employers offer maternity packages more generous than the statutory minimum, in terms both of pay and benefits, including maternity leave, but where they do not, women choose to work until the birth or shortly before the birth to maximize their earnings, since the statutory sums are very low.

Some women also work as late as possible because they feel (rightly or wrongly) that no one else can do their work and know that what they leave undone they will come back to later. Others take as little time off as possible in order not to prejudice their chances of promotion, etc. Increasingly, women want to achieve as much as men in the work-place and to minimize the effects on their work of having a family. However, more often than not, even when they have a partner, it is women who are responsible for arranging childcare and dealing with illnesses both of their children and the providers of their childcare. Employers of men rely on this, so perhaps it is only fair to yourself to take your full entitlement to maternity leave if your financial situation allows.

Many women feel extremely fit throughout their pregnancy, but find that by 34 weeks they become more tired and find travelling to work more difficult. At this time the baby is growing fast and the woman's body is 'living for two'. It is important that you get enough rest so that you are fit for labour and able to make a quick recovery afterwards: in this way you will be more able to enjoy the early days with your baby. Much depends on the nature of your work: working in a factory, serving in a shop or working in a busy office-based job, perhaps with travel, is different from sitting at a desk at home. However, working at home is not always the most restful choice. Research has shown that many women 'at home' with no domestic help (especially if they have other children or relatives to look after) have to work much harder, and therefore get less rest, than women in paid employment outside the home; if women work outside the home, they are more likely to get help from their partners with cleaning, shopping and childcare. Research has shown that women with three or more children and no domestic help are at risk of giving birth to babies 'small for dates' (see Glossary).

Won't I get bored sitting around if I give up work at 34 weeks?

The last six weeks can be a busy time, with weekly antenatal check-ups and antenatal classes. Many women get in touch with their local NCT postnatal support group so they meet women who have already had their babies. This can be a pleasant way of making new friends and learning what equipment you do and do not need for your baby.

Many women find, perhaps after an initial bout of guilt, that they enjoy this time alone at home. In the past they may have spent all their holiday travelling or going to stay with relatives or doing DIY with their partner, so that they have never had an extended period of time at home on their own just to please themselves and/ or catch up with all the jobs there is never time to do.

Some women use this time before the baby to 'nest', buying things and getting their home ready for the baby's arrival. Even if you choose to order larger items such as a pram and cot to be collected after the birth, time needs to be spent choosing which to buy. Making physical space for the baby in this way helps many women (and their partners) make mental space for him/her: as they make up the baby's bed and put away the newly-washed clothes and supply of nappies, they start to make the transition from having a baby inside them to having a baby they will hold, look after and get to know in a different way. Women (and their partners) who have lost a baby in the past may find this difficult and prefer not to make any preparations until the baby is safely delivered: if this is the case, they might use the time before the baby comes to talk over their anxieties with their GP, midwife, NCT antenatal teacher or a counsellor.

What happens to maternity benefits if anything happens to the baby?

The benefit rules are carefully phrased to take account of the fact that some babies are born early, some late and that sadly a small number of babies die. The amount of benefit you receive stays the same. However, where you gain or lose is with your statutory maternity leave which will be adjusted according to the actual date of the baby's birth: difficult if the baby is born prematurely.

7: Choosing antenatal classes

*I would much rather read some books than go to
antenatal classes. Isn't that as good?*

The two are not necessarily mutually exclusive. Many people who
enjoy going to antenatal classes find reading appropriate books
reinforces what they have learned and gives them additional
information on topics of individual interest or concern. They also
enjoy relevant TV and radio programmes, videos and magazines
for parents. Conversely, people who have read many books by the
time they go to antenatal classes find they learn things you cannot
learn from books which include: what having a baby is really like;
what looking after a new baby is really like; routine procedures in
local hospitals; practical methods for coping with labour; different
experiences of labour, home birth, Dominos and individual
hospitals. One can never be completely prepared for the reality of
parenthood, but learning about it in different ways can help.

The other benefits of antenatal classes include the chance to be
with a group of people at about the same stage of pregnancy;
opportunities to ask questions; and being able to discuss different
aspects of labour, birth and parenthood with other prospective
parents. Antenatal classes can be enjoyable social occasions,
giving the members the opportunity to share worries, make new
friends and to discuss the details of all aspects of birth without
boring friends who have not yet had children or who are too
experienced to interact in the same way.

*How do NHS and National Childbirth Trust
classes differ?*

NCT classes tend to be smaller (a maximum of eight couples or 12
women per teacher) so they can be tailored to the needs of the
group. They are often held in the evenings and include fathers.
They are usually held in the teacher's home, and are private so
there is normally a fee payable ranging from about £30 to £60 per
course of eight classes. Subsidized places are usually available for
those who have difficulty meeting the cost. Most NCT teachers are

not medically qualified, but all have undergone a thorough training which includes learning teaching skills. All NCT teachers have had a baby themselves. Parents automatically receive help with breastfeeding and postnatal support. By hearing about routine procedures in different hospitals, parents can obtain an overall view. There is an emphasis on self-help methods for coping with labour combined with reliable information on the advantages and disadvantages of artificial pain relief and obstetric procedures. The NCT encourages its teachers to maintain a balance between information, discussion and physical preparation. Parents are encouraged to think about the choices open to them in labour and birth and to choose for themselves on the basis of the factors which are most important to them. NCT classes are very popular and so you need to book early: look in your local telephone directory or contact NCT headquarters.

NHS classes are taken by midwives, health visitors, or occasionally obstetric physiotherapists and doctors, who have not necessarily had any training in teaching skills. They usually take place in hospitals, but may also be held in local clinics by community midwives. There is usually not as much time available for discussion as in NCT classes because classes are larger. They are one way of finding out the hospital procedures and policies on specific aspects of labour and birth. Good NHS antenatal preparation is consistent with what actually happens in the labour ward of a particular hospital and prepares women for early discharge after the birth. Many NHS classes teach women how to change nappies, bath the baby, etc, and have more of a 'parentcraft' emphasis. There is often a tour of the labour ward, organized separately from the other classes, which women and labour partners can attend, even if they choose not to go to hospital classes. Most hospitals try to provide antenatal classes for all first-time mothers. You will be told when they are or you can ask at the hospital antenatal clinic.

Do I need to go to hospital classes if I am booked into NCT classes?

Many women like to attend both, welcoming the opportunity to learn as much as they can and to meet more women having babies at the same time. For others, perhaps with less time, and who are attending NCT classes with their partners, they may be less important. You can choose, but most women and their labour partners find it very useful at least to go on the tour of the labour ward which usually forms part of NHS classes: this is a way of finding out exactly how to get there at all times of day and night (when the main door of the hospital may be closed) and what extra equipment you may want to take in to make you as comfortable as possible during labour.

What are active birth classes?

They are private classes (for which a fee is payable) run by teachers trained by the Active Birth Movement (see Useful Organizations). They are usually held for groups of women at different stages of pregnancy (which gives different learning opportunities) and concentrate on physical preparation for labour, combining yoga-based stretching exercises, breathing and relaxation with positions for labour. Some active birth teachers also hold fathers' evenings and full antenatal courses, covering similar ground to NCT classes.

Active birth classes may be particularly useful if you are hoping to achieve a drug-free labour and/or having a home birth. Many women find they are complementary to NCT classes, as they concentrate almost entirely on physical preparation. As most active birth teachers hold a weekly class which women join at any time during their pregnancy, when vacancies are created by other women having their babies, members can obtain the benefits of group support as well as the exercises for a larger part of their pregnancy, not just during the last three months, as is the case with NCT and NHS classes. Many NCT antenatal teachers include elements of active birth in their classes.

How do I choose classes?

Ask other people what they thought of the classes they attended. Questions you could ask the teacher or Parentcraft Coordinator at your hospital include:

Is there time for discussion?
Do you talk about hospital procedures?
Do you teach relaxation, positions and breathing for labour?
Do you talk about the postnatal period?
Do you have any expectations about the sort of birth your clients should aim for?
How big are the classes?
Are fathers welcome and included?
What about breastfeeding?
What happens if I miss a class?
Will I meet other women having a home birth or a Domino?
Is everyone a first-timer?
Are postnatal exercise classes available?

How do I book classes?

The hospital (usually the antenatal clinic) will tell you which course of NHS classes is available for you, but ask if they are not mentioned. For NCT classes, look in your local telephone directory or ring the HQ number (081-992 8637) for your nearest branch: a bookings secretary will put you in touch with a local teacher. NCT classes get booked up very quickly, so book as soon as you can. The Active Birth Movement (see Useful Organizations) may be able to put you in touch with a local active birth teacher. You may hear on the grapevine about independent antenatal teachers, or sometimes they advertise in the local newspaper. If they do not belong to a recognized organization, it is important to check out their credentials locally. Ask to speak to other women who have already been to classes or ask a local midwife.

I can't get into antenatal classes, what can I do?

Unfortunately, some NHS hospitals do not have enough classes for everyone and some private maternity units do not offer classes at all. You may be able to find an active birth or independent antenatal teacher in your area by asking your friends, your GP or a community midwife. Sometimes, people drop out of classes and you might be able to get a waiting-list place.

If there really is nothing available, read this book and the NCT's *Pregnancy and Parenthood* which describes in detail ways of coping with labour and gives a lot of information about all aspects of pregnancy, labour, birth and after, including hospital procedures. You could read some of the other books in the Bibliography, and popular magazines for parents are a good way of learning about other people's experiences. There are many TV and radio programmes and videos (see Bibliography) which are useful.

Try to spend some time every day trying out positions, relaxation and breathing awareness for labour and also practise them in your daily life; the techniques are useful for any stressful situation. Also try to spend some time once or twice a week practising with your labour partner and talking about your hopes and fears for labour.

8: When the unexpected happens: special needs

I had bleeding at eight weeks and now at twelve weeks. My GP says it is all right to carry on as normal, but would it be safer to have bed-rest?

You can choose which course of action you feel happier with. The true miscarriage rate is thought to be one in five, including miscarriages which are often perceived by women to be a period which has come late and is heavier than usual. It is also thought that many of these miscarriages are due to there being something wrong with the fetus, so that a miscarriage is nature's way of taking care of the problem. Therefore current thinking is that if there is something wrong with the fetus and if you carry on as normal, you are letting nature take its own course. Moreover, there is no evidence to show that in otherwise healthy women bed-rest prevents miscarriage. It is very common for women to bleed at the times when they would have had periods during the first three months: it seems that the pregnancy hormone does not entirely outbalance the hormones of the menstrual cycle. In such cases, the rest of the pregnancy usually proceeds normally and they produce healthy babies.

I've just discovered I'm having triplets. How on earth shall I cope?

Giving birth to 'super twins' (another name for multiple births) brings its own joys and problems. The number of multiple births has increased appreciably during the last decade with the increasing availability of *in vitro fertilisation* (IVF) and *gametes intra-fallopian transfer* (GIFT). In 1982 70 sets of triplets were born; in 1989 there were 183 sets of triplets.

As you are an 'interesting' case, you are likely to receive good antenatal care, with high involvement from your consultant. As triplets are often born prematurely, it is important that you are booked for delivery in a hospital with a grade one special care baby unit, that is one where, if necessary, babies can be artificially ventilated for as long as they need. In this way, if any of your triplets are born with problems, they will get the best possible care from the start.

You can use the time of your pregnancy to work on strategies for coping with the babies once you get home. It may help to ask yourself and your partner the following questions: Will your house or flat be big enough for the sudden influx of three new family members? Do you have family, neighbours and friends who could help with feeding and changing the babies? Can you afford paid help? What help is available from your local council? Can you get hold of second-hand equipment and clothes for the babies? Do you qualify for any benefits from the Department of Social Security? You can contact TAMBA and the Multiple Births Foundation, both of which can help with practical information and put you in touch with other parents of triplets for informal support (see Useful Organizations). TAMBA local groups recycle clothes and equipment. There are also a number of books on the subject of multiple births (see Bibliography). You might also like to talk to an NCT breastfeeding counsellor about breastfeeding triplets.

> *At 30 weeks my blood pressure has risen sharply and they want to admit me into hospital. I feel I could rest more effectively at home – my mother could come and look after me. Can I choose to stay at home?*

It is your choice whether you stay at home or go into hospital, but the hospital may feel they can look after you better and monitor you more efficiently if you are there. However, it may be possible for a community midwife or your GP to take your blood pressure once or twice a day at home or at a nearby clinic or surgery; or the hospital may be able to supply a machine whereby your blood pressure reading could be transmitted over the telephone. Even fetal heart rate monitoring can be done over the telephone if the right equipment is available. Another possibility is that the hospital has a day-care ward where you could be admitted for one or two days a week, going home at night, for special monitoring: many women, especially those with young children at home, find this an acceptable compromise if they are able to make arrangements to go in just for a day. You can ask if any of these alternatives is available for you.

> *If the baby is going to be handicapped, what are our choices?*

If you have had amniocentesis or chorionic villus sampling with a positive result, you can choose whether or not to have a termination. In some hospitals parents are shocked to find they are automatically expected to have a termination. Even if you choose this form of fetal screening on the basis that you would terminate the pregnancy if the result turned out to be positive, you (and your partner) may feel differently once you confront the choice in reality. The voluntary organization SATFA (see Useful Organizations) gives information and support both before and after late termination for fetal abnormality.

The hospital may arrange for you to see a geneticist or other counsellor to help give you information about the condition. If you need time to consider your decision, take it. You may find things become clearer for you once you are at home and in your own surroundings. You can speak to an appropriate consultant who will advise you as to the probable outcome of the pregnancy if it continues, and the quality of life for the child. Some conditions are easier for parents to decide about than others. If you need general counselling, ask for it if the hospital has not offered it; some maternity units have an obstetric counsellor, while others have members of their psychiatric department who have a special interest in counselling people with obstetric problems.

If the condition of the baby is one that would be 'compatible with life' – sadly, not all are – it may be helpful for you to contact a self-help group who can talk to you about life with such a child and often have useful literature for you to read: this is certainly the case with Down's syndrome and certain other conditions. Your hospital should have a list of such groups (see also Useful Organizations).

Even though certain conditions mean that the baby will die during or shortly after birth, some women decide to continue the pregnancy and 'let nature take its course', allowing the baby to live as long as he or she is able without life support. It has been found that women who choose this course and then give birth, may find it easier to grieve than those who terminate the pregnancy earlier.

What if the condition becomes apparent only at birth?

The choices will depend on whether the baby's condition is compatible with life. Appropriate consultant doctors will be on hand to give information about the prognosis for the baby and to discuss the advantages and disadvantages of different courses of action. A hospital with a good neonatal unit will give a very ill baby maximum intensive care from the start, since immediate care has been shown to achieve a better outcome for babies.

If there is nothing to be done for the baby, parents are given the time they need to assimilate that news and then, in their own time, if they choose, give basic care to the baby, and, if appropriate, let him or her die in their arms. Witnessing a baby's death in this way may for some parents be the best ending for their short relationship with the baby.

There are many conditions which, while being a shock and disappointment for the parents, nevertheless can be treated with good results. Conditions such as club foot, cleft palate and dislocated hips can be treated very effectively. Parents, supported by good information from consultant doctors, can join in choosing when their children should receive surgery or other treatments. Some parents choose to go to another hospital for treatment from a particular specialist or for private care. There are many self-help groups which offer networks of informal support and excellent practical information on coping (see Useful Organizations). NCT breastfeeding counsellors support women feeding babies with conditions such as cleft palate and the NCT postnatal support network includes special support and resources for parents with disabled children or who are themselves disabled.

Can I breastfeed if the baby is in special care for weeks or even months?

If babies are very small or very ill they cannot suck at the breast, but they can be fed your own breastmilk (expressed using an electric breast pump) through a tube. If you maintain your milk supply in this way, eventually the baby will be able to breastfeed. Breastmilk is very good for ill or premature babies, protecting them against potentially fatal infection. Mothers who express milk feel that at least they are able to do something for their babies which no machine can do.

Where possible, holding the baby next to the skin also helps keep the milk supply going, even if the baby is still too small to feed (the sucking reflex may not yet have developed). The NCT has a national network of agents who hire out electric breast pumps for mothers to use at home; the agents are often breastfeeding counsellors. All NCT breastfeeding counsellors are trained to support mothers wishing to breastfeed babies in special care and can be an invaluable support when a baby is ready to establish proper breastfeeding.

9: When the baby dies

Why did this happen to me?

There is no answer to this question and nothing anyone can say can make it feel better. Feelings of confusion, denial, guilt and anger are normal parts of the grieving process. It is easy to feel isolated too, but the experience is more common than any of us care to think. Parents who have lost babies and use the opportunities they have to talk and express their feelings, to each other, relatives, friends and professional counsellors and therapists, as appropriate for them, will eventually be able to resolve the experience and take up the reins of normal life again. This takes time; bereaved parents can choose to grieve for as long as it takes them to mourn the loss of their child. Some parents find it therapeutic to write an account of what happened; this can be destroyed or kept with family papers for the future. Parents do not always grieve at the same pace; it is important to be aware of this and at certain times it may be easier to talk to an outsider about certain aspects than to your partner.

What do we say to our other children?

SANDS (see Useful Organizations) produces an excellent leaflet called *What to tell your other children*. Generally, to tell them that the baby died and, if appropriate, that it didn't grow properly or that no one knows why it died, will be enough. The children will ask questions as needed, provided they are given the opportunity. They will want to share your grief and to comfort you if you let them. Children need to know that babies are especially vulnerable and that they themselves are old enough and healthy enough not to be at risk of dying.

The baby was only 24 weeks, can we have a funeral?

Yes, you can; funerals are usually possible for babies from 20 weeks' gestation. There is usually someone in the hospital who will be able to talk to you about the practicalities and what the hospital can offer: it may be the chaplain, the bereavement officer or someone else. Sometimes hospitals have a special burial place in a local cemetery for small babies, which is cheaper than paying for your own plot (unless your family already has a plot). The hospital will be able to make arrangements for you, unless you choose to make these yourselves.

Although it is a painful task, many parents derive great satisfaction from arranging, usually with a minister of their religion, an appropriate service and cremation or burial. This can give parents a ritual which they may choose to share with family and/or friends to mark the sad end of a pregnancy or short life and can become something good to be remembered. The hospital bereavement officer or your minister of religion will have details of undertakers with experience of funerals for small babies. You can take time over your decision; the hospital will keep the baby in the mortuary until you decide what to do.

At what gestation does the baby have to be registered?

Since the new legislation, 24 weeks. Before that time, the loss of a baby is legally a late miscarriage.

My baby died at 26 weeks, the day after she was born. Why couldn't I choose a Caesarean section?

Although the Caesarean section rate is rising (see Birth Statistics), it still remains a major operation which carries risks for the mother. General anaesthetic is nowadays the main cause of maternal death in childbirth. It has been shown that women who have a Caesarean section have greater problems dealing with their grief and may be more likely to have their grief compounded by postnatal depression, since Caesarean delivery is a predisposing factor for this. (All major operations can cause depression.) Performing a Caesarean section safely is also problematic when a woman is less than 30 weeks pregnant. The uterus is still relatively small and it is difficult to avoid damage to blood vessels and other tissue. The scar tissue resulting from early Caesarean section can reduce fertility. Therefore, it is considered good obstetric practice to avoid Caesarean section whenever possible.

When a baby as young as 26 weeks' gestation is born, the chances of survival are low. It is often felt that if a baby is well enough to survive the first stage of labour, it will be born in as good a condition as possible in the circumstances. Forceps may be used to protect the head. If the baby does not survive the first stage, its death is considered to have been probable even with all possible interventions. The doctors providing care weigh up the costs and potential benefits to the parents and the baby very carefully, taking all the known factors into account. If in their clinical judgement a Caesarean section is not advisable, a choice will not be offered. There are some occasions when the knowledge and experience of doctors is invaluable. If you have any doubts or queries, it is your right to ask and their duty to explain.

I've just heard my baby has died inside me. I just can't face going through labour now.

Giving birth to a baby you know is going to be born dead is a very difficult experience, but there are ways of minimizing the distress to both parents. Unless labour starts spontaneously, the parents can choose when to go in for the induction. Most parents choose to induce the birth fairly soon so the appearance of the baby does not deteriorate or because they don't want to leave it too long. Parents can ask for a room in a quiet part of the delivery ward. Sometimes it is possible to give birth in the gynaecology department of a hospital, but there may be problems if there is an emergency or if the woman wants to have an epidural. The hospital should assign an experienced midwife to be present throughout the whole labour, so as to build up a relationship with the parents and give them appropriate support. As a Syntocinon drip (see Glossary) is often needed to induce or accelerate the labour, women may choose to have an epidural (see page 97) or other artificial pain relief. Before the birth, both parents can choose whether they want to see the baby straight away or after he or she has been washed and dressed.

Many parents choose to hold and examine their babies so they have some memory as a basis for their grief. Whatever the parents decide, polaroid photographs are usually taken of the baby and kept with the hospital notes so they are available for the parents to have at any time, even years after the birth. Some parents choose to have a photograph taken of themselves holding the baby, which may become a treasured family possession. Some parents like to have a portrait drawn from a photograph.

Hospitals generally like to keep the mother in for one night for observation and are usually able to find her a room to herself which her partner can share: a camp-bed is often kept for this purpose.

Some women choose to return to the antenatal ward (if perhaps they had spent a length of time there) to benefit from the support of the midwives and doctors they know, and the other women. Other women are able to stay on the labour ward. Hospitals try to be flexible in the way they accommodate women after the loss of a baby: how exactly they do it will depend on the facilities and geography of each hospital. SANDS (see Useful Organizations) can be very helpful immediately after the birth as well as later.

Is it true that women produce milk after a stillbirth?

This must be one of the cruellest things that nature does. Many women produce milk even after a late miscarriage and it appears to be more likely if they have breastfed in the past. Women are often offered a drug by the hospital to take for 14 days or so after delivery to prevent their milk coming in. In practice, this suppresses lactation which may then occur when the woman stops taking the drug. Distressing though this is, some women find it easier to cope with lactation two weeks or so after the birth rather than two days or so after: it is a personal choice for the woman. Current evidence shows that the most effective and safest drug is bromoergocriptine and that women can themselves help suppress lactation (either with or without the drug) by limiting their fluid intake and binding their breasts: experienced midwives can usually show a woman how to do this.

Is there someone I can talk to?

You may find it sufficient to talk to your partner, to relatives or to friends. Some women talk to the people who looked after them during the pregnancy and birth: their GP, hospital doctors and midwives, community midwife, health visitor or sometimes their NCT antenatal teacher. Other people prefer to go to a trained counsellor or psychotherapist. There may be counselling or psychotherapy services available at your hospital, at your GP's practice (some practices have psychiatric nurses who support families in many ways) or you may be referred elsewhere. Some local authorities run free or subsidized counselling services. (See also Useful Organizations)

Why don't you leave us alone? We want to forget about it and get on with the rest of our lives.

Everyone copes with loss in their own way, but it has been shown that people who do not complete the grieving process are likely to suffer depression or other psychological problems in the future. Talking about the experience over and over again can help resolve it; the expression of feelings which often accompanies the reliving of the experience can be therapeutic. You may find that you are too close to the experience to talk about it now, but that in a few weeks' or months' time you are distanced enough from the experience to look at it again and deal with any unresolved feelings.

They say we should wait six months before trying again. Why is this?

There is no universally agreed best time to try for another baby and much will depend on the stage of pregnancy at which you lost your baby. Six months is quite frequently given as a gap long enough for the woman's body to have got back to normal and for her to have regained her menstrual pattern, but for some women even this is physically, not to say emotionally, too early. It is often said that it takes a woman a year to get completely back to normal after childbirth, but for some couples, particularly if they feel time is running out, this may be too long to wait. Many couples become pregnant again quite quickly, often unintentionally, because there is a great need to prove to themselves (sometimes unconsciously) that they can produce a live, healthy baby.

From a psychological and emotional point of view, couples are often advised to wait a year before trying again so that they are able to cope with the baby's due date (if born before term) and the anniversary of the death without the distraction of another pregnancy, or even a baby, if the woman becomes pregnant again very quickly. It is well established that a pregnant woman cannot grieve fully, so the danger is that if she starts another baby too early, once he or she is born, she may find herself depressed and unable to enjoy her new baby because she is now doing the grieving work for her previous loss.

Each couple should feel able to decide what is the right choice for them. Provided they remain aware of the possible consequences of their choice and seek and/or accept support as it becomes necessary, they are likely to cope.

10: Self-help and natural therapies

There are many ways in which women can help themselves cope with labour, but always one of the great unknowns is how long labour will last. 71 per cent of the respondents to the *Good Housekeeping* Survey were in labour for 12 hours or less; 18 per cent for 13 to 24 hours; and 6 per cent for over 24 hours. At some stages during labour 32 per cent coped with contractions by sitting upright; 26 per cent squatted; 8 per cent went on all fours; 5 per cent used a bath or birthing pool; and 4 per cent used a birthing stool. In 1990 the National Council of Women did a survey called, *Are we fit for the 90s?*, to which over 9,000 women responded: 53 per cent of them said they had insufficient information on natural childbirth.

> ***I want to avoid drugs and medical interventions in labour as far as possible. How can I best prepare myself?***

First, it is important that you inform yourself about the process of labour, including the complications that can occur, and about the wide range of experiences which are possible. You can do this by reading books (see Bibliography), attending good antenatal classes and talking with other women and couples about their own experiences, but beware of the horror stories which some women seem to delight in telling to newly pregnant women. It may also be helpful for your partner to talk to other people, both men and women, who have supported a woman in labour. In this way you can acquire a realistic idea of what may happen, of women's experiences of the pain of labour, artificial pain relief and medical interventions, routine and otherwise.

Secondly, it is important for you to prepare your body physically by practising relaxation, breathing awareness, different positions and touch, both on your own and with your labour partner. These techniques may by learned at NCT, active birth, yoga and other antenatal classes and from books. However, classes are not enough, particularly if your labour partner does not attend: the bodywork needs to be practised a few times a week, so the techniques become second nature. Just as pelvic floor exercises can become automatic, something you can do every time you make a telephone call, boil a kettle or wash your hands, so relaxation techniques can be used every time you find yourself feeling tense in a traffic jam, at a difficult meeting or waiting for an antenatal appointment. Use the Braxton Hicks contractions (see Glossary), if you are aware of them, and the aches, pains and twinges many pregnant women experience to practise your coping techniques for labour. Labour contractions will feel different, but if the techniques are second nature, you will be able to respond to labour in a way that maximizes your own resources.

Thirdly, you need to integrate all your knowledge of labour and the ways of coping with it, by rehearsing in your head, or verbally with your labour partner or other pregnant women, various situations which might happen in labour, normal and abnormal, and the ways in which you would prefer to deal with them. For instance, one woman might decide that although she would prefer to do without drugs for a normal labour, if she had a Syntocinon drip for induction or acceleration of labour, she would probably choose to have an epidural (see Glossary) to cope with the extra, synthetically-produced pain. Another woman might decide that even if there was time to put up an epidural for an emergency Caesarean section, she would prefer to be unconscious for the operation. It is tempting in pregnancy to go through the motions of antenatal classes, exercises, etc, and not do any of this thinking, assuming 'it will be all right on the night'. The chances are that it will be, but if you are unlucky enough for complications to occur, you will be better able to meet them confidently if you have spent some time preparing yourself for the unexpected.

Will the hospital help us with our self-help techniques?

This varies from hospital to hospital, from midwife to midwife and doctor to doctor. Many hospitals now offer equipment to assist upright positions for labour, such as special low beds, birthing chairs, birthing stools, bean-bags and large cushions. Some hospitals have large baths for waterbirths. Ask your hospital what is available and how likely your chosen equipment is to be free on the day. Try it out on the labour ward tour: some women are surprised to find their feelings about different sorts of equipment confirmed or overturned by seeing and trying them. Very often women are expected to use equipment such as a birthing chair just for delivery or the second stage of labour, so if you want to try, remember to ask to use them in the first stage also. Even if equipment is proudly displayed on the labour ward tour, it may be forgotten when you are admitted in labour, so make sure you or your partner ask for what you need, particularly if only some of the delivery rooms have the specially adaptable beds.

More and more midwives and doctors are becoming tolerant of self-help techniques and more upright positions and are prepared to examine and deliver women however and wherever they feel most comfortable, be it on a bed, on a birthing chair, on a mattress on the floor or in a birthing pool. Some midwives and doctors will also offer creative support by becoming one of the team with you and your labour partner, encouraging you in your chosen relaxation and breathing techniques, suggesting changes of position (perhaps when you and your labour partner have run out of ideas) and generally using their knowledge, experience and confidence to assist you in your chosen way of dealing with labour. Sometimes student midwives, nurses and doctors are thrilled to attend an active labour and come in very useful for physical as well as emotional support, for example when a woman needs to be held in some form of supported squat!

Other midwives and doctors have been trained to care for women in labour in a more conventional way and are concerned about their ability to examine a woman in a position they are not familiar with, such as on all fours, or to deliver her baby whilst she is standing on the floor.

Once you know the sort of methods you want to use for coping with labour, ask at antenatal classes and appointments about staff attitudes to them. Your preferences can be put in a birth plan (see Chapter 14), discussed with a doctor and attached to your notes. When you are admitted in labour, if there are enough midwives on duty, you may be assigned a midwife who will feel positively about the opportunity to care for a woman wanting to rely as far as possible on her own resources.

Will the hospital let us bring in our own cushions and other equipment?

It is useful for both you and your labour partner to go on a tour of the labour ward. Some hospitals have available large cushions, bean-bags and extra pillows, while others are less well equipped. On the whole, hospitals are tolerant of people bringing in their own equipment, so you may choose to supplement what the hospital has to offer, provided there is room. Many hospitals do not allow large items like portable birthing pools because small delivery rooms do not have enough space. Taking in your own possessions is a way of making yourself and your labour partner as comfortable as possible and also of making the delivery room your own territory. Some people find music helps them to relax, but be prepared for every person who comes through the door to comment on your choice!

Can I have a water birth in hospital?

More and more women are choosing to give birth in this way and, gradually, hospitals are installing large-sized baths and birthing pools. If your local hospitals do not offer this option, ask if you can take in a portable birthing pool (see Useful Organizations). If not, you may have to compromise by using an ordinary bath for pain relief in the first stage of labour. You can use your own bath at home, before you go into hospital. With help, even in a standard-sized bath you can get into an upright position for contractions and lie down and relax in between. If you use an ordinary bath in hospital for pain relief, ask your labour partner to clean it thoroughly with a cleanser or disinfectant and your own personal cloth (taken in specially for the purpose – also useful for your postnatal hospital stay) to reduce the risk of infection. The hospital may advise you against a bath once your waters have broken. If having a bath in hospital is not an option, taking a long warm shower may be beneficial. (See Bibliography)

I always practise my breathing for labour to a relaxation tape; supposing we can't play it?

It is unlikely that anyone, either at home or in hospital, will prevent you from playing your tape. If anyone does object, you could always ask them the reason. More important, though, you may find that the tape, whilst perfect for practising, does nothing for you in labour, or for some parts of labour, so it is probably wise to practise your breathing without the tape in all kinds of situations so you are not exclusively dependent on it to relax.

Do homoeopathic remedies interfere with artificial pain relief?

So far as is known they do not, but there have been no studies to demonstrate whether this is so. Many people who use homoeopathy, either on their own or with a qualified practitioner (see Useful Organizations), choose to do so in labour. As with other conditions and processes, both physical and psychological, homoeopathic remedies will not take the pain away nor have any dramatic effect, but *if properly chosen* may enhance the woman's own physical and psychological abilities for giving birth using her own resources. However, among certain homoeopaths, there is concern that unqualified people are using remedies for labour, in potencies that are too high and therefore running the risk of adversely affecting the normal course of labour if wrongly chosen. Some homoeopaths have prepared lists of remedies in high potency for individual women which are then passed around among women who do not understand their effects and who have not consulted a homoeopath to see if the remedies are suitable for them. You and your partner may choose to consult a qualified homoeopath experienced in prescribing for labour who will give you a list of remedies tailored for your needs.

Although commonly advised, it is unwise to take Caulophyllum or any other homoeopathic remedy prophylactically; all remedies for labour should be taken only if they are needed and match the woman's symptoms. If the homoeopath will not be attending labour, and you and your partner want to use remedies, it may be a helpful safeguard to take no potencies stronger than six so that if you choose the wrong remedy, the effects will wear off quickly. Some homoeopaths stay in touch with labour partners over the telephone, being consulted as necessary. The right choice of remedy is said to assist with interventions such as induction or assisted delivery but there have been no controlled trials. You can check with the hospital that no one will object to your taking homoeopathic remedies during labour.

Would the hospital allow me to bring in my acupuncturist to assist with pain relief?

It is unlikely that they will object since acupuncture is recognized by the medical profession as giving effective pain relief. You will have to discuss it with a doctor or midwife at an antenatal appointment and have his/her permission written into your notes, so whoever attends you during labour will see that you have gone through the proper channels.

In China, where acupuncture is a very popular system of medicine, women rarely use acupuncture for labour. In this country, some acupuncturists find that clients of theirs who have received treatment during pregnancy tend to have fairly quick, straightforward labours which they manage to cope with on their own, using self-help techniques.

The father of my baby won't be around, could I bring a friend as well as my mum to the birth?

Even if the father of their baby is to be present at the birth, women often find it helpful to have a second labour partner. At some home births (and a few hospital ones), whole families are present because it is part of their culture or personal preference. Hospital midwives often look after more than one woman at once, so it is in the interests of the hospital that you are well supported, since it is unlikely that a midwife will be able to be with you all the time. It is advisable to write in your birth plan, or have it written into your notes at a hospital antenatal appointment, that you intend bringing in two labour partners. You might also think about how you intend to use your two partners. Some women like their mothers just to be present and observe the labour and birth whilst their other labour partner takes a more active supporting role, assisting with relaxation, breathing awareness and touch, etc. Other women use their labour partners interchangeably, the labour partners taking it in turns to have breaks.

I don't want to be induced, but I'm a week overdue. Can I do anything about it?

If all is well with you and the baby, the hospital or your midwife should give you the chance to go into labour spontaneously up to 42 weeks, or even longer. Meanwhile, there is a whole range of things you could try to get the labour going. Many women have found a combination of long walks, hot curries, making love so they have an orgasm and even a dose of castor oil taken in a glass of orange juice does the trick if their bodies are ready to go into labour. If you use a qualified homoeopath or acupuncturist, they may be able to help you. If your cervix is soft, your midwife or doctor may give you a 'sweep' to stimulate labour while giving you an internal examination. A finger is gently inserted into the cervix and swept around between the uterus and the membranes: it is painful, so breathing techniques learned for labour can be helpful.

I am very extrovert; will they mind if I shout?

On the whole, you can assume that doctors and midwives experienced in supporting women in labour will be used to women making a noise. In some cultures, women are positively encouraged to vocalize and their attendants may join in with songs, chants, etc. Most people find it difficult to watch a person in pain, even in labour when pain is more often part of the process than a sign that there is something wrong. Many midwives and doctors have resolved their own feelings about this and allow the woman to express herself in any way she likes. Others find witnessing evidence of pain so difficult that they may strongly encourage women to have Pethidine or an epidural, regardless of any lack of request for artificial pain relief.

It is sometimes difficult for people present at a labour to remember that for many women making a noise is a way of coping. This is an issue not only for the professional attendants but for your labour partner as well, so it is important that he/she has the chance to discuss it both with you and people who have been labour supporters in the past. It is worth remembering that labour partners are themselves a form of pain relief; studies have shown that women whose partners support them in the self-help techniques learned antenatally need less artificial pain relief than women without this valuable form of support.

Is it possible to avoid tearing at delivery?

The idea of your delicate tissue tearing may sound alarming. Most women who experience a tear find the time taken for the tear to heal painful, but the moment of the tear of relatively little significance. As the baby's head is born some women experience a burning feeling as the tissue of the perineum is stretched; many women are vividly aware of the baby's head coming down the vagina, while others have no particular sensation, the tissue being numb, due to the pressure of the baby's head. Sometimes a tear is unavoidable if the baby's head or shoulders are very big or if the baby is born quickly, but there are several ways in which you can minimize the risk of tearing.

By practising pelvic floor exercises during pregnancy you will build up strength, suppleness and awareness of the perineum and be more able to relax that part of you during the second stage. Some women massage their perineum with vegetable oil, such as Vitamin E or olive (not mineral) oil, for the last few weeks of their pregnancy and, sometimes with their partner, practise stretching the vaginal opening to make it more elastic for birth. There is no formal evidence that this works, but many women believe it has helped them avoid perineal injury and many couples enjoy incorporating the massage and stretching into their lovemaking at a time when the growing baby may make their usual ways of making love uncomfortable.

During the second stage of labour, it is important that you work with your midwife (who will take a professional pride in delivering you with an intact perineum) to deliver the baby's head in a controlled way in an upright position. Research shows that getting into an upright position during the second stage not only reduces the number of tears, but also shortens the second stage and reduces the rate of assisted deliveries. (The only exception to this is when a woman sits on a birthing chair, for which there is evidence that tears in the labia, the tissue in front of the vagina, are more common.) When the baby's head is about to be born, if you have practised panting for labour, you will be more able to cooperate with the midwife when she instructs you to 'stop pushing, pant' and allow the uterus to push out your baby unaided. Some midwives 'guard' the perineum by holding it as the baby's head is born; others massage the perineum with vegetable oil during second stage to help it stretch, or hold a hot pad or compress against it; others believe that to touch the perineum in any way increases the risk of a tear. Probably any method the midwife is happy and experienced with is likely to be effective if you work with her.

SUMMARY OF CHOICES FOR SELF-HELP AND NATURAL THERAPIES IN LABOUR

Relaxation Being aware of physical tension and being able to relax consciously both during and between contractions helps prevent or reduce pain or makes it easier to cope with and allows your body to work efficiently, as well as keeping up your energy.

Upright positions Your body will tell you which position is most comfortable at each stage of your labour.

Changing position and moving When a position stops working, change it and don't get stuck into any one position for too long. Hourly visits to the lavatory while you feel mobile are helpful. Many women find pelvic rocking and other rhythmic movements help with the pain.

Breathing awareness Concentrating on breaths out, letting the breaths in take care of themselves and breathing as slowly and deeply as you can aids relaxation, ensures plenty of oxygen for the baby, efficient working of the uterus and good energy levels for you. Antenatal teachers teach various techniques.

Touch and massage Maintains contact between you and your labour partner so long contractions do not feel lonely. Massage can be a great aid to localized pain in the lower back, hips and thighs.

Darkness It has been shown that darkness enhances the production of endorphins in labouring women and some women automatically close their eyes when a contraction comes. If you prefer, lights can be dimmed and curtains or blinds closed. Remember to dim the lights again if they have been switched on for a vaginal examination.

Visualization Some women find picturing a scene far removed from their labour, or visualizing their cervix opening, a good way of getting through contractions.

Making a noise Moaning, grunting, singing and chanting are time-honoured ways of coping with labour. Some people learn songs backwards for use in transition!

Eye contact and focussing Many women find focussing on their partner's eyes, on flowers, a picture or something else in the room, helpful for dealing with strong contractions.

Food and drink Essential for the labour partner, who in hospital may not be offered even a cup of tea. Many women are not hungry or thirsty during labour (the digestion slows down, although metabolism rises to 700 to 1,000 calories per hour) but just need sips of liquid to moisten their mouths. However, you may find yourself ravenous after delivery, with hours to go before the next meal, so make sure there is food in the labour bag for you too.

Many hospitals discourage or forbid eating and drinking during labour in case a general anaesthetic is necessary, because inhalation of stomach contents may damage the lungs. Research has shown, however, that inhalation does not occur if the anaesthetic is properly administered and that the acid juices of an empty stomach are more damaging than partially digested food. If you are hungry, you can choose to eat. Even if you are sick later on in labour, you may feel better having something to be sick on.

Props and equipment Using some of the following may help you: large cushions; a bucket to sit on; a rubber ball for massage; an upright chair on which to sit astride; a rocking chair; a birthing stool; a foot stool; a child's plastic step; a Gardosi cushion (see Glossary); a birthing chair; a special hospital birthing bed. Also, a sponge for mopping your brow, an ice pack and a flannel to use as a hot compress.

Music Music in a hospital delivery room has a miraculous effect on the atmosphere and many midwives and doctors appreciate it too. You may find you want different sorts of music at different times, or that, having carefully chosen a balance of tapes, music during contractions is too distracting. Some women take in special yoga or relaxation tapes to encourage slow, relaxed breathing.

Warm bath or shower Many women find warm water very soothing, especially in early labour at home.

Birthing pool More and more women are enjoying using these for labour, even if they decide to give birth 'on dry land'. If your hospital does not have a special pool or bath, you can hire one for use at home or in hospital (if the hospital agrees).

Natural therapies Many women find them helpful, although their use in labour has not been scientifically tested. Properly qualified practitioners may be found from the appropriate professional register (see Useful Organizations).

Homoeopathy: you can either pay a homoeopath to attend you during the labour or ask your labour partner (with instruction from a qualified homoeopath) to administer remedies. A homoeopath may also be willing to be consulted during labour over the telephone. Some midwives administer remedies.

Acupuncture: used for pain relief. Sometimes the acupuncturist inserts a needle connected to a machine which stimulates the needle to pulse and give more effective relief.

Hypnotherapy: hypnotherapists usually work with women from the beginning of pregnancy, teaching them self-hypnosis so they can induce a pain-distancing trance in themselves either for the duration of labour or for each individual contraction, whichever the woman finds more helpful.

Herbal remedies: best used in consultation with a qualified herbalist or naturopath.

Aromatherapy: some essential oils are said to enhance the progress of labour and help a woman to relax and cope with pain. A qualified aromatherapist will recommend a range of oils for use by each individual woman.

11: Routine medical procedures

A number of procedures are often carried out routinely during the course of a woman's labour. These and their timing will vary from hospital to hospital. There is sometimes an assumption underlying hospital policies that because some medical procedures carried out for high-risk women and babies improve the outcome of birth, if they are carried out for all women and babies they will improve the outcome overall. This is not borne out by research. Whilst certain procedures such as vaginal examinations, listening to the baby's heart rate periodically, temperature and blood pressure checks play an important part in observation and preventive care in every labour, this is not the case with all the procedures. Some are unnecessary and others may affect the course of labour and the woman's and baby's ability to cope.

One of the most controversial areas is routine continuous electronic fetal monitoring in labour. Research shows that this does not improve outcome unless accompanied by fetal scalp blood sampling, a more invasive procedure. In *The Guardian* of 1 May 1990, Dr Norman Davies, research fellow at the Harris Birthright Centre for Fetal Medicine at King's College, London, was quoted as saying: 'In an ideal world the machines would not be necessary. But in this country we are desperately short of trained midwives and a woman in labour will often have several different people looking after her. In these circumstances, it's safer to have a continuous record of what's happening. The big advantage of the electronic monitors is the trace, the hard copy that shows us what's happening. We're watching for shortage of oxygen and if you look at the worst possible interpretation of the trace, 50 per cent of women would need Caesareans. This is ridiculous, so another test is needed to interpret the trace.' In other words, he is saying staffing constraints in hospitals make electronic monitoring 'necessary' but that its use leads to intervention in too many cases – in many normal labours – unless further tests and careful evaluation follow.

Another controversial procedure is artificial rupture of the membranes (ARM) which sometimes needs to be carried out if it is feared that the baby is in distress. Breaking the waters will reveal whether the baby has passed meconium (see Glossary) and enable a fetal scalp electrode to be fastened to the baby's head if its heartbeat needs to be continuously and accurately monitored. However, in many hospitals, ARM is performed routinely on a woman's admission into hospital in labour, even if she is only two or three centimetres dilated. This is easily done, since it is a 'low-tech' procedure which can be carried out by a midwife on her own initiative or in accordance with hospital policy. The effect of ARM is usually to make the contractions more painful than they need to be. Following ARM, labour may be perceived to progress more quickly, but there is no guarantee that the labour will be shorter. Indeed, as a result, a woman may choose to have more artificial pain relief than she would otherwise have done, which in turn may affect the course of her labour and her baby's condition. For example, a woman may, after ARM, choose to have an epidural. This in turn may damp down the contractions so that a Syntocinon drip needs to be administered. The Syntocinon may make the baby tired and able to cope less well during the second stage; or the epidural may prevent the woman from being able to push the baby out herself; in both cases forceps may be needed to deliver the baby – the use of forceps is not a routine procedure. A procedure becomes an intervention when it changes the course of labour. The sort of sequence of events just described is sometimes referred to as a 'cascade of intervention'. (See Bibliography)

The number of routine procedures carried out may be affected by whether a woman's case is considered to be normal or abnormal. Another factor is at what stage of labour a woman chooses to go into hospital: a woman who is admitted towards the end of the first stage will have time to experience fewer routine procedures and interventions than a woman who chooses to go in earlier.

At a home birth, Domino scheme birth or GP unit birth, the midwife and/or GP attending the woman will usually have a more flexible and more conservative approach to the use of routine procedures.

SUMMARY OF ROUTINE PROCEDURES FOR LABOUR IN HOSPITAL

PROCEDURE	TIMING	REASONS
Vaginal examination	On admission and periodically until delivery	To check dilatation of cervix and position of baby. Kept to a minimum, usually every four hours, because of the risk of infection if done too frequently
Taking woman's temperature	On admission and periodically until delivery	Raised temperature could be sign of infection
Checking woman's blood pressure	On admission and periodically until delivery	Severely raised blood pressure could indicate pre-eclampsia, a dangerous condition for both mother and baby
Shaving woman's pubic hair	On admission	Intended to prevent infection. Full shaving is now rarely done because it does not prevent infection and the regrowth of hair is uncomfortable. Hair around the perineum may be clipped short to make stitching easier should it prove necessary
Giving an enema or suppositories	On admission	To reduce soiling and speed up labour. (Rarely done now because hazards outweigh benefits unless woman seriously constipated.) Some women may choose an enema so as to avoid feeling anxious about soiling the mattress
Bath or shower	On admission	To ensure woman clean. Risk of infection from bath if waters broken/unbroken: clean bath first
Monitoring baby's heartbeat for 20 mins using belt monitor or Sonicaid or fetal stethoscope	On admission and periodically until delivery	To check condition of baby and for insurance reasons

PROCEDURE	TIMING	REASONS
Monitoring strength of contractions for 20 mins using belt monitor	On admission and periodically until delivery	To check for effective contractions
Monitoring baby's heartbeat using belt monitor or fetal scalp electrode	Continuously until delivery	To give a printed record of baby's heartbeat, sometimes because of shortage of midwives
Asking woman to fast from food and drink	Until delivery	To prevent inhalation of stomach contents if general anaesthesia necessary: no evidence to support this practice which may make women weak
Giving woman antacid tablets, eg magnesium trisilicate	Periodically until delivery	To neutralize acid juices of empty stomach before or in case of general anaesthesia: not always effective
Artificial rupture of membranes (ARM)	On admission or at some other time before delivery; often as early as 2 cm dilatation before progressive labour has become established	Frequently performed to speed up labour or to see if baby has passed meconium (could be sign of distress)
Episiotomy	Before delivery	Frequently performed to speed up delivery or to prevent tearing of perineum
Injection in thigh of Syntometrine	After delivery of baby's first (anterior) shoulder	To speed up delivery of placenta and reduce risk of postpartum haemorrhage
Clamp and cut baby's umbilical cord	Immediately after delivery	To help deliver placenta quickly and prevent overtransfusion of baby with blood from placenta after strong contractions following giving of Syntometrine

NB It is important to read the discussions in this chapter about the pros and cons of each of the above procedures.

ROUTINE PROCEDURES EXPERIENCED BY RESPONDENTS TO
GOOD HOUSEKEEPING SURVEY

Monitoring baby's heartbeat
using fetal stethoscope	41 per cent
using belt monitor	51 per cent
using scalp electrode	26 per cent

Artificial rupture of membranes	43 per cent
Episiotomy	41 per cent
Syntometrine *(some women may have been unaware of the procedure)*	63 per cent

Those women having first babies experienced more routine procedures than those women who had other children. 63 per cent of the respondents thought the amount of intervention was about right.

Do I have to be examined every two hours?

The frequency of vaginal examinations will depend on the policies of the hospital, the usual practice of the midwives and doctors attending you, the course of your labour and the condition of yourself and your baby. It is good practice to maintain a balance between avoiding unnecessary invasion, with the attendant risk of infection, and carefully monitoring progress of labour and well-being. It is usual for vaginal examinations to be done every four hours.

It can be discouraging for you if there has been little progress in dilatation between frequent vaginal examinations. On the other hand, if you feel you want to use some form of artificial pain relief a vaginal examination may inform your decision. You might be encouraged to go on a bit longer without extra pain relief if you feel you are making real progress. Some women find vaginal examinations during labour very uncomfortable. The doctors and midwives will generally avoid examining you during a contraction, but you might ask to be examined in a position other than lying on your back, such as on all fours or in whatever position you happen to be. Alternatively, you may find it helps to have a little Entonox (gas and air) for the duration of the examination.

Another way for the midwives and doctors to assess dilatation of the cervix is to observe the red line that in most women (91 per cent) appears above the anus and extends upwards between the buttocks as the cervix dilates (it is thought to be caused by pressure on blood vessels as the baby's head descends).

Do they still shave you and give you an enema?

This is now very rare. If the procedures are still current in your hospital, you can choose to refuse them, since studies have shown that they are usually unnecessary and most women find the experience unpleasant.

I am worried about relieving myself during labour. What can I do?

It is very common for women, often while they are still at home, to evacuate their bowels in early labour quite spontaneously. Some women also vomit at the beginning of labour and it is as though their bodies were clearing out so they can concentrate on the task of labour. If you find this does not happen early on in labour you can choose if you wish to have suppositories to encourage evacuation of the bowel while you can still walk to the lavatory. Interestingly, in a study on enemas for labour, it was found that when women who had had enemas soiled the bed, the faecal matter was more difficult to clean up than from women who had not. Very rarely, now that more people are conscious of the importance of dietary fibre, a woman is so constipated that the hard faecal matter in her rectum prevents the descent and birth of the baby's head. In such a case she would be advised to have an enema at the beginning of labour to remove the obstruction.

I have a dread of episiotomy. Can I avoid it?

It is a sad fact that only about 20 per cent of women have an intact perineum after birth and some women have as great a dread of tearing as you do of having an episiotomy.

There are some occasions when episiotomy is medically necessary: when a baby is delivered by forceps or Ventouse (see Glossary); when a baby needs to be delivered quickly because it or its mother are showing distress in second stage; when a baby is born very premature and episiotomy can reduce the pressure on its head; and when the size of a baby makes a third-degree tear a high risk. If you found yourself in one of these situations, you might find yourself choosing to have an episiotomy.

On other occasions, midwives and doctors choose to perform routine episiotomy for the following sorts of reasons: they find episiotomies easier to stitch than tears; they prefer to cut the perineum rather than see it tear; the woman's consultant does not allow women in his/her care to tear; they believe a small episiotomy will prevent a large tear; their hospital policy is for every woman having her first baby to have an episiotomy. In one of these situations you might choose not to have one, on the grounds that episiotomy is not medically necessary.

Some women refuse a routine episiotomy on the grounds that they prefer to tear only as much as is necessary rather than have an episiotomy which may be larger than needed; an episiotomy cut always goes through all the layers of the perineum whereas it is possible for a tear to be superficial, affecting just the skin or the skin and the first layer of muscle underneath; many women find that tears heal more quickly than episiotomies, are less likely to become infected and are less likely to affect lovemaking later on.

Having established the hospital policy on episiotomy, you could write in your birth plan or have written in your notes that you would prefer not to have a routine episiotomy and that you would prefer to have an intact perineum after delivery. By preparing yourself for labour (see previous chapter) and working with your midwife in the second stage to deliver your baby in an upright position and in a gentle, controlled way, you have a good chance of ending up with an intact perineum.

Does breaking the waters speed up labour?

Research has shown that artificial rupture of the membranes (ARM) reduces the length of the first stage of labour by about an hour. However, women generally find that when the waters are broken contractions suddenly become stronger, more frequent and more painful. Once the cushion of amniotic fluid in front of the baby's head is removed, there is increased pressure on the baby's head. Some people believe that as, in the majority of women, the waters do not break if left alone until the latter part of the first stage, nature perhaps intended the cushion of waters to protect the baby's head from experiencing too much pressure. Medical staff tend to be tempted to break the waters to speed things up when labour is progressing normally but slowly; if all is well with the baby, you can choose whether or not to take their advice to break your waters. As the membranes cannot be put back together once they have been broken, if in doubt, it may be a good idea to decline the offer of ARM. The earlier in labour you are, the longer you will have to cope with the consequences of your decision. For further information, see the NCT study, *Rupture of membranes in labour* (see Bibliography).

I hate needles. Do I have to have the injection to deliver the placenta?

It is almost universal policy in UK hospitals for an injection of Syntometrine to be given to speed up the delivery of the placenta, so that if you choose to refuse the injection, you must include this in your birth plan or have it written in your notes. A midwife or doctor will probably want to discuss your decision with you at an antenatal appointment. If you have booked a home birth or Domino, you can discuss the matter with your community midwife and/or GP.

Many midwives and doctors are reluctant to omit Syntometrine for the third stage of labour because the research, as it stands at present, shows that Syntometrine, as part of a 'managed third stage', reduces the risk of post-partum haemorrhage, although it is not a fail-safe guarantee against its occurrence. Many health professionals say how frightening it is to witness a post-partum haemorrhage.

Some women, though, feel that if they have a drug-free labour, they would prefer to have a drug-free third stage also and to deliver the placenta physiologically. If you choose to have a 'physiological third stage' it is important that you understand the differences between a physiological and a managed third stage. It is also important that your midwife knows how to look after a woman having a physiological third stage. The essentials are as follows:

Physiological third stage	Managed third stage
No drugs	Syntometrine or Syntocinon if there are medical reasons why the woman should not have ergometrine
No time-limit	7-minute time-limit before drug clamps down uterus and closes cervix
No intervention, that is no touching of abdomen or cord, but midwife/doctor to stand by to observe cord stop pulsating and signs of placenta having detached itself so woman can be encouraged to push out placenta if uterus does not do so itself	Clamping and cutting cord immediately after delivery
Upright position so gravity can aid delivery of placenta	Midwife/doctor may rub abdomen to encourage uterus to contract and placenta to detach itself

Physiological third stage	*Managed third stage*
Mother holds baby and allows it to suckle to increase oxytocin which will increase contractions to reduce size of uterus, detach and expel placenta	Midwife/doctor gently eases out the cord (with other hand on abdomen to hold uterus) to remove placenta

A more detailed discussion of physiological and managed third stages appears in *Pregnancy and Parenthood* (see Bibliography).

Will a midwife be with me all the time?

Unless you have booked a home birth or Domino (when a community midwife will join you once labour is established and stay with you until after delivery), it is unlikely for two reasons. First, there are often not enough midwives on duty, particularly if it is a busy time on the labour ward; secondly, now that fathers are increasingly present during labour and able to take an active part in supporting women, it is recognized by many midwives that many couples prefer to be alone together for large parts of labour and that women are sometimes unable to derive much support from a succession of midwives changing shift and moving between two or more women in labour.

It is recognized by some enlightened midwives that intervention and complication rates rise when labour wards are overstretched and understaffed, but there is little they can do about it. In practice, what happens is that they try to give time to each woman when she is most in need of it, that is if she does not have a labour companion and towards the end of the first stage and throughout the second stage of labour. Student nurses, midwives and doctors are sometimes used to give support when a woman would otherwise be alone or to give a couple extra support.

Do I have to be hooked up to a machine for the baby's heartbeat to be checked?

Electronic fetal heart rate monitoring is being used increasingly, so that midwives do not have to check the baby's heart with a fetal stethoscope or Sonicaid but can look at a printout as and when they have time. A printout obtained from 20 to 30 minutes' monitoring on admission gives information about the strength of the woman's contractions and the baby's reactions to them, providing a base line with which to compare any changes later on in labour. However, the information obtained needs to be interpreted by staff with the appropriate skills and experience.

Electronic fetal monitors are often used as substitutes for the personal care of a midwife and their use can give a delivery room a technological atmosphere and divert attention away from the woman and her specific needs for support in labour. Some women and their labour partners are comforted by the use of electronic fetal monitoring, others are made nervous. One of the results of increased electronic fetal monitoring is that midwives may be becoming less confident in their own ability to listen to and interpret a baby's heartbeat in the traditional way.

Research has shown that electronic fetal monitoring improves outcome (that is it reduces the risk of a baby dying in labour) only if accompanied by fetal blood scalp sampling, and that periodic checks using a fetal stethoscope or Sonicaid can be as effective. What matters is that the interpretation of the information should be correct and acted upon quickly if a baby is shown to be in trouble. It is suggested in *A Guide to Effective Care in Pregnancy and Childbirth* (see Bibliography) that there is a case for more intensive monitoring of this kind when there are indications for increased risk of neonatal seizures, that is multiple births, induction or acceleration of labour or the amniotic fluid is stained with meconium, indicating possible fetal distress. It goes on to say, 'For the majority of labours for which no such indications apply, the current evidence suggests that more intensive monitoring increases obstetric intervention with no clear benefit for the fetus. Regular auscultation [listening to the baby's heart using a fetal stethoscope or Sonicaid] by a personal attendant... therefore seems to be the policy of choice in these labours.' (Page 198)

As with any other form of routine procedure, if your labour is normal, you could choose to refuse electronic fetal monitoring and ask for your baby's heartbeat to be checked in other ways. Alternatively, you might prefer to be less challenging by agreeing to electronic fetal monitoring for 20 minutes on admission and then asking for checks using a fetal stethoscope or Sonicaid at agreed intervals during the rest of your labour.

I feel awful when my blood-sugar gets low. Do I have to fast during labour?

If you are having a home birth, or alternatively while you are at home before going into hospital, you can do as you please. Many women find themselves eating when hungry and drinking when thirsty during early labour to keep up their energy. Some women do not feel hungry during labour, others would like to eat.

12: *Artificial pain relief*

ENTONOX (gas and air)
50 per cent oxygen and 50 per cent nitrous oxide inhaled by woman through rubber mask or plastic mouthpiece. Gives mild analgesic effect and can make mother feel 'high' so pain easier to cope with. Inhaling it for more than two hours can make a woman pass out, so it is usually kept for the latter part of first stage, say from 8 cm dilatation. Some women use it for second stage pain relief, including it in their rhythm for pushing; other women find this too complicated and concentrate on pushing. Some women use it during vaginal examinations or while waiting for an epidural. It may be available at a home birth.

Advantages
For mother: In control, timing so relief obtained at height of contraction has distraction value. Effects stop as soon as inhalation stops.
For baby: drug metabolized in mother's lungs so cannot cross placenta unless use continued for more than two hours.
For partner: woman seen to be in less pain and in control; can help woman with its administration and continue other forms of support.

Disadvantages
For mother: some women feel nauseous and dislike effect of drug.
For baby: can be affected if mother inhales for too long.
For partner: may not perceive mother's pain to have been greatly relieved.

PETHIDINE
Synthetic narcotic which does not remove pain but alters woman's perception of it and helps her relax. The drug crosses the placenta and has a depressive effect on the baby, making him or her sleepy if born with the drug still in his or her system. The baby's liver cannot break down the drug or its by-products, so if the mother's liver does this before delivery, there are fewer side-effects for the

baby after the birth. The effect is to send a woman to sleep between contractions and lose her sense of time: she may feel 'high' or peculiar and may like or dislike that feeling. The dosage can be varied between 50 and 125 mg (midwives tailor it to build of mother but the smallest dosage may achieve the desired effect and can be topped up or repeated if more relief is needed). It gives relief for one to two hours, depending on the dosage, but should not be given in the two hours before delivery. An antidote is usually available for resuscitation of the baby. Woman should not receive more than two doses because the baby's liver cannot metabolize the by-products. Therefore the maximum relief available from drug is for about two to four hours during first stage; it is not an option for second stage.

Advantages
For mother: can give her a break in first stage. Good for women who are very tense or who have not learned relaxation techniques.
For baby: may derive benefit from mother being more relaxed.
For partner: can give him/her a break to gather energy for remainder of labour.

Disadvantages
For mother: she may feel nauseous/vomit. Drug once administered takes at least an hour to wear off (longer if more than 50 mg given), if woman dislikes effects. Mobility will be limited. May be knocked out so she experiences each contraction as agonizing cramp waking her from a drugged sleep.
For baby: may make baby sleepy at delivery and for first few days after birth, may thus affect establishment of breastfeeding and relationship with mother.
For partner: may dislike seeing mother under effects of drug; may have to feel for contractions and wake mother to deal with them.

MEPTID
Some hospitals offer Meptid as an alternative to Pethidine. The newborn baby's liver can metabolize Meptid (unlike Pethidine) so it is safer to give close to delivery and does not make the baby so sleepy. For the mother, it is very similar to Pethidine in its effects (including the possible side-effects of nausea and vomiting), and for her appears to offer no advantages over Pethidine. The effects of its use have not been so well studied and documented as those associated with Pethidine.

EPIDURAL ANAESTHESIA
Local anaesthetic is injected into the epidural space around the

spinal cord via a fine tube inserted between two vertebrae in the lower back. Intended just to numb abdominal area; in practice it usually also numbs her legs so the woman stays in one position, lying on her side or propped up. A drip is always set up in case of a severe drop in blood pressure; there is continuous electronic monitoring of the baby's heartbeat and contractions; sometimes a urinary catheter is inserted (see illustration). It is a skilled procedure (taking about 40 minutes) requiring an appropriately trained experienced anaesthetist: it should not be performed by a doctor more junior than a registrar (see Glossary). There is a risk of a dural tap if the dura (the sheath round the spinal cord) is pierced by mistake, causing leakage of cerebro-spinal fluid. This leads to a severe headache unless the mother lies completely flat for at least two days following delivery. Epidural anaesthesia can be used for Caesarean section (except in an emergency when general anaesthesia is quicker) as well as routine pain relief. For good pain relief the epidural should be 'topped up' (the dose repeated) every $1\frac{1}{2}$ hours rather than when the woman requests it. Because of the increased risk of delivery by forceps if the epidural is continued for the second stage, the epidural should not be topped up after 8 cm dilatation. The relaxant effect of the drug can make the pelvic floor floppy and prevent the baby from turning or the woman pushing it out, or the urge to push may not be felt. The aid of gravity may be lost too, if the woman is unable to get into an upright position. It is not appropriate pain relief for second stage (except for medical reasons, such as high blood pressure) and is only available in hospitals.

Advantages

For mother: can give total pain relief, some obstetricians recommend them for long, slow labours. Many women choose epidural

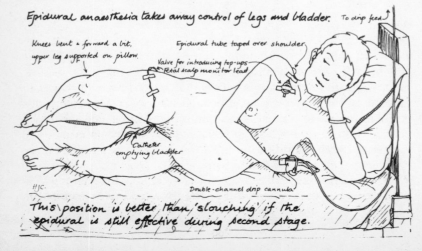

Epidural anaesthesia takes away control of legs and bladder.   To drip feed

Knees bent + forward a bit, upper leg supported on pillow.

Epidural tube taped over shoulder.

Valve for introducing top-ups
Fetal scalp monitor lead

Catheter emptying bladder

HJC.

Double-channel drip cannula

This position is better than 'slouching' if the epidural is still effective during second stage.

if labour induced/accelerated using Syntocinon drip. Popular in private hospitals. Woman can be awake for Caesarean section and hold baby soon after birth. Tendency to lower blood pressure can be useful if mother's blood pressure high.

For baby: may derive benefit from mother being more relaxed.

For partner: does not have to witness woman in pain.

Disadvantages

For mother: not possible for some women (eg if back injury or very obese); does not work at all for about 10 per cent of women (skill of anaesthetist may be a factor); sometimes works only partially, eg on one side. Procedure unpleasant, especially if contractions frequent and strong. Being in one position may prevent baby in unusual position from turning. Drug may damp down contractions so Syntocinon drip needed to stimulate them. Catheter may be necessary to empty bladder which may lead to urinary infection postnatally. May have to wait a long time for anaesthetist to be available. Increased risk of forceps delivery and episiotomy. Woman may feel distanced from birth and unable to relate to baby. A recent study showed an 18.6 per cent incidence of long-term backache following the use of epidural in labour (though not following epidural used for elective Caesarean section) compared with a 10 per cent incidence of long-term backache following labour in all women.

For baby: has slight depressive effect, strongest immediately after administration. May become distressed as result of Syntocinon drip being necessary. Increased risk of forceps delivery. If long epidural, may be perceived to lose a lot of weight after delivery (drug makes baby take on extra fluid during labour which is lost after birth) and, rarely, become dehydrated before milk comes in; establishment of breastfeeding may be affected or formula needed.

For partner: may feel redundant or distressed at sight of woman connected up to so many tubes.

TENS (transcutaneous electrical nerve stimulation)

A small machine (hung over shoulder, hand-held or clipped to garment) sends small electrical impulses between four electrodes taped to the woman's back. The strength of the impulses can be varied by turning a dial. It reduces pain in labour by interfering with the pain messages to the brain and also by increasing production of the woman's endorphins (natural painkillers). Women often do not realize how effective the pain relief given is until the electrodes are removed and then they have to wait for the effect to build up again. Women are often advised to start using it early in labour to get maximum relief, but it can work well used later. Machines are lent by some hospitals or can be hired (see Useful Organizations).

Advantages

For mother: she can start and stop using it at will and be in full control. Can be used throughout labour. Mobility is retained so it does not interfere with positions, etc. Can be used at home.

For baby: mother's mobility can help babies in awkward positions.

For partner: can continue supporting mother with self-help techniques and help with TENS machine if mother chooses.

Disadvantages

For mother: some women find the pain relief inadequate.

For baby: there may be unknown side-effects; none have been shown so far.

For partner: mother's pain may not be perceived to be greatly relieved.

PUDENDAL NERVE BLOCK

Injection of local anaesthetic at either side of the pudendal nerve at the top of the vagina to numb pelvic area before forceps or Ventouse.

LOCAL ANAESTHETIC IN PERINEUM

This is given usually before performing an episiotomy and repairing the perineum. Not all hospitals give it automatically for episiotomy: you can ask to be sure of having it.

SPINAL BLOCK

Injection of local anaesthetic into base of spine to numb pelvic area before forceps or Ventouse; sometimes used as alternative to pudendal nerve block. May also be used before emergency Caesarean if a woman is keen to avoid a general anaesthetic or should not have one for medical reasons. There is a risk of severe headache following the procedure, but this may be avoided by a skilled anaesthetist using a very fine gauge needle.

PAIN RELIEF CHOSEN BY THE RESPONDENTS TO THE *GOOD HOUSEKEEPING* SURVEY

Entonox (gas and air)	48 per cent	General anaesthetic	5 per cent
Pethidine	21 per cent	Other (may include spinal	
Epidural	20 per cent	and pudendal blocks)	4 per cent
TENS	11 per cent	No pain relief	12 per cent

Which is the most effective kind of pain relief?

Epidural anaesthesia, provided it works, is the only artificial form of pain relief which can give 100 per cent pain relief, but it bears out the maxim, 'There is no such thing as a free lunch' because of its disadvantages, which are not always widely advertised, even in antenatal classes. The other forms of pain relief vary in their effectiveness from woman to woman but never give complete relief. The usefulness of the various forms of artificial pain relief can be affected both by their timing and the woman's expectations. For example, if a woman chooses to have 50 mg of Pethidine at 6 cm just so she can sleep between contractions and get some rest, not expecting it to take her pain away, its use can be very effective.

It is important to balance the relief of pain during labour with the avoidance of pain after delivery. An epidural may increase the chances of an episiotomy which can lead to painful sex for several months afterwards. A woman who has realistic expectations of what the different forms of artificial pain relief have to offer is likely to find them more effective than one who does not. Many women find self-help ways of coping with pain extremely effective. By giving her full attention to coping with contractions as they come, a woman who knows what to expect and is well supported can find the natural dynamics of the process of labour give her huge personal resources for dealing with pain.

How do I choose the best form of pain relief?

If you build up a good knowledge of the range of possibilities for labour; the advantages and disadvantages of the different forms of pain relief (you can read more in *Pregnancy and Parenthood* – see Bibliography); and other women's experiences of artificial pain relief in labour, you will gradually form your own preferences in your mind. When the time comes, circumstances may dictate otherwise or you may change your mind, but if you have realistic expectations about the pain, you are likely to have realistic expectations of what you will need and choose.

Some women decide in advance that if labour is normal they will not have any drugs at all but rely instead on all the self-help options and a well-prepared labour partner to deal with the natural pain, but that if a Syntocinon drip is necessary for good medical reasons, they will have an epidural to give relief from the artificially increased pain. Other women choose to have an epidural as soon as they go into hospital, but allow it to wear off for the second stage when they use Entonox to help with contractions.

Some women hire a TENS machine which they can start using at home and take into hospital where they promise themselves Entonox when the going gets really tough at the end of the first stage. Other women cannot bear the thought of a needle in their back for an epidural, so choose to have a small dose (50 mg) of Pethidine if they need a break during the first stage and Entonox for the end of the first stage and perhaps for second stage; they may decide that if a Caesarean section were to be necessary they would prefer general anaesthesia to an epidural.

Whichever form of artificial pain relief you choose, you can ask for a vaginal examination immediately before it is administered. Occasionally it takes so long for an anaesthetist to be available to give an epidural, that a woman may be 8 cm or more dilated and the need for it passed.

Are the different forms of pain relief given in a certain order?

What often happens is that as the contractions become longer, stronger and closer together with the progress of labour, women turn to stronger forms of artificial pain relief if they feel they need increasing help in order to cope. For example, one does hear sometimes of a woman in labour trying some gas and air, then trying a dose of Pethidine and then having an epidural in a sort of reverse order of acceptability. On the other hand, some women prefer to move directly to an epidural as soon as they feel pain in order to get the benefit straight away.

You can see from the summary on pages 96 to 100 that the only form of artificial pain relief suitable for use throughout labour is TENS. Pethidine should not be given in the two hours before delivery so that it is best not to have it later than, say, at 6 cm or 7 cm dilatation. An epidural can be given until 8 cm; after this there is an increased risk of forceps delivery if it is not allowed to wear off. Entonox should not be used for more than two hours so it is probably best left for the end of the first stage so that you have something left to fall back on. Some women use Entonox for the second stage and possibly vaginal examinations if they are very painful.

There is therefore some flexibility in terms of the order in which the various forms of pain relief may be used, but there are also specific considerations to take into account for each method.

Can I have more than one form of pain relief at the same time?

Given that their use is limited, you might find it better to spin out what is available by having one at a time. Some women use a TENS machine for the whole of their labour because, although the effect does not appear very strong, they have heard other women say they didn't believe the electrodes were having any effect until they were removed! If you choose to use TENS continuously, you could have Pethidine or Entonox at the same time. The administration of an epidural would make TENS redundant.

Which kind of pain relief has fewest side-effects for the baby?

Entonox, provided it is not inhaled over a period of more than two hours, seems not to affect the baby. The use of TENS appears to be safe, though as yet it has not been studied in detail with a long-term follow-up.

I think my wife ought to have an epidural because she has a very low pain threshold. How do I make sure she can have it?

If she knows before labour that she definitely wants an epidural, she can check on its availability at the hospital and put her preference in her birth plan or have it written into her notes. There are many men who would have preferred their wives to have had an epidural in labour because they found it extremely distressing to see them in pain. For many people, health professionals and laymen alike, witnessing the experience of pain and being unable to alleviate it is very difficult. Have you discussed the issue of pain with your wife? Is she keen to have an epidural, or would she rather keep an open mind?

In any maternity unit the anaesthetist on duty has to give priority to emergency Caesareans before routine epidurals, so it is as well to be prepared for a wait and to use self-help techniques such as appropriate positions, relaxation, breathing awareness and massage until an epidural is administered. If your wife would rather wait and see whether she needs an epidural, do not underestimate your ability to help her to use her own resources by supporting her with the techniques you can learn at antenatal classes. Bear in mind that it is often the women who give full expression to their feelings who are in fact 'coping' best with their pain.

What pain relief is available at a home birth?

All community midwives carry Pethidine and the antidote to it and some of them carry TENS machines. Alternatively, you may hire your own TENS machine or borrow one direct from the hospital. Entonox should also be available. Usually, women planning a home birth are confident in the process of birth and in their ability to cope with it. They are in their own home with their own possessions, supported by a midwife and/or a GP committed to home birth and prepared to use their skills to help women give birth using their own resources. Labour partners (there are sometimes several at a home birth) often feel more comfortable and able to use what they have learned in a familiar environment and thus also be a valuable support to the mother; studies have shown that women supported by partners in their use of self-help techniques learned antenatally need less artificial pain relief. Some women who spend only some of their labour at home before going to the hospital they have booked for delivery, find the contractions were easier to cope with at home, even if they were very painful.

I'm petrified of the pain, can I request a Caesarean under general anaesthetic?

There is nothing to stop you requesting a birth of this kind, but it is unlikely that you would be given a Caesarean section under general anaesthetic in an NHS hospital unless it were necessary for medical reasons. Most obstetricians go to great lengths to avoid Caesarean section because, if the pregnancy and position of the baby are normal, a vaginal delivery is safer for both the mother and the baby. Moreover, routine Caesarean sections under general anaesthetic would use up resources needed for emergencies. If you were to need a Caesarean section for medical reasons, you could discuss your preference for a general anaesthetic rather than an epidural.

Another, perhaps more fruitful, approach would be to grasp the nettle and think about the pain and ways of dealing with it. The majority of women fear the pain of labour when expecting their first baby. You might find it reassuring to talk to other pregnant women in NHS or NCT antenatal classes and at your antenatal clinic. You are likely to find that you are not alone in your fear.

Unlike many other forms of pain, labour pain is experienced as the result of a normal physiological process. It comes from the dilating cervix and from the uterus pulling on the ligaments holding it in the abdomen. Just as an athlete feels pain during a long run, some women find labour contractions painful, but they need not be frightening or overwhelming if you are well prepared both mentally and physically and are supported by experienced and caring attendants. Pain is not experienced throughout labour, only during contractions. There is often a build-up in the length, strength and frequency of contractions so you have time to get used to them.

Many options for dealing with pain, natural and artificial, are summarized in this chapter and the previous one. Think about how and where you would be best spending your labour. Would you be most comfortable staying at home for as long as possible, using your bath or a TENS machine, for example? Or would you choose to go into hospital at the first sign of real labour and have an epidural? Or would you choose to see how it goes, using all the self-help ways of coping, promising yourself some artificial pain relief if the pain gets really bad?

Think about having a labour partner with you; it can be very reassuring to have someone there just for you, whether it is your baby's father, a relative or a friend. You could both go to antenatal classes and work together on strategies for coping with labour. Learning about the process of birth, practising relaxation techniques and sharing feelings about what labour means could be helpful. Years ago it was found that fear of childbirth leads to tension which in turn causes or increases pain, and this is the basis of most modern antenatal preparation for birth.

Labour sounds so painful. Do women really manage without any pain relief? How?

Labour does seem to be less painful for some women than for others. It may be of comfort to know that it is not just a question of 'pain thresholds', although the extent to which women are prepared to tolerate pain is a factor. It has been shown objectively by the use of the McGill pain questionnaire that the degree of pain actually experienced by different women varies. The questionnaire works on a system of adjectives, giving any pain (not just labour pain) a score on a scale up to 80, according to the adjectives used to describe it, such as 'mild', 'severe', etc. Reported pain in labour ranges from 10 to 65 on the scale, 5 to 10 per cent of women showing a pain score of 65 which is very severe. 80 per cent of women fall somewhere in the middle. Therefore some women do seem to experience less pain than others.

The second important factor is the degree and nature of support and encouragement that women in labour receive from labour partners, midwives and doctors. Research has shown that women need less artificial pain relief if they are supported by labour partners in self-help coping techniques learned antenatally; if they receive continuity of care from midwives in a team midwifery scheme; and if they have home births where they are in familiar surroundings and continuity of care usually plays an important part. It is obvious that if a woman experiences painful contractions she is less likely to choose artificial pain relief if everyone around her is positive, encouraging, helping her into upright positions, massaging her back, etc, *and if they believe she can cope*, than if all they can do is check how the baby is doing on the electronic fetal heart rate monitor and suggest she has Pethidine or an epidural. The choice of place of birth is therefore also important.

The third important factor is women choosing to do without artificial pain relief and concentrating all their energies on all the other ways of coping. They may choose to do this because they want to give the best possible start in life to their baby or because they feel that having done without drugs throughout their pregnancy, they do not want to start having drugs now; or because they want a natural, drug-free labour. Some of those women who know that the intense sensation of contractions in labour is normal, safe and signifies progress, do not perceive them as painful. Another approach is for some women to promise themselves particular kinds of pain relief 'when it gets really bad'. Such women may find themselves requesting an epidural when contractions are extremely intense, only to discover that they are 8 cm or 9 cm dilated and the first stage is nearly over. Having got so far, they then feel proud and encouraged to do the rest without artificial pain relief as well or they might choose to have some Entonox. Yet another approach is for a woman to choose to do without artificial pain relief if the labour progresses normally, on the basis that for any pain she experiences naturally, she feels she will be able to find her own natural resources for coping.

The fourth important factor is good antenatal preparation, factual, physical and psychological; it is even more helpful if the labour partner shares in this too. Ignorance of what to expect and how to cope sets up the fear-tension-pain syndrome and makes labour harder to cope with than it need be. (See Bibliography)

Why should women suffer in labour?

Many people, among them many midwives and obstetricians, believe that because artificial pain relief is available, women should not suffer. Health professionals have been known to be very scornful of women who try to rely on their own resources, find the pain too great and then choose artificial pain relief. Recently, an experienced anaesthetist in a large teaching hospital, summoned to perform an epidural, on catching sight of the TENS machine and large pile of cushions in the delivery room said sarcastically, 'Another satisfied customer!' This was in ignorance of the fact that the TENS machine and self-help coping methods had worked well for over 12 hours and up to 6 cm dilatation before an awkwardly positioned baby and artificial rupture of the membranes made the pain too great for that particular woman to bear.

The issue is not whether women should suffer in labour, but that they should be well prepared for labour. Women who are well prepared and well supported may simply never feel the need for artificial pain relief. If this is the case, then many difficult decisions and unwanted side-effects can be completely avoided. If it is not the case, women should be in a position to make free and informed choices about which artificial pain relief to use. Many women choose forms of pain relief, the possible side-effects of which they have been told nothing about. For other women, conditions in modern obstetric units are such that a high-tech environment and approach to labour, no continuity of care, a fear of the labour process, an inability by some midwives and doctors to trust women's ability to cope with pain, and a failure to treat women with dignity and respect, makes artificial pain relief a virtual necessity rather than one of several options.

Just as women and men who run marathons, climb mountains, sail single-handedly around the world, etc, test their physical endurance to the utmost as part of their particular achievement, often experiencing physical pain in the process, so some women set out to achieve a natural, drug-free birth, the endurance of pain becoming afterwards part of their sense of achievement. Fathers who can put aside their own feelings about witnessing the evidence of strong labour pain are often amazed at what their partners are capable of enduring and are left with a deep sense of respect and admiration. Women are often full of praise for their partners' practical and emotional ability to support them in their aim to cope with labour contractions on their own.

Women have the right not to have artificial pain relief as well as the right to have it. Therefore it is for each individual woman to choose what is best for her in each labour, and she should be able to make her choice in the full knowledge of the implications, not only without feeling under pressure, but with constructive support.

13: Medical help for complications

Sometimes complications occur during pregnancy or labour. They may be relatively minor or they may be serious. Any complications will have implications affecting who provides care, where it is best for the baby to be born and how much choice about care can be made by the woman having the baby. For example, complications will probably mean a woman is referred to an obstetrician who will remain quite closely involved with the management of her care. It may be decided that the birth should take place in a consultant unit rather than at home, in a GP unit or continue under the Domino scheme. It may also be that the element of choice for management of the pregnancy and labour is taken out of the woman's hands. If complications do occur, the feeling of your plans being overturned and a sense of losing control of the situation can be demoralizing at best and frightening at worst. However, when complications do arise, there are often more choices for a woman than she might realize. For example, if your labour has to be induced because you have developed pre-eclampsia, although you might be unwise to prolong your pregnancy, you have choices for coping with the induction which you can discuss with the medical staff and make for yourself. For example, you can consider the extent to which you wish to rely on self-help coping techniques or use artificial pain relief.

It is possible to think of the different situations of women and babies at the end of pregnancy and during labour as being ranged along a sliding scale. At one end is the altogether normal pregnancy and labour being experienced by a fit and healthy woman and baby; at the other end are situations where immediate action is needed to save the life of the woman or her baby. An emergency Caesarean section may be needed, or a blood transfusion or administration of a stabilizing drug. At the normal end of the scale, a woman has the full range of choices open to her with plenty of time in which to discuss, make and exercise them. At the abnormal end, there is no time for discussion, and decision-making has usually to be left in the hands of the medical staff who are trained to deal effectively with such emergencies. Ranged along the scale between these two extremes are all the other situations where there is at least some time and scope for choice, consideration and decision-making by the woman. How much of these she exercises will depend partly on how much responsibility she wants to take for her birth and partly on how particular situations are presented to her by the midwives and doctors caring for her.

To develop the idea of the sliding scale of complications further, situations nearer the abnormal end will require more obstetric procedures and interventions than those nearer the normal end. Where on the scale the woman is regarded to be and which procedures and/or interventions may be appropriate is partly a matter of judgement by midwives and medical staff. For example, a woman who has conceived naturally, had a totally normal pregnancy and gone into labour spontaneously may be viewed as further away from the normal end of the scale if she is carrying twins; is over 40 years of age; has had infertility treatment in the past; has had a previous stillbirth; or is having a straightforward but very slow labour. The judgement of midwives and medical staff may be affected by their own feelings about and experiences of birth, by their attitudes to hospital policies and to each individual woman. Women can influence their carers' views by questioning and by expressing their own views and preferences.

In a situation where a woman may feel that her body has failed her, her baby and, perhaps, her partner, it is important that midwives and medical staff make special efforts to explain the situation carefully and their proposed way of dealing with it. It is equally important for the woman and her labour partner to ask questions about anything they do not understand and to make sure the woman is involved in any necessary decision-making.

If you are faced with the prospect of, for example, an assisted delivery, you may wish to discuss the pros and cons of different methods with your obstetrician. However, studies have shown that obstetricians, in common with other doctors, are not always guided by the latest research or lack of it, but often more by their own training and preferences. Some women, therefore, may choose to be guided by the choice of their obstetrician. A person doing what he/she is used to doing and is most comfortable with may be more reliable than one doing something on request with which they feel less confident. Occasionally, should a woman's choice not coincide with the preferred practice of her obstetrician, she might ask to be attended by a different obstetrician, though the loss of continuity may be a high price to pay.

CAESAREAN SECTION

Much controversy surrounds the rapidly rising rates for Caesarean section. In 1980 the rate was 9 per cent, in 1985 the rate had risen to 10.5 per cent (see Birth Statistics). Though more recent national statistics are not available, studies suggest the rate is continuing to rise. The Caesarean section rate for the respondents to the *Good Housekeeping* Survey was 13 per cent, not uncommon in many hospitals, and in at least one NHS hospital the rate for one month in 1990 was 20 per cent. The USA Caesarean section rate is 25 per cent and it is well established that one of the main reasons for this is the fear of litigation; if an obstetrician performs a Caesarean section they can say they did all that they could to save the baby. A survey carried out for the Maternity Alliance and published under the title *Changing Childbirth* (see Useful Organizations) asked obstetricians to explain the reasons for the rising Caesarean section rate in their maternity units. The main reasons given for the change were improved facilities for neonatal intensive care; more breech babies being delivered by Caesarean section rather than vaginally, particularly in first-time mothers; fear of litigation; avoidance of longer labour or difficult delivery; the interpretation of fetal distress from electronic fetal heart rate monitoring; and repeat Caesarean sections. However, it is not clear that the increase in Caesarean sections is either necessary or, on balance, beneficial to women and their babies.

Birth has not changed: only the ways of managing it. In the May 1990 edition of *Good Housekeeping*, the obstetrician Wendy Savage was quoted as saying, 'There is no justification for a national Caesarean section rate of more than 6-8 per cent – it depends on whether or not one believes that breech presentation is best dealt with surgically, and this is an area fraught with difficulty.' Wendy Savage and others critical of the extent to which birth has been medicalized are aware that the British and American ways of managing maternity care are not the only ways. In Holland, there is a 6 to 8 per cent Caesarean section rate, a third of women still have their babies at home, women are booked for care by midwives unless and until complications occur, and the perinatal mortality rates are lower than those in Great Britain.

When women are recommended by their obstetricians to have a Caesarean section, if the situation is not an emergency there may be a choice. Some women may feel strongly that they wish to avoid a Caesarean if at all possible, not least so as to be physically fit for the difficult days and weeks ahead. Some women who feel strongly are able to persuade their obstetrician to agree to a 'trial of labour' – a commitment to let labour begin and to review its progress with a view to performing a Caesarean section only if there are problems. Some have a trial of labour which ends in a vaginal delivery and some culminate in a Caesarean section. Women who have a trial of labour feel they have done all they could to achieve a normal birth, they enjoy knowing what the experience of labour is like and have a good chance of achieving a vaginal birth in the future. Other women prefer not to risk a long, tiring labour culminating in an emergency Caesarean section (although there is often time for an epidural unless the baby suddenly becomes distressed) and choose to have an elective Caesarean, giving themselves time to get used to the idea and choosing an epidural so that they are awake for the birth and able to hold and feed their babies more easily afterwards. Each woman should feel able to choose what she is most comfortable with, having heard all the relevant arguments.

FETAL MONITORING

Sometimes in complicated labours it is necessary to monitor the baby's heartbeat continuously throughout labour using an electronic fetal heart rate monitor linked to the baby via a fetal scalp electrode. Sometimes a woman may be able to choose intermittent monitoring, say 20 minutes in every hour, so that the rest of the time she is not restricted in her movements. It may also be necessary to back up the readings of the electronic fetal monitor with fetal blood sampling from the baby's scalp. The woman usually has to lie on her back for this procedure, but afterwards she can get into a position more comfortable and more helpful for labour. The strength of contractions can be monitored as well as the baby's condition. The most straightforward way is with an electrode held on the abdomen with an elastic belt. This can be uncomfortable and not very reliable. Sometimes a catheter will be inserted through the cervix into the woman's uterus to measure the strength of contractions: this may give a more accurate result than using the belt monitor. A woman can ask to get into the most comfortable position for her before undergoing this procedure.

SPECIALIST ADVICE

Women with particular medical or other conditions pre-dating pregnancy need the advice of specialists when making choices about their labour and delivery. In the case of some medical conditions pre-dating pregnancy, it may be difficult for a woman to find either a specialist of the condition who knows enough about obstetrics or an obstetrician who knows enough about the medical condition. Women in such a situation often find it helpful to contact other women who have the same condition and have had babies. There are many specialist self-help organizations (see Useful Organizations or try your hospital or local telephone directory) or the NCT Parents with Disabilities Group may be able to help. The NCT holds, for example, research on the maternity experiences of mothers affected by epilepsy, multiple sclerosis and Thalidomide.

A detailed account of obstetric procedures for complications can be found in *Pregnancy and Parenthood* (see Bibliography).

MEDICAL HELP FOR COMPLICATIONS RECEIVED BY ALL RESPONDENTS TO THE GOOD HOUSEKEEPING SURVEY

Induction using pessaries	13 per cent
Induction using Syntocinon drip	14 per cent
Forceps delivery	15 per cent
Ventouse delivery	4 per cent
Caesarean	13 per cent
(elective 6 per cent, emergency 7 per cent)	

> *I am 34 weeks pregnant and my waters have broken. Do I have any say in the way my baby should be delivered?*

Although the onset of premature labour is usually a shock to parents, modern neonatology can achieve a great deal for babies who are born early. Unfortunately, the best way of managing labour is not altogether clear, since no randomized controlled trials have been carried out to compare premature babies born vaginally with those born by Caesarean section. Retrospective studies have often been biased or unable to compare like with like in an environment where delivery vaginally and by Caesarean section are managed with equal skill. Sometimes the fact that a premature baby is also breech makes obstetricians choose Caesarean section, because the complications are doubled. Although pre-term breech babies have been shown to do better after Caesarean sections, the research which shows this has been questioned. The soft and overlapping bones of the very premature baby's head can lead to problems associated with the compression and expansion which occur during a vaginal birth. In an attempt to protect premature babies' heads being delivered vaginally, it is common practice to perform a large episiotomy and, in some cases, use forceps.

However, *A Guide to Effective Care in Pregnancy and Childbirth* states, 'There is no evidence to suggest that either an elective forceps delivery or performing an episiotomy reduces this risk. The routine use of both of these procedures should be abandoned, except in the context of controlled trials' (page 94). As you are faced with the prospect of a pre-term delivery, you may want to discuss the pros and cons of a vaginal or Caesarean delivery with your obstetrician.

I am having twins. How likely am I to achieve a normal delivery?

Many women carrying more than one baby go into labour spontaneously before 40 weeks. If this does not happen, many obstetricians will recommend that they induce labour or perform an elective Caesarean at 36 or 37 weeks. If the pregnancy is the result of in vitro fertilization (IVF), it is very common, particularly in private hospitals, for elective Caesarean section to be performed at 37 weeks. (37 weeks is chosen as the time when the baby's lungs should be mature but when spontaneous labour is unlikely.) Strictly speaking, IVF babies are no different from naturally conceived babies (though there may be a tendency for labour to start earlier than 40 weeks), but there is a strong feeling among obstetricians working in the infertility field that 'precious' babies should not be subjected to the risks of vaginal delivery and this feeling appears to be shared by many of their clients. (Many people dislike this use of the concept of a 'precious' baby since it implies that some babies are to be valued more than others, but it is a reality that women who have conceived by IVF or who are over 40 may feel that they have fewer chances of conceiving again in the future.) However, Caesarean section has associated risks both for mothers and babies. When one or more of the babies in a multiple pregnancy is breech or in an awkward position, Caesarean section may be a safer choice. The factors in each individual woman's case need to be carefully weighed up by both the woman and her obstetrician when choices are being made for delivery.

Provided that you and your babies are well, you can choose to let labour start spontaneously and use your own resources, with good support from your labour partner, to achieve a normal delivery. It is very important that the midwives and medical staff attending you use their skills to help you. Discussing all contingencies with your obstetrician will help you prepare for all eventualities.

> *They are going to do special tests to see if my*
> *pelvis is big enough for the baby. Does this*
> *mean I might have to have a Caesarean?*

It is possible that you may have a Caesarean, but it may not be necessary, depending partly on the results of the tests and partly on how you decide to deal with the situation.

What the doctors will be looking for is cephalopelvic disproportion. The easiest way for a baby to be born vaginally is if it is head down, with its neck well flexed, that is chin down on chest, and facing the mother's spine (see illustration). If the baby is facing another way or does not have its head well flexed, a vaginal birth may be more difficult or occasionally impossible. Very rarely, a woman's pelvis is too small or an unusual shape (sometimes due to disease or injury) and even an optimally positioned baby cannot be born vaginally.

When cephalopelvic disproportion is suspected before term, x-rays are taken to estimate the size and shape of the woman's pelvis and a detailed ultrasound scan is performed to estimate the size and position of the baby (clinical pelvimetry). An alternative to taking x-rays is to measure the woman's pelvis (particularly the distance between the ischial spines) using a detailed physical examination. (There have been reports of an association between pre-natal irradiation and childhood leukaemia, although minimum doses of radiation are used and it is thought that the baby is protected by being within the bony pelvis.) Whereas it was once thought that a woman's shoe size was a reasonably reliable indicator of the size of her pelvis, this is no longer accepted. It is the internal size and shape of the pelvis which are significant, not the overall size.

If cephalopelvic disproportion is thought to be the case, the woman can choose between a trial of labour (that is going into labour spontaneously and giving the baby a chance to be delivered vaginally) and elective Caesarean section. *A Guide to Effective Care in Pregnancy and Childbirth* states, 'Neither X-ray nor clinical

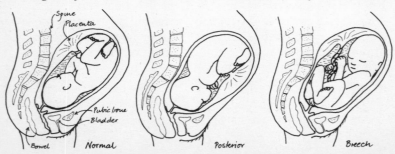

114

pelvimetry have been shown to predict cephalopelvic disproportion with sufficient accuracy to justify elective Caesarean section
for cephalic presentations. Cephalopelvic disproportion is best
diagnosed by a carefully monitored trial of labour, and x-ray
pelvimetry should seldom, if ever, be necessary' (page 68). One of
the reasons why pelvimetry is often inaccurate is that during
labour the pregnancy hormones enable the woman's pelvis to
increase in size slightly as the baby's head moves through it, and
the bony plates of the baby's head overlap to make it smaller.

If your baby is lying head down, you may therefore choose not to
have clinical pelvimetry, but instead allow your labour to start
spontaneously and see what happens. On the other hand, if you
have the pelvimetry and the results are good, you and the hospital/
midwife/GP may be more relaxed during labour. However, if you
have the pelvimetry, the results may be unfavourable. In this
instance, you can end the uncertainty by opting for an elective
Caesarean or you can allow yourself to go into labour spontaneously on the basis that your pelvis may enlarge sufficiently
during labour. During any trial of labour, you can maximize the
size of your pelvis by taking up favourable upright positions with
your knees slightly bent and your coccyx free. If you choose a trial
of labour, you may be recommended to have an epidural 'in case
you need a Caesarean', but being immobilized by an epidural
would prevent you from using gravity fully and the most favourable positions for birth. If your baby is in a breech position, the
need to assess the capacity of your pelvis in advance of labour is
more pressing. With a cephalic presentation, if the head does not
descend through the pelvis a Caesarean section can be performed.
With a breech, by the time the largest part of the baby – the head –
reaches the pelvis, the body has already passed through. If there is
any obstruction at this stage, remedial action is problematic.

> *There is a chance that I may be developing pre-*
> *eclampsia. If I do, how will this affect my*
> *choices in labour?*

This would depend on the severity of the disease. It is worth doing
all you can yourself at this stage to prevent it becoming serious or
from developing at all (see page 39). If the pre-eclampsia is mild,
you might be allowed to go into labour spontaneously and your
blood pressure would be checked more frequently than usual;
labour would be accelerated or an assisted delivery performed only
if your blood pressure started to rise dramatically. If the pre-

eclampsia is more serious, your obstetrician might recommend your being induced. This might not be the way you envisaged labour, but it might pre-empt a dramatic rise in your blood pressure and the need for an emergency Caesarean section. You might be recommended to have an epidural which would reduce your blood pressure as well as giving you total pain relief. If the illness were to become severe very suddenly, you would have to have a Caesarean. Depending on the time available, you might be able to have an epidural rather than a general anaesthetic.

I am diabetic. Do I have to have a Caesarean?

It is routine to advise diabetic women to have an elective Caesarean section at 37 weeks, but this advice may change for a number of reasons. It is becoming common practice for pregnant diabetic women to be encouraged to control their disease very carefully so that their babies develop at a normal rate and are less likely to have the respiratory problems experienced by babies of diabetics in the past. Provided a diabetic woman has been able to control her disease well, the baby appears to be of a normal size (a detailed ultrasound scan may be able to help with this assessment) and there are no obstetric indications for early elective Caesarean section, *A Guide to Effective Care in Pregnancy* states, 'There is no valid reason to terminate an otherwise uncomplicated pregnancy in a diabetic woman before term, and probably not before the expected date of delivery' (page 109). Therefore it may be possible for you to prepare for a spontaneous labour and vaginal delivery, rather than an elective Caesarean. Talk to your diabetic specialist and to your obstetrician and see what they have to say.

I've heard Ventouse is better that forceps. Do either of them hurt the baby?

Some assisted deliveries can be performed only with the help of forceps, for example for protection of the aftercoming head in a breech delivery; for others either Ventouse or forceps may be used, depending on the preference of the woman and the obstetrician.

Ventouse as a method of assisted delivery is less invasive than forceps, because the obstetrician merely has to fix the cup to the top of the baby's head and hold it there, rather than having to fit forceps round the baby's head within the woman's vagina and pelvis. As the Ventouse does not add to the circumference of the baby's head, the woman may need a smaller episiotomy than with forceps, or may not need one at all if the baby has made a full descent down the vagina. There is also a choice of a hard or soft cup: where not much traction is needed, a soft cup can be used and causes as little as possible trauma to the baby's head. Many women, given the necessity of an assisted delivery, prefer the idea of a Ventouse for these reasons, and in some maternity units the proportion of assisted deliveries performed using Ventouse rather than forceps is rising. Ventouse delivery is still not available in every UK maternity unit, largely because not all obstetricians are trained in its use. As the *Good Housekeeping* Survey results show (see page 112), forceps are used more often than Ventouse.

It is difficult to say how much discomfort the baby suffers in an assisted delivery. If you want to have an idea of what assisted delivery might feel like for the baby, lie down on the floor and ask someone to hold your head between their hands and pull gently. The amount of bruising seen on babies delivered by forceps varies greatly. After Ventouse, babies have a swelling from the site of the cup which subsides soon after delivery. For a few days after a forceps delivery, some babies need very sensitive handling.

Which is better, Caesarean under epidural or general anaesthesia?

Unless a woman prefers to be unconscious for the operation, an epidural is better for mother and baby. The mother can be awake for the operation and birth; have her labour partner present; hold and feed the baby more quickly; be less tired after the operation; and have the benefit of the epidural for pain relief for the first 24 hours after birth. The baby has fewer drugs; can be held by the father or labour partner immediately after delivery; can hear the mother's voice immediately after delivery; and has the benefit of a mother who is not drowsy after general anaesthesia and can hold and feed him or her (with help) very soon after delivery. The father can see his child being born and hold him or her immediately after the paediatrician has checked all is well; he does not have to see his partner drowsy and disorientated after general anaesthesia. An epidural must be totally effective for a Caesarean section; this can be very disappointing for the 10 per cent of women for whom epidurals do not work.

How do I decide whether to agree to an induction?

It is important that the medical staff give you all the relevant information about yourself, your baby and their concerns in order for you to make an informed choice. Obviously if you are 42 weeks pregnant and there is evidence that the placenta is beginning to function less well, you may be readier to choose induction than if you are 41 weeks pregnant and everything seems to be fine.

The majority of pregnancies last beyond 40 weeks; only 5 per cent of babies are born on their due date. Unless there is some medical reason for inducing labour, most hospitals allow pregnancies to last up to 42 weeks. Some private hospitals suggest induction at a time earlier than 42 weeks, to avoid the weekend, since the obstetrician is committed to attend the woman in labour. Some women feel happy to be induced whenever the obstetrician suggests it and may even suggest it themselves, being fed up with the discomfort of heavy pregnancy. Others put off induction as long as possible, provided there are no adverse signs, in order to give themselves every chance of going into labour spontaneously.

By waiting the full 42 weeks (if all is well) a woman has the chance to use self-help techniques for inducing labour (see page 81). If induction is necessary, less intervention may be needed if a woman's body is that much readier for labour. Some hospitals are prepared for or even encourage women to continue pregnancy beyond 42 weeks. Some women refuse induction at 42 weeks, particularly if they know the menstrual cycle in which they conceived was a long one (most midwives and doctors will only take account of the date of the last period, not the date of ovulation, even if the woman knows when it was) and they know they are only in fact 40 or 41 weeks pregnant. It should be remembered that 40 weeks is only the estimated length of pregnancy: some women's gestation periods are as short as 38 weeks or as long as 42 weeks or longer, and expected dates of delivery can go awry if a woman's menstrual cycle is either very long or very short. Only 51 per cent of respondents to the *Good Housekeeping* Survey gave birth to their babies at 40 weeks: 16 per cent were born 'early' and 32 per cent were born 'late'. The babies of first-time mothers were more likely to be born early than those of women with other children.

If the pregnancy continues 'beyond term', that is past 40 weeks, the way the woman and baby are monitored varies from hospital to hospital and can include the usual antenatal checks on mother and baby; extra ultrasound scans; internal examinations to assess the state of the cervix; electronic fetal monitoring to check the baby's heartbeat for a length of time; Doppler scanning (see Glossary) to assess the blood flow through the umbilical cord; amnioscopy and amniocentesis. Sometimes a 'sweep' is done (see page 82).

Provided the mother and baby seem well, the balance of

evidence does not suggest that any or all of these methods of monitoring, or induction itself, improve the outcome of pregnancies which continue beyond the estimated date of delivery. Therefore a woman post-term may choose the degree of monitoring she feels most comfortable with and whether to ask for or agree to induction.

It is very common for hospitals to admit women the night before induction is to take place and then to telephone the labour partner to come in 'when you are needed'. Some women choose instead to admit themselves early on the day of induction accompanied by their labour partner who can then support the woman throughout: this may also be a way of ensuring a better night's sleep at home than might be the case in hospital.

The usual procedure for induction is to insert prostaglandin pessaries (such as Prostin) to soften and 'ripen' the cervix, followed by artificial rupture of the membranes to bring the baby's head directly down on to the cervix, and a Syntocinon drip to initiate or strengthen contractions. If the baby's head is not engaged, the membranes might be left intact. Prostaglandin pessaries cannot be used if the waters have broken spontaneously, because of the risk of infection, but some hospitals use oral prostaglandins. Research has shown that induction is most effective if all three steps are used, but it is usual practice to allow time between each step for the woman to accustom herself to the effects of each procedure. Sometimes one or two of these procedures are sufficient to tip the woman's body over into labour.

How do they decide that your labour needs speeding up?

The acceleration, stimulation or augmentation of labour (terms often used interchangeably in different hospitals, and sometimes with specific nuances) are undertaken because a woman's labour is considered to be progressing too slowly. This may be because the woman and/or the baby are observed to be tired and/or because the labour is too slow according to hospital policy. Hospital policies on the maximum desirable length of labour vary widely for a number of reasons. Midwives and doctors (as well as women and their labour partners!) start timing 'established' or 'active' labour (as opposed to 'pre-labour' or 'the latent phase') at different stages; timing may start from the first strong contractions, from the beginning of dilatation, or when progressive dilatation is established. Women's labours vary greatly in length and some labours take a long time to become established with a long phase of regular

Braxton Hicks contractions which may come and go but do not increase in strength. Both women and their babies vary in their ability to withstand a long labour; some hospitals favour active management of labour and prefer to intervene sooner rather than later.

Ways of speeding up labour are breaking the waters, putting up a Syntocinon drip and, occasionally (not all obstetricians are in favour of this), inserting prostaglandin pessaries. If speeding up labour is suggested, it is important for a woman to be given the reasons for the suggestion so that she may make an informed choice as to whether or not to accept the advice.

Breaking the waters is a simple procedure which can be carried out by a midwife and is generally painless in itself, although as uncomfortable as any vaginal examination during labour. However, it is often remembered as being painful because of its effects: the procedure usually results in contractions being more intense and often more painful, because the baby's presenting part, usually the head, is pressing directly on the cervix. Whilst this may produce the desired result and help the labour progress more quickly, it is important that the woman is prepared for the change in intensity of the contractions. She will certainly need extra support with self-help coping techniques. Sometimes, waters are broken late on in the first stage by a midwife who knows from her experience and from her examination of the woman that full dilatation and the second stage will quickly follow the procedure. In such a case, a woman can choose to accept the midwife's recommendation that she break the waters, or let her labour take its natural course. Breaking the waters at the end of the first stage may be followed by a very strong sensation as the cervix dilates fully and the baby's head descends, for which the woman should be prepared.

Putting up a Syntocinon drip is a more invasive procedure and also requires the baby to be monitored more intensively, so the woman may find it more difficult to change position and may be forced to choose an epidural to deal with the artificially intensified pain. If there are good medical reasons, speeding up a labour may prevent the need for a Caesarean section; but if it is done because arbitrary time-limits have run out, a woman may choose to refuse the procedure.

Whether or not a woman agrees to having her labour speeded up, there are things she can do, supported by her labour partner, to help labour progress. Changing position, having a warm bath or shower to aid relaxation or having something to eat can all help.

Nipple stimulation (rubbing the nipples between thumb and forefinger for two minutes in every five) can also stimulate the woman's natural oxytocin levels.

I overheard them saying the baby is posterior. Is this normal?

It is quite normal for babies to be in a posterior position, that is facing towards the front of the mother's body rather than her back, up to the end of pregnancy. Usually they turn into the anterior position, that is facing towards the mother's back, before labour begins (see illustration on page 114). For some reason some babies stay in the posterior position, and this may make labour more difficult. During labour, the baby will either remain in the posterior position for delivery, or turn through 180 degrees, either of which may make the second stage longer. If the baby gets stuck after turning 90 degrees, so it is facing towards the mother's side as its head comes through the mother's pelvis, Caesarean section will probably be necessary, because the widest measurement of the baby's head is being pushed through the narrowest measurement of the woman's pelvis.

Many women find that when the baby is in a posterior position they have what is commonly known as a 'backache labour' when the contractions are felt as strong pains in the lower back. The most comfortable position for contractions is often on all fours having lots of massage from a labour partner directly on the site of the pain. An ice pack in between contractions may help too. Some women combine these techniques with using a TENS machine, which because its electrodes are attached to the woman's back, may also give direct relief while not interfering with the woman's freedom of movement. Other women choose other artificial pain relief. When the second stage is protracted, being in an upright position and moving about can help the second stage progress normally. Enlarging the pelvis by squatting or half-squatting or half-kneeling with one knee up, one knee down can also help.

I have been told my baby is breech, how will this affect my choices in labour?

Depending on the policy of your particular hospital and the preferred practice of your obstetrician, you may be strongly encouraged to have an elective Caesarean.

Only 3 to 4 per cent of babies are in the breech position at the onset of labour. One risk of vaginal delivery is that if there is cephalopelvic disproportion (see page 114), the baby's head will get stuck in the pelvis once the baby's body has already passed through. Despite the use of ultrasound scans, there have been no real advances in assessing the possibility of cephalopelvic disproportion with any accuracy except in a very few obvious cases. There has been an increasing trend to deliver breech babies by elective Caesarean section, often at 37 weeks. Since dilatation of the cervix may depend as much on pressure from the baby's correctly positioned 'presenting part' as on the contracting uterus, the nature of the breech position may be taken into account when choosing between vaginal and Caesarean delivery: it is much more likely that a curled up baby with its legs tucked up and its buttocks pressing neatly on the cervix will be delivered vaginally than a baby who is stretched out with its head under the woman's ribs and its feet tucked into one side of her pelvis. Evidence from a detailed ultrasound scan to ascertain the size and position of the baby and from an x-ray to measure the woman's pelvis is therefore important when making the choice, although its accuracy cannot be guaranteed. If vaginal delivery or a trial of labour is chosen, *A Guide to Effective Care in Pregnancy and Childbirth* recommends that a further ultrasound scan be performed during early labour to ascertain the exact position of the baby then, since it may have changed position since 36 or 37 weeks, when assessment for cephalopelvic disproportion is normally carried out (page 69).

External cephalic version can be used to move the baby into a more favourable head-down position by manipulating it through the wall of the mother's abdomen. Obstetricians vary in their readiness to perform the procedure and the time when they do it. It may be done at any time between 32 and 37 weeks and babies frequently turn themselves to the breech position again. *A Guide to Effective Care in Pregnancy and Childbirth* therefore recommends that external cephalic version be performed at term or at the beginning of labour to prevent this happening and to minimize the (small) risks involved in the procedure (pages 70-72). External cephalic version at term or at the beginning of labour has clear benefits because it can reduce the frequency of breech presentation and Caesarean section.

A woman with a breech presentation diagnosed before labour therefore has a number of choices: whether to ask for external cephalic version at about 36 weeks or at term or to refuse it; whether to have a detailed ultrasound scan and x-ray of the pelvis to assess for cephalopelvic disproportion at about 36 weeks; whether to have a further ultrasound scan at the beginning of labour; whether to have an elective Caesarean at 37 weeks or a trial of labour.

If a woman chooses to have a trial of labour, she can try different positions to help the cervix dilate and the baby to descend. She can maximize her pelvic measurements for delivery by getting into positions which are particularly favourable, such as squatting, semi-squatting and sitting with legs hanging down at the end of a bed. Some women find standing on the floor, leaning forward slightly and holding on to something or someone, with knees slightly bent, is a very good position for breech delivery. An equally active midwife or doctor can then lie on her or his back on the floor between the woman's legs and help deliver the baby.

The fact that your baby is breech may affect who delivers your baby and where. If you have booked a home birth, your midwife and/or GP will (almost certainly) recommend you to have your baby in hospital so you do not have to risk a traumatic transfer to hospital in an ambulance if the baby cannot be delivered vaginally: you may choose to accept or reject their advice. If you have booked a Domino birth, you may or may not be able to be cared for in labour by your designated community midwife/midwives: many hospitals take women out of the Domino system when complications arise. The same may apply if you have booked your birth in a GP unit. If you have booked a conventional consultant unit birth, there will be no changes, except that the condition of the baby will be monitored more carefully during labour.

> *I am 36 weeks pregnant and my baby is breech.*
> *My consultant is happy to let me choose to have*
> *a trial of labour but is not in favour of trying to*
> *turn the baby. Is there anything I can do in the*
> *meantime to encourage the baby to turn?*

The self-help options you can choose from are: touching and talking to your baby, encouraging it to turn; crawling around on all fours like a cat for half an hour every day; lying on the floor with your feet propped up on a bed or sofa (as in *The New Active Birth* – see Bibliography); getting into the knee-chest position for a few minutes every day; consulting a homoeopath or acupuncturist.

Do Caesareans and breeches run in families?

There is no evidence to suggest that this is generally the case. The only exceptions are when women in a family inherit an unusually small or awkwardly shaped pelvis, in which case Caesarean section may be necessary or babies may be breech because of the shape of the pelvis. If your own mother had a Caesarean section because of the size or shape of her pelvis, it may be helpful to remember that you have inherited genes from your father's family as well. Some women have problems with their pelvis because of poor nutrition or injury: if your mother had a Caesarean section, it might be worth asking if these factors are relevant. (See also Useful Organizations)

Is it true that they don't use high forceps any longer?

Now that Caesarean section is safer than in the past, it is often performed instead of high forceps when the cervix is fully dilated but the baby has descended only a little way or not at all in the second stage. Many obstetricians prefer to perform Caesarean section because it may carry fewer risks for the baby. However, it should be remembered that Caesarean section is a major operation and, as such, carries the usual risks for the mother and requires time for recovery afterwards.

Obstetricians usually look at the need for assisted delivery on an individual basis, trying to do what is best for that particular mother and baby: much depends on the exact position of the baby and the method of assisted delivery preferred by each obstetrician. One obstetrician may be very skilled at using high forceps, another may not. Some obstetricians use Ventouse followed by low forceps to deliver a baby rather than high forceps: it is a matter of training, skill and preference. For some women, high forceps may be very traumatic and so a Caesarean section may be preferable.

I had a long labour culminating in an emergency Caesarean. Why didn't they give me a Caesarean straight away, or at any rate earlier?

It is generally considered to be good obstetric practice to give a woman every chance to deliver a baby vaginally because a Caesarean section means a woman has a major operation to recover from at a time when she is going to be more busy than she has ever been before in her life, and because Caesarean section, although safer than in the past, carries certain risks for the woman and her baby. It can be very frustrating to reach full dilatation after a long, slow, painful labour and then have to have a Caesarean section, but some women find they have got some satisfaction out of experiencing labour, and the physical dilatation may make a vaginal delivery of a subsequent baby more likely.

14: Negotiating a birth plan

At least 59 per cent of the respondents to the *Good Housekeeping* survey had made a birth plan. For 35 per cent the birth plan was adhered to; for 13 per cent it was changed because of a medical emergency; 6 per cent changed their minds; and for 4 per cent the staff were unsupportive.

What is a birth plan?

A birth plan is a letter or statement in writing of a woman's preferences for labour and delivery. It should be discussed with a midwife or doctor at some time during pregnancy. It is usually attached to her notes, so that all the midwives and doctors attending her in labour are made aware of her wishes when they read her notes. It is wise to retain a copy of the birth plan as a record and to take it into labour as a reminder of what has been agreed.

What do you put in a birth plan?

You may choose to write down all the things you intend or would like to do to make yourself and your labour partner as comfortable as possible during labour. This may, for instance, include self-help coping techniques such as comfortable positions, eating and drinking, and all the things you would prefer the midwives and doctors attending you to do and not to do.

By finding out in advance about policies and routine procedures in the areas of concern to you, you will save time by omitting the aspects of routine hospital care you are happy with. Showing that you have done your research in this way, will also show the hospital staff that your choices are informed.

Choosing the style and presentation of your birth plan carefully can also help: phrases such as 'I should prefer' and 'if possible, I should like' are more likely to be favourably considered than 'I want' and 'I will'. It is wise to say that you may change your mind about what you have put in your birth plan, depending on how labour progresses and whether any emergencies arise. It can be tempting to adopt a more assertive approach. However, it is often better strategically to assume the staff will be sympathetic to your wishes. Many midwives and doctors are ready to take a woman's preferences seriously, particularly if they are presented in a tactful way. By using this approach, the option is still open to become more assertive if your wishes meet with unjustified or unreasonable opposition.

The Maternity Alliance has published a pack called *Your baby your choice* to be used by women in NHS antenatal classes taken by midwives. If it is being used in your classes, it will give you the chance to discuss the general topic of birth plans and what could go in them with a midwife and other pregnant women. If it is not being used, your midwife can obtain copies through the Maternity Alliance (see Useful Organizations).

Is a birth plan necessary?

Women who have booked a home birth under the NHS or with an independent midwife or a Domino under the NHS often find a birth plan is unnecessary. As the person/people who have been giving them their antenatal care will be delivering their babies, there is ample time during the pregnancy to talk about the sort of birth they would prefer. Moreover, the community and independent midwives and the GPs who attend home births tend to trust the natural process of birth and to have confidence in the ability of women to cope with labour and give birth naturally: this tendency causes them to listen to the preferences of women and give them positive encouragement to do it their own way, with professional support.

Women who have booked their birth at a private hospital may or may not find a birth plan necessary. Some women have such confidence in the private obstetrician they have chosen that they feel whatever the consultant and his/her team suggest will be right; other women wish to write down and discuss with the consultant their preferences for birth. As intervention rates are higher in private hospitals, women who have booked this kind of care may wish to discuss issues such as induction, episiotomy and assisted deliveries with their doctor.

Some women who have booked their birth at a conventional consultant unit are happy to accept whatever the hospital staff suggest and make any necessary decisions about labour as they go along; they may feel that midwives and doctors are the experts and know what is best for them and their babies. Other women have preferences and want to make them known.

The hospital has its own birth plan, so there's no need for me to do my own is there?

You can either use theirs or prepare one of your own. Some hospitals offer women a form to fill in with their choices and this may be sufficient for your particular preferences; on the other hand it may not. If it does not cover all your preferences, you might add a list or letter setting out the remainder, or you might choose to write a single letter or birth plan of your own. It is possible for a hospital birth plan to steer women in the direction of their policies and protocols, rather than informing women of all the choices actually available to them. Look out for the things that have been left out as well as what is listed. Remember to look for what you want to happen as well as what you want to avoid.

Who do I give my birth plan to?

It is usual for a woman to discuss her birth plan with a midwife or doctor at an antenatal appointment. If necessary, you can ask for a slightly longer appointment than is usual at the antenatal clinic or arrange to see a midwife or doctor (either your consultant or a registrar in his/her team) at a time outside usual antenatal clinic hours. It is not satisfactory to talk with a Senior House Officer (SHO) for this purpose, since SHOs may only have been practising for a few months and therefore have relatively little experience. If it is at an ordinary antenatal clinic appointment, make sure you are fully clothed and sitting or standing rather than lying down so you are in a position to discuss the birth plan as an equal. (You could ask the midwife or doctor to read your birth plan while you get dressed.) Some women choose to have their (labour) partner or a friend with them for moral support.

The midwife or doctor may wish to discuss or clarify particular points with you and may refer to hospital policies, protocols, guidelines and routine procedures. It is important to remember that policies, etc, are not legally binding, only a way of giving coherence to the way that hospital staff care for women, particularly in a large maternity unit delivering a large number of babies every year. You can choose to have an individual pattern of care during labour. After discussion with the midwife or doctor, you may choose to amend the birth plan; make sure that both copies are amended so that you too have a record of what was agreed. The hospital's copy of the agreed birth plan should be signed by the midwife or doctor and attached to your notes with a statement to the effect that the plan was discussed and agreed by [the named doctor] on [date]. Even if your hospital has a scheme whereby you carry your own notes, the midwives attending you will read the plan when you are admitted during labour.

Once your birth plan has been agreed, the hospital midwives and doctors attending you during labour will be aware of your preferred choices. If either you or the staff should feel a need to alter any part of the birth plan either before or during labour, further discussion will be necessary.

Supposing the hospital doesn't agree with what I want in my birth plan?

If reasons for the refusal are given, you may choose either to follow or reject the midwife's or doctor's advice. If no reasons are given for the refusal, ask them to give reasons and offer evidence to back up your request and your arguments. If the reasons given are rather vague, a good way of pointing this up is to ask the midwife or doctor a question like, 'What does the latest research say about this?' You may decide not to get involved in fruitless arguments with the midwife or doctor and ask to see a senior midwife or senior registrar or your consultant.

Some consultants are extremely helpful when a woman's case is complicated and although care in pregnancy for a particular condition might be clear, the management of labour is less clear; they may supply a woman with copies of research reports, so she can see for herself the current state of knowledge and make an informed choice about her preferences for labour.

It is important to remember that many midwives and doctors find it a refreshing change to care for a woman who takes an enlightened interest in her care, and view positively the challenge presented by a woman who has thought about what is best for her, her baby and her partner. Remember also that maternity care is the professional speciality of midwives and obstetricians. Their training, experience and sensibilities should be borne in mind.

Since discussing my birth plan I now realize this hospital is not for me. What can I do?

You may find that you can obtain your preferred approach to care in labour by changing consultant within the same hospital: ask the midwife sister in charge of the antenatal clinic and explain the problem to her.

If there is another hospital you would prefer, ring the supervisor of midwives to see if they have room for you. Although not widely known, there is movement in bookings during the latter stages of pregnancy. Sometimes women have to change hospital for medical reasons or because they move house. There may be a place for you now, when there wasn't a place at the beginning of your pregnancy.

If there isn't another hospital, or one that is better for you, or you no longer wish for a conventional consultant unit birth, it may be possible for you to be booked with the community midwives either on the Domino scheme or for a home birth. Places on the Domino scheme are limited but in some health districts are not always taken up (difficult to believe but true) so it is always worth ringing up the community midwives. They usually have an office either at the hospital or in a clinic – the hospital switchboard will know. You may decide finally to have your baby at home: the legal position is that the community midwives are obliged to attend you at home, and no quota exists, unlike the Domino scheme. Most maternity units have an emergency obstetric team (often called 'the flying squad') to provide back-up not only for home births, but also for pre-term and precipitate births not planned to take place at home.

It is also worth examining your feelings honestly and discussing them with your partner or a close friend. Are your feelings of discontent based on valid considerations (they may well be) or are they an expression of anxiety about the forthcoming labour or of feelings about past experiences?

CHECK-LIST OF CHOICES FOR BIRTH PLAN

To be treated with respect and dignity at all times
To have every procedure explained to you
To be able to change your mind
Having more than one labour companion
Routine inductions; whether partner there from beginning
Induction, elective Caesarean section or spontaneous labour and delivery for diabetic mother
Routine admission procedures
The right to return home if in early labour and waters unbroken or broken
Routine artificial rupture of membranes early in the first stage
Food and drink during labour
Wearing own clothes for labour
Using own equipment for labour, including music
Positions for first and second stages of labour

Positions for vaginal examinations

Routine acceleration, such as artificial rupture of membranes and Syntocinon drip

Management of breech labour

Management of twin or super-twin labour

Birthing pool: wish to use hospital's or bring in portable one

Routine offering of artificial pain relief

Availability of epidural anaesthesia for pain relief and Caesarean section and availability of suitably skilled anaesthetist

Availability/acceptability of TENS machines and/or midwives trained in their use

Policy towards use of alternative methods of pain relief, such as homoeopathic remedies, Bach flower remedies, acupuncture, self-hypnosis

Time-limits for first, second and third stages of labour

Management of second stage: whether woman allowed to await urge to push before being expected to push; whether epidural allowed to wear off after 8 cm

Care of perineum during delivery; routine episiotomy and policy re tearing, especially in primigravidae

Availability of local anaesthetic for episiotomy and/or stitches

Choice of pudendal/spinal block for forceps

Availability of spinal block for emergency Caesarean

Positions for delivery

Management of third stage: whether midwives trained in and confident about physiological management if woman chooses not to have managed third stage

Management of baby immediately after delivery: sucking out of mucus; Leboyer-type delivery; whether handed to mother immediately; midwife/mother/father to determine sex of baby; mother/father to cut cord; help with first breastfeed in delivery room; vitamin K injection/drops

Availability of suitably skilled midwife/doctor to sew tear or episiotomy

The stay in hospital: how long; whether/not have to stay in bed for six hours after normal delivery; availability of amenity room; support for breastfeeding; policy re extra fluids for breastfed baby; breastfeeding if baby in special care; rooming-in; visiting; privacy

15: Choosing from the options during labour

I have written a birth plan, but can I change my mind?

Yes, of course you can. Some midwives and doctors are rather cynical about birth plans because of the number of women who change their minds. However, it is your birth plan, your birth and up to you whether you need to change your mind. One way round the problem is to reserve the right to change your mind in the birth plan and to be realistic about emergencies, etc.

How do I choose when to go into hospital?
Several women I know found their contractions
stopped as soon as they got there.

Unless you have booked a Domino (when a midwife usually comes to assess you at home), you will have to decide yourself when to go into hospital, without having had a health professional examine you to see whether your cervix is at all dilated. If you are not in established labour, the hospital, especially if they are very busy and your waters are still intact, may encourage you to go home and keep in touch by telephone. Many women (and their labour partners) find this approach helpful and enjoy the opportunity to spend more of their labour at home, in their own surroundings. If, as many first-timers do, you find you have gone in too early, you could ask to go home again: this option could even be put into your birth plan. Unfortunately the luxury of such choices may be eroded for those women who live in rural areas far from their nearest maternity unit or who have to travel through congested cities or coastal areas popular with tourists in the summer months.

Even when they are in established labour, many women find that their contractions stop when they get to hospital, but then start again after an interlude. If this happens to you, you could use this break in your labour to make yourself at home in the delivery room assigned to you, to go for a walk round, or you can rest and relax, gathering your energies for when the contractions return.

Is it possible to combine self-help with artificial pain relief?

Entonox and TENS can be used in conjunction with positions, massage, breathing and relaxation techniques, etc. An epidural, if it works, obviates the need for such techniques. Pethidine sometimes puts a woman to sleep between contractions and for the early part of them so she suddenly wakes up to the peak of a contraction for which she has had no preparation; the labour partner can help by feeling her abdomen and waking her for each contraction. However, effects vary from one woman to another and may be influenced by fatigue and hunger.

Supposing the midwife makes me have Pethidine?

Neither a midwife nor a doctor should make you submit to any procedure, be it an injection of Pethidine or an episiotomy, without your permission. To do so would be an assault. It is your choice whether to accept or reject professional advice and all proposed procedures. It is also up to you to request any treatment or attention you would like. The midwife or doctor will make a clinical decision. If you cannot agree, you may choose to ask for a second opinion. There is a school of thought that by booking your care with a particular hospital you have given consent for all procedures deemed necessary during your labour and delivery. This concept is known as 'implied assent'. Legally, it is a grey area. You may choose to make your wishes known in advance or to be vigilant during your labour.

Sometimes a midwife or a doctor may believe, from their observation of a woman and from their own professional experience, that she might benefit from an injection of Pethidine. They might feel, for example, that Pethidine would help a woman relax and enable her cervix to dilate more quickly. Even if this were true, a woman might prefer not to have the drug and allow labour to take its natural course, using her self-help techniques to relax as much as possible during and between contractions: it is her choice.

Sometimes Pethidine is offered in a very gentle, subtle, albeit insistent way so a woman ends up believing it is best for her, even when she had decided before labour that she would not use that particular form of artificial pain relief. These things happen, and she should not blame herself or feel guilty.

How do I assess the reasons given for any
medical procedure, routine or otherwise, if I am
not medically trained?

It always helps if you feel able to trust the health professionals attending you. However, whatever procedure is being proposed, any midwife or doctor should be able to give you reasons for carrying it out in a way that you are able to understand and evaluate for yourself.

Ask other women how they found the midwives and doctors in the hospital you are going to. When wanting to carry out a procedure, do they say something like, 'So and so is happening, and we should like to do so and so. How do you feel about that?' or do they launch in and say, 'We're going to do this'? In the latter situation, you and your labour partner can choose to assert your right to be told what is happening and why they believe a particular procedure is necessary.

I have told my husband not, under any
circumstances, to let me have artificial pain
relief, but what if I change my mind?

Some women and their labour partners agree to work as a team to do their utmost to avoid artificial pain relief and any other procedures interfering with the natural progress of labour. However, as neither of you know what you will feel like during labour, it is best to approach it with an open mind, albeit prepared to use some options before others. If your partner works with you, giving you positive support and encouragement throughout, he will know why you wish to change your mind and support you in your request for artificial pain relief.

My friend asked them to let the epidural wear
off for the second stage so she could push the
baby out herself, but when it came to it she
ended up with forceps. How can I prevent this
happening to me?

One obvious way is not to have an epidural at all. Another way is to state in your birth plan that if you decide to have an epidural, you want it to be allowed to wear off after 8 cm dilatation and to use other ways of dealing with the pain (such as positions, Entonox, etc). Once this has been agreed with a midwife or doctor antenatally, in labour you and your labour partner can refer staff to the agreed birth plan. Though some women and some doctors and midwives are concerned about whether feeling the full power of contractions after having had no sensation at all will produce pain which is too much to bear, many women find that after a break from their labour provided by an epidural, they have the mental and physical energy to cope very well with a natural second stage. It is very common for the dynamics of second stage to be quite different from the end of the first stage, giving a woman a new lease of energy and the strength to deliver her baby herself. Many women also find that the second stage is often less painful than the end of the first stage. Being in touch with the sensations of labour can help a woman take up the positions which feel most comfortable and are likely to be the best for her to give birth to her baby.

I have stated in my birth plan that I would prefer to avoid an episiotomy unless it is medically necessary, for example if the baby is in distress and needs to be delivered quickly. How do I know they will respect my wishes?

However well informed you are, there does come a point at which you have to trust the midwives and doctors attending you. However, there are times when your birth plan can be a useful negotiating tool. For example, your second stage may progress normally, but the midwife might say to you, 'I'm going to give you an episiotomy because otherwise you will tear'. At this point you can choose either to discuss the matter with her in detail, asking her how she knows this, and how badly she thinks you will tear, and then decide whether or not to agree to the procedure; or you can choose to avoid such discussion, saying that it has already been agreed that you will not have an episiotomy as an alternative to tearing, that you have learned breathing techniques for delivery and that you welcome her skills and experience in helping you not to tear by controlling delivery. If you do not have confidence in her ability or willingness to do this, you can choose to have an episiotomy after all, or ask for another midwife to help you deliver your baby. During this interchange, you may choose to let your labour partner negotiate, depending on the attitude of the midwife to using an intermediary. Such a delay may of course make an episiotomy redundant!

How do I make sure my birth plan is put into action? So many friends have done birth plans which have gone by the board during labour.

It is important that both you and your labour partner prepare yourselves mentally and physically for labour, maintaining realistic expectations about the possible range of experiences within which your own labour might be. With this attitude, you will have a realistic birth plan (in which you reserve the right to change your mind and the right not to be challenged about it during labour) on which you can rely in labour. When you are admitted into hospital and each time there is a change of shift, ask any midwife and doctor attending you to read the birth plan. If a midwife or doctor makes some suggestion that does not take account of your birth plan (even if they have read it) you, or, if you prefer, your labour partner, may tactfully point out that the suggestion is inappropriate, reminding them of the specific item in the birth plan. Some women are surprised at how amenable the hospital staff can be to their wishes, encountering no opposition during labour; others find themselves encountering constant persuasion, in the most subtle manner, to accept routine procedures contrary to their original wishes.

Ideally, a birth plan properly used by both the woman and her attendants, should, if labour progresses normally, prevent the need for unexpected decision-making in labour, leaving the woman and her labour partner free to concentrate on coping with contractions; and the midwives and doctors free to channel their skills and energies into supporting the woman in the way she finds most helpful.

> *I've heard that I can change consultant or midwife or ask for a second opinion. Won't this just put everyone's backs up and make things difficult for me?*

This is something that is probably best considered with the facts before you at the time. It may also depend on how tactfully you approach the problem and how serious your difficulties with your existing doctor or midwife are. In obstetrics, as in other fields, it is recognized that not everybody can get on with each other and the fact that you want to change doctor or midwife or get a second opinion may be a relief to the professional concerned. If you have serious reasons for wanting a change of attendant or a second opinion, you might blame yourself afterwards if you do not try at the time to ask for what you want. You may make things better for yourself and for those women following you.

16: The first few hours

Can I hold the baby immediately after he or she is born?

It is usual for the midwife delivering the baby to hand him or her to you immediately after birth so you are the first person to hold and cuddle your new baby. However, if there are any complications such as a Caesarean section or the baby having passed meconium during labour, the baby is given to a paediatrician to check, perhaps to have his or her air passages sucked out and, if necessary, oxygen administered to help him or her breathe. A woman who has a Caesarean section under general anaesthetic may not be able to hold her baby for several hours.

Most midwives and doctors are well aware of the need for parents to hold their babies as soon as possible after birth and check for themselves that their baby is 'all right'. However, sometimes they need reminding of this, especially if they are very busy or if the baby needs special checks. Some parents are shy about asking to hold their baby in such a situation, forgetting that the baby is theirs: you can ask to hold your baby if the staff do not let you do it automatically.

What procedures do they carry out in the delivery room?

The midwife may or may not suck out the mucus from the baby's mouth and nose to clear the airways; some midwives prefer to let the mucus drain out naturally. You may be able to choose which you prefer, but in some cases it may be a necessity.

The umbilical cord is clamped and cut either before or after delivery of the placenta, depending on whether you are having a managed or physiological third stage; if the latter, you or your labour partner may choose to cut the cord as a symbolic ending of the pregnancy.

The midwife gives the baby an Apgar score out of 10 which is recorded in the notes – anything over five is generally all right – and repeats the procedure five and ten minutes after delivery; the score takes into account how quickly the baby breathes, his or her colour, muscle tone, etc, and if the score is low, the baby is looked after extra carefully.

Babies are often born with vernix and some maternal blood on their skin. Sometimes they are only wiped, sometimes bathed, in the delivery room, depending on hospital policy. You may be able to choose. After the first cuddle and feed, midwives like to dress babies, because their temperature control is not yet fully developed. You and your labour partner may choose to do this yourselves.

Before you leave the delivery room, or before the midwife leaves your home if you are having a home birth, the baby is usually given vitamin K. A deficiency of vitamin K may lead to a disorder of the blood clotting mechanism. Whilst the deficiency occurs in only a very few babies, the condition is potentially so serious that it is a very common procedure to give vitamin K to all babies. Recently there were reports of a study which found that children with childhood cancer had received Pethidine during birth and vitamin K immediately after. What the reports omitted to say was that no causal connection between childhood cancer and Pethidine and vitamin K had been proved and that the study asked for further research to be carried out. Some people are beginning to question the routine administration of vitamin K and other substances and tests to all babies as a way of reaching the few babies who are in need of them.

Vitamin K may be given either as an injection or drops and sometimes fathers are invited to administer the drops to their new son or daughter. Although drops are less invasive than an injection during the first hour of life, there is sometimes doubt about how much the baby swallows. Some hospitals get around this problem by administering a second dose of drops before the baby leaves hospital to make sure (presumably the same could be done by a community midwife at home if there were any doubt). Some people might question the safety of giving a baby two doses of vitamin K if he or she is not deficient. It is worth remembering that colostrum also contains vitamin K.

If you have had an episiotomy or tear, this will be sutured (sewn up) either by the midwife (more and more midwives are being trained to do this) or by a doctor. This is a skilled procedure, the success of which will determine the rate at which you heal and may affect your sex-life. If stitches are necessary, you might want to ensure that the midwife or doctor is sufficiently experienced (this could be discussed tactfully with the midwife or the sister in charge of the labour ward if it is not in your birth plan). Sometimes it is necessary to wait for some time before a sufficiently experienced doctor is available for suturing. At a home birth, suturing will be performed either by the community midwife or the GP. *Effective Care in Pregnancy and Childbirth* (pages 241-242) recommends polyglycolic acid sutures (Dexon or Vicryl) as the best material for repair. Doctors conventionally tend to use silk, the easiest material to work with. However, recent research recommends that from the point of view of the woman's comfort during healing, polyglycolic acid is better. It might be a point to raise and to be firm about. The procedure is traditionally carried out with the woman's feet in stirrups, but some professionals are happy for a woman to lie with her legs apart, as for a vaginal examination.

If a woman has Rhesus negative blood, the baby may have a blood test in the delivery room to see if he or she is Rhesus positive. If so, the mother must be given an injection of anti-D within 72 hours of delivery to protect any future Rhesus positive babies. If you are not told the result of the test during this time, it is worth checking so that if you need the injection you can ensure it is given within the time-limit.

If you have a preference about any of the above procedures, you may wish to discuss them before the end of your pregnancy and put them into a birth plan.

Supposing there is a problem with the baby?

Much depends on the nature and severity of the problem. If babies need special medical surveillance, immediate surgery or extra help with breathing, they are usually transferred without delay to the special care baby unit (SCBU) or neonatal unit at the hospital. New mothers are emotionally very vulnerable and are likely to find any separation from their new baby upsetting. Sometimes a baby is transferred in an incubator to a different hospital with superior facilities, which can be especially distressing for the mother if she has to stay in the hospital where she gave birth for a few days before being discharged. If this happens to you, it is worth asking if you could be transferred as soon as possible as well: some neonatal units have beds so mothers can stay near their babies all the time. Some babies need just a few hours in an incubator if they have had a difficult birth.

SCBUs are often some way from the normal postnatal ward, so it is worth asking if your labour partner could take you in a wheelchair to see your newborn baby. (Hospitals don't like women walking around too soon after labour and sometimes they are too busy to release a midwife/call a porter to escort a woman.) If a baby does have to spend a short time in a SCBU for observation, it is worth reminding the staff if you intend to breastfeed. This should prevent them feeding the baby by tube. You can ask them to help you put the baby to the breast when he or she is hungry.

Can my partner stay with me after the birth?

For women having their babies at home, the question doesn't arise; for many families, all going back to bed together after the birth is one of the high-spots of the whole experience. Most hospitals allow women and their partners time with the baby in the delivery room to get to know each other and will often leave them alone for a time in privacy. However, the time comes when a woman has to be helped with washing, dressing in a clean nightdress or day-clothes and moving to the postnatal ward. If it is outside visiting-hours or at night, partners are asked to leave so as not to disrupt the ward. If a woman has booked a Domino which includes six-hour discharge, the partner may be able to stay until it is time for her to go home, depending again on the time of day and also on whether there is a special short-stay ward. If your partner is asked to leave but you would prefer him to stay, you could ask for the three of you to be together either in the day-room or nursery.

How soon can I breastfeed my baby?

Some women feed their babies immediately after birth, others leave it until a little later. Babies vary in their readiness to take to the breast straight after the birth, but once they have got used to the bright lights and noise and recognized their mother's voice, some babies are ready for their first feed in the delivery room. Other babies choose to wait longer for their first feed but may lick and nuzzle the nipple. Many parents find themselves moved to see the baby's rooting and sucking reflexes enabling him or her to feed so soon and are amazed at the strength of the baby's suck. Some women having a physiological third stage put the baby to the breast to assist delivery of the placenta.

Do I have to stay in bed for six hours after the birth? Is it hospital policy?

Hospital policies are rules, not laws. The policy of making women stay in bed for six hours after birth dates back to the time when more women were recovering from the drugs administered during labour and unsteady on their feet. For safety reasons, it was thought that each woman should be escorted by a midwife or auxiliary if she walked around; restricting women to their beds except for vital visits to the lavatory made the staff's job easier. This is yet another area where no research has been done to evaluate the effectiveness of widespread hospital practice for all women. Therefore, there is no need for you to stay in bed if you do not want to. Once they are on the postnatal ward, many women find they need to empty their bladders quite frequently, as they begin to lose the extra fluid taken on during pregnancy to support the baby.

How tired am I likely to be after the birth?

If you have a general anaesthetic or a lot of other drugs and a difficult labour, you might be quite tired after the birth. However, often women who have had a good birth feel euphoric and full of energy. A woman who has drawn on every last ounce of her strength and energy to cope with contractions and push the baby out, may undergo an extraordinary change after birth and suddenly look fresh and ready for anything. It is common for such women to become quite frustrated about not being able to sleep during the first 24 hours or so after delivery. Babies who have not had drugs are usually alert and look around them after birth, perhaps have a feed and then once all the fuss has died down, settle to sleep to recover from the rigours of labour. The woman, tucked up into a clean bed on the postnatal ward or at home, may be ready for a sleep herself, particularly if she has missed a night's sleep, but she is all too likely to find herself wide awake, unable to sleep and with nothing to do, because her baby is dozing peacefully beside her. Research on this has led some people to believe that it is hormones which keep a newly-delivered mother awake to watch over her baby. If this happens to you, you could use the time to have a shower or bath, wash your hair or even write down an account of your labour or ring a friend or relative. Or you might just want to gaze at your baby and look forward to a good night's sleep once the first 24 hours is up!

Can I have my baby with me after the birth?

Unless a woman is very ill, when the baby will be kept in the nursery, it is usual practice nowadays for babies to 'room in' with their mothers so they are never separated. It is recognized that this helps mothers and babies build up their relationship and makes breastfeeding easier. In some private hospitals it is still policy to take babies away to the nursery, particularly at night, to give the mothers a rest. However, you can choose to keep your baby with you all the time if you wish.

If you were to have a Caesarean under general anaesthetic, you could ask to have your baby brought to you when you wake up for the second time. Waking after general anaesthesia can be a disorientating experience for many women. As a result of the general anaesthetic they may have forgotten seeing their baby in the recovery room. If the labour partner stays until the woman wakes up, he or she could perhaps ask to keep the baby so the woman sees him or her immediately on waking.

Can I eat after the birth?

Many women are ravenous after labour and pack food and drink in the labour bag to eat after the birth. Hospitals often provide a cup of tea and toast after the birth, but only for the woman.

Do hospitals cater for minority diets?

Yes, they often cater for special dietary needs, providing, for example, vegetarian meals, kosher meals and meals prepared using Halal meat. Before your birth, you can ask about what is available at hospital antenatal classes or telephone the hospital administrator. If they do not cater for your needs, they usually do not object to relatives and friends bringing in special food. If the latter is not possible, you can ask the hospital to arrange special food just for you.

I am having my baby in an NHS hospital. Is it ever possible to have a room to oneself?

Many hospitals have 'amenity beds' which are reserved for women needing extra peace and quiet after a difficult birth or special nursing. They are often allocated to other women after a normal birth in return for a usually reasonable fee, on the understanding that if the room is needed for a special case, it will be vacated. You can ask about amenity beds at hospital antenatal classes or telephone the hospital administrator.

Many modern NHS hospitals have small postnatal wards for four women who share their own bathroom. This accommodation is much more comfortable than the old-style long wards, and women enjoy each other's company, often making friends.

17: Staying in hospital

70 per cent of the respondents to the *Good Housekeeping* Survey who had their babies in hospital found the length of their stay in hospital just right; 14 per cent found it too long; 7 per cent too short. 14 per cent stayed in for one day or less; 15 per cent for two days; 10 per cent for three days; 12 per cent for four days; 15 per cent for five days; and 22 per cent for six to ten days.

> ### The hospital are asking women to go home after 24 hours, but can I choose to stay in longer?

Some hospitals are beginning to ask all women following a normal delivery, including first-time mothers, to go home at the end of 24 hours to release beds in order to cut costs. They may also take into account the amount of support a woman has at home and how she and her baby are getting on with breastfeeding. Some hospitals are holding joint mother and midwife breastfeeding workshops before the birth, so women are better informed about breastfeeding and have built up a relationship with a midwife whose support they can seek by telephone after the birth.

Many first-time mothers are alarmed at the thought of going home so early, but find that once home, they are glad to be there. There is a risk of catching postnatal infections from dirty hospital bathrooms; many postnatal wards are understaffed and there is still much conflicting advice given on breastfeeding. Thus life in hospital, despite the fact that some women manage to get more rest than they would at home, is not always all that one would wish. Many women find they are unable to gain confidence in their ability to look after their baby until they are settled at home. Once home, each new mother is visited at home by a community midwife who, for the duration of her visit, gives the woman her undivided attention, can help with cleaning the baby's umbilical cord, breastfeeding, etc. The community midwife can visit for longer (up to 28 days after the birth) if necessary for either mother or baby before handing over to the health visitor. It is thought by many midwives that women who stay in hospital for too long may become too dependent on the midwives and lack confidence in their own abilities to look after their babies.

You can ask to stay in longer than 24 hours if you feel that is right for you and see what they say. Be prepared to put a good case!

The hospital likes women to stay until the third day, but can I go home earlier if the baby and I are OK?

Legally, you can discharge yourself whenever you like, and the district health authority has the statutory duty to provide you with care from a midwife for as long as you and your baby need it, up to 28 days following delivery. In practice, it is not a good idea to discharge yourself unless there is a real emergency and usually it is not necessary if you make your needs known before and immediately after the birth. In some hospitals, because most people go home after a set time, say two, three or five days, the staff may not be used to getting all the paperwork and 'phone calls done within a shorter time. Before you can go home it may be hospital policy for you to be discharged, that is passed as fit, by a doctor; the baby is usually seen by a paediatrician; and the community midwives serving the area where you live need to be told that you will be coming under their care. If you know before the birth that you are likely to want to go home before the third day, you could choose to put this in your birth plan and discuss it either at an antenatal appointment or with the supervisor of midwives; this way, they will be alerted as soon as you reach the postnatal ward that you are going home early and will start the administrative ball rolling.

How can I decide on the length of my hospital stay now, when I have no idea what I shall feel like after the birth?

It is difficult for many women to decide, but most women choose to go along with what the hospital suggests and find themselves quite happy with that once the baby is born. It can be quite enjoyable to be with other new mothers all experiencing more or less the same transition into parenthood. Other women find themselves miserable and desperate to go home very quickly. If the latter is the case, you may find it helpful for your partner or a friend to negotiate an earlier discharge: if you burst into tears, they may be even more reluctant to let you go!

> *Do we have to keep to the official visiting*
> *hours? My partner works odd shifts and my*
> *mum wants to come from quite a long way*
> *away just for the day.*

The visiting hours are generally designed to ensure women get enough rest before going home, particularly in these days of increasingly early discharge. However, there is no reason why you cannot explain the situation to the midwife sister in charge of the postnatal ward and ask to see your partner and mother in the day-room or nursery to minimize disruption to other mothers. The sister is likely to appreciate your consideration for the other women, and grant your request.

Can I keep the baby in bed with me at night?

Some hospitals and individual midwives are more relaxed about this than others. Many of them are very nervous of babies being dropped on the floor and of mothers rolling on to their babies. Research shows that both men and women are born with an instinct not to roll on top of babies, but it is important that no alcohol or drugs are taken. Even paracetamol (often given in hospital to relieve perineal pain) can alter a woman's natural reactions. Some midwives take pleasure in tucking up new babies snugly with their mothers. You could ask your hospital what their policy is or choose not to ask, but just do it!

Can I leave the baby in the nursery so I get a good night's rest before going home?

This is something you could negotiate with the night staff on duty; some are quite happy to keep an eye on the baby and bring him or her to you if he or she needs feeding. Some women find this more restful than having the baby next to them, particularly if they have missed two nights' sleep. Others may refuse, perhaps because they are too busy, or because they are too far from the nursery for a baby's cries to be heard. You could choose to go home earlier and ask whoever is looking after you to listen for the baby.

Do I have to wear a nightie in hospital? I never wear one at home.

Many women confront their list of 'what to take into hospital' in this situation! You can choose to wear whatever feels most comfortable for you. More hospitals are encouraging women to wear lightweight comfortable day clothes such as leisure suits and T-shirts which help them remember they are not ill. However, there is a school of thought which suggests women do wear nightdresses, pyjamas and dressing-gowns so they get the rest and support they need and so that visitors don't stay too long! Whatever you decide to pack, make sure it is thin (but not transparent!) because postnatal wards are very hot, and that it can be pulled up or opened at the front for breastfeeding.

How can I avoid getting a postnatal infection?

Ten per cent of the respondents to the *Good Housekeeping* Survey had a postnatal infection. Women are particularly prone to postnatal infection after episiotomy, Caesarean section, forceps delivery and a longer stay in hospital, so achieving the most natural birth you can and staying in hospital for as short a time as possible may minimize the risk.

While you are in hospital, always wipe loo seats and the rims of bidets with antiseptic wipes (available from chemists if the hospital does not supply them – some do) both before and after using them, making sure you leave bathrooms and loos as you would wish to find them. You should wash your perineum with clean water (a bidet makes this easier, but your own small washing-up bowl is quite all right) every time you empty your bladder or bowel. Hospital bidets should be cleaned carefully before use. Showers are more hygienic than baths, but if you prefer a bath or if there isn't a shower, clean the bath with cream cleanser and a cloth that you have packed in your hospital bag. Even, and especially, if you have had a Caesarean, you must clean the bath before using it – or perhaps your partner or a friend could do it and then hold the baby while you have a bath. Any wound must be kept as clean and dry as possible: the best way is to dab it gently with a clean towel or sanitary towel and let it finish drying by exposing it to the air. The use of a hairdrier (sometimes recommended) to dry the perineum is inadvisable for three reasons: first, the risk of airborne infection; second, the risk of a drop of blood falling into the hairdrier; and third, excessive drying of the perineum may inhibit healing.

Many women find homoeopathic remedies and other natural therapies aid healing, but it is probably wise to avoid any kind of poultice which may lead to breakdown of the repair. Salt or antiseptics in the bathwater have been shown by research to make no difference to the healing process or to the incidence of infection.

Pelvic floor exercises promote healing dramatically: start doing them gently as soon as you can and build them up day by day.

The hospital says I should not open my bowel for three days so as not to damage my episiotomy repair. Is that right?

Many women find that if they have thoroughly emptied their bowel during labour and missed several meals before the birth, they do not need to empty their bowel again for a couple of days. Once the faecal matter builds up again, the thought of passing a stool through a sore perineum may be alarming. To minimize the discomfort of the stitches and to allay any worries, you could hold a clean sanitary towel or a pad of lavatory paper over the episiotomy while you empty your bowel. Generally speaking, the longer you wait to pass a stool, the more uncomfortable it is, so go when you have to and keep the stools as soft as you can by eating plenty of fibre (some women pack muesli and dried apricots and other dried fruit in their hospital bag) and by drinking plenty of liquids; it is easy to become dehydrated in a hot postnatal ward. Some pain relieving drugs can cause constipation, so check with a midwife if this becomes a problem.

I never wear sanitary towels. Is it all right to use tampons after the birth?

The blood loss from the site of the placenta in the uterus lasts for about three to four weeks. It is heavy only for the first week or so and gets lighter more quickly if you breastfeed, since the hormones stimulated by breastfeeding cause the uterus and therefore the wound from the placenta to reduce in size more quickly. Doctors advise against the use of tampons because of the risk of infection from introducing anything into your vagina, and you might find inserting a tampon after the birth uncomfortable anyway. You will probably find that as the blood loss decreases the sanitary pads you use can be very discreet. Sanitary pads enable midwives to gauge the blood loss and assess its nature and they may ask you whether the blood loss is brown, red or rust colour.

NCT (Maternity Sales) Ltd (see Useful Organizations) sell special nylon pants for use before and after birth; they are very stretchy, so hold pads firmly in place without the need for belts, pins etc, and increase and decrease in size with you! They are especially comfortable after an episiotomy or a Caesarean section, when normal pants may rub uncomfortably on the wound: the NCT pants avoid this by reaching to the waist. Their other virtue is that they dry very quickly after washing.

18: Breastfeeding and bottle feeding

Only 1 per cent of the respondents to the *Good Housekeeping* Survey had problems with breastfeeding, but 23 per cent would have liked to have had more information about it.

Which is better for the baby, breastmilk or formula?

Breastmilk is better for the baby, because it is always available, at the right temperature, of the right consistency and differs to suit the developing baby's needs. Breastmilk also contains many valuable immunoglobulins which help reduce the risks of respiratory and gastric infections beyond the period of actual breastfeeding. The only exception is when a baby has a lactose intolerance, but this is extremely rare. Breastfeeding also gives a baby a unique experience which cannot be replicated.

Which is better for the mother?

Breastfeeding, because it is convenient (no sterilizing or waiting for bottles to cool down or warm up); the oxytocin produced by the baby's sucking helps the uterus return to its non-pregnant size more quickly; some women seem to lose weight more easily; and it is cheap (a mother has to eat very little more in order to produce enough breastmilk). Also, the nappies of breastfed babies are less smelly than those of bottle-fed babies! The mother knows she is giving her baby the very best possible start and there is a special closeness.

Which is better for the father?

Breastfeeding. Many men find it very rewarding to see their partner breastfeed their baby; it is cheap; he does not always have to get up in the night but may choose sometimes to keep his partner company or fetch the baby for her; and he knows it is best for his baby. Some people attach too much importance to the fact that fathers cannot share breastfeeding, but there are many other things they can do, both for the mother and the baby. It is possible for men to get close to their babies in many pleasant ways: by giving them baths; going for walks; cuddling them; talking and singing to them; smiling at them; and playing with them.

What if I fail to breastfeed or choose not to?

It is better for a baby to be happily bottle fed than unhappily breastfed. Often women who do not breastfeed try to deal with their guilt by saying formula milk is as good as breastmilk: this is not the case and never will be. If women have chosen not to breastfeed because that is best for them and their family situation, they can also choose not to feel guilty: they must make their decision and stick to it. When women have tried but failed, it is possible that their lack of success is due to having been given the wrong information or conflicting advice.

Isn't breastfeeding much harder than bottle feeding?

Not everyone finds this, but because breastfeeding was out of fashion for so long, new mothers are no longer always surrounded and supported by midwives or other women who are skilled in the art of breastfeeding. However, there is an increasing interest in breastfeeding and many midwives and health visitors are becoming better informed. There is often an assumption that because breastfeeding is natural, it must be instinctive. Although a baby is born with rooting and sucking reflexes to help him or her learn to breastfeed, he or she and their mother need to learn to breastfeed together. Even an experienced breastfeeding mother has to re-learn with a new baby: every baby is different and she may also have forgotten how to breastfeed a newborn baby.

Another important aspect is that women see very little breastfeeding around them or in the media so that the way a baby is positioned for breastfeeding has not been imprinted on their memory in the way the image of a mother and baby bottle feeding has. The Joint Breastfeeding Initiative (see Useful Organizations) carried out a survey on people's attitudes to seeing breastfeeding. This showed that the majority of people are in favour of breastfeeding as long as they don't have to see it, particularly in public, but even at home! There is little appreciation of the needs of young babies to feed frequently and of new mothers to get out of the house; it may be impossible to do the shopping or have a meal out within the short interval between breastfeeds.

Even if a woman has problems to begin with, once breastfeeding is established, it is easier than bottle feeding because there are no bottles to be made up, etc. If every woman choosing to breastfeed her new baby had access to the well-informed support and positive encouragement she deserves, breastfeeding would be easier than bottle feeding from the beginning. Contacting an NCT breastfeeding counsellor in the early days can help this happen.

What is the minimum time you should breastfeed a baby for?

Successful Breastfeeding, the Royal College of Midwives' handbook on breastfeeding (see Bibliography) says, '...unless individual circumstances make it impossible, all babies should be exclusively breastfed until they are at least four, and preferably six months old.' The Department of Health also makes this recommendation. From the age of three months onwards babies are increasingly able to build up their own immunities and between four and six months onwards most babies begin to eat some solid food: this can be a good time to introduce formula milk as well if that is what the mother wants, but many mothers (and their babies) prefer to breastfeed for much longer, giving their babies a mixed diet of solid food and breastmilk. If breastfeeding goes on for some time, there may be no need ever to wean on to a bottle: many babies graduate from breast to trainer cup. There is some evidence that longer avoidance of cow's milk reduces the risks of allergies developing.

How can I succeed at breastfeeding?

During the end of your pregnancy get to know someone who can support you with breastfeeding. If you attend NCT antenatal classes, one class will be devoted to breastfeeding and you will meet an NCT breastfeeding counsellor who will support you after the birth. NCT breastfeeding counsellors are available 24 hours a day, free of charge to *everyone* and you may choose to contact one through your local branch or group of the NCT.

Some hospitals have midwives or nurses given a title such as 'breastfeeding counsellor', 'lactation sister' or 'feeding advisor', etc, and they are usually available during normal working hours to women during their postnatal stay in hospital. At other times you are dependent on the availability, attitudes and knowledge of the other postnatal ward midwives. Once you go home, or throughout the ten days if you have booked a home birth or Domino, you will have the support of community midwives. Once the community midwives have discharged you, you will have access to a health visitor, many of whom give excellent support to breastfeeding women. The community midwife can visit for longer if there are problems with breastfeeding.

You might find it helpful to read about breastfeeding (see the NCT's leaflets in the Bibliography), but in the end you and your baby will teach each other to breastfeed. It is not always easy to maintain a positive attitude but it helps to get support from a reliable source as soon as there are any problems: the sooner you seek help, the sooner any problem can be sorted out. Breastfeeding should not hurt: if it does, there is something wrong which a community midwife or NCT breastfeeding counsellor can help you sort out before it escalates into a bigger problem.

> *I had decided not to breastfeed but the hospital*
> *says I should try it and see. What if I hate it,*
> *but the baby won't give it up?*

It is possible that a baby might reject a bottle, but fairly unusual. If it does happen, there are strategies to try, such as someone else offering a bottle to the baby when you are out of the room. You could give breastfeeding a try and see how it goes. You may surprise yourself. If you decide it is not for you, you can use the support of the hospital community midwives, your health visitor or an NCT breastfeeding counsellor to help you stop. It is important that mothers do not stop breastfeeding abruptly but allow their milk to dry up gradually.

chest to chest
chin to breast

If you feel you would like to discuss the matter with someone in a neutral manner, you could contact an NCT breastfeeding counsellor who would not pressurize you in any way, but would listen, answer your questions and give you a chance to explore your feelings about breastfeeding. The act of breastfeeding can feel a very primitive one in our society where people prefer to see breasts bared to titillate on page three rather than a baby being breastfed on a bus: you are not alone in your doubts and worries.

I would have liked to breastfeed, but is it worth it, as I have decided to return to work after three months?

Three months is not as long as the minimum time recommended by the Royal College of Midwives, but breastfeeding would give your baby the benefits of colostrum and the immunities from three months' worth of breastmilk, and your uterus would more quickly return to its non-pregnant size. Research shows that breastfeeding exclusively for 13 weeks confers benefits in the form of fewer respiratory and gastro-intestinal illnesses for far longer than the actual period of breastfeeding. It would give you and your baby the unique closeness experienced in the breastfeeding relationship. Indeed the closeness could be maintained by keeping on the first and last breastfeeds of the day and any that occur at night. Many women returning to work obtain great pleasure from partially breastfeeding and their bodies obligingly produce milk at the times of day their baby needs it. Some women are able to take it further and fully breastfeed after returning to work by expressing milk to leave at home; by using a crèche which they visit for breastfeeds; or, in a few cases, finding a childminder near work or arranging for their nanny to bring the baby into work so they can give their babies a breastfeed and a cuddle in the lunch-hour. Once breastfeeding is well established, many babies gracefully accept what they are offered, happily switching from breast to bottle at different times of day with different people, so you can choose the pattern best suited to your needs. More information can be found in the NCT booklet, *Breastfeeding – returning to work*.

Supposing the baby won't take the bottle when I return to work?

This is rarely a problem, but if it is, consult an NCT breastfeeding counsellor or your health visitor. Babies are extremely sensitive to the moods and emotions of people around them, so it is important that you sort out for yourself the best time to return to work and whether you will return full-time or part-time. You may have no choice in this respect for financial or other reasons, but if you do, make sure you are making the right decisions for you, your baby and your family.

It is true that bottle-fed babies sleep through the night earlier than breastfed babies?

Most babies wake at least once in the night for feeding because their stomachs are very small. As they grow older, breastfed as well as bottle-fed babies begin to sleep through the night, but this is an individual thing and may depend on their milk intake during the day. For every bottle-fed paragon sleeping through the night from early on (the kind every mother envies at postnatal groups!) there is a breastfed paragon too, but both are quite rare. Formula milk is less easy to digest than breastmilk, so it often enables babies to go longer between feeds than breastfed babies, depending on their individual digestion and capacity, and this can help some bottle-fed babies to sleep through the night at a younger age. However, this advantage is disappearing now that manufacturers are making formula milk more like breastmilk and babies are not going so long between feeds.

There is a myth that babies who wake up at night for breastfeeds become toddlers and children with sleep problems, but this is not true for all breastfed babies. All babies are physiologically capable of sleeping through the night by around five months, but whether or not they do may depend on their parents' management of bedtime routines, etc, and, more difficult, on their own personalities! Between six and eight months many babies become unsettled at night due to 'separation anxiety' which is the newly acquired knowledge that the mother is a separate person and may not come back again. If this is handled sensitively and confidently, babies can learn eventually how to put themselves to sleep both at the beginning of the night and whenever they wake during the night. There are a number of excellent books setting out useful strategies for parents to help their children become good sleepers (see Bibliography).

Will the hospital give the baby formula or Dextrose without telling me?

This rarely happens nowadays, since midwives understand much better how important it is for breastfed babies to get all their food at the breast so the milk supply is properly stimulated and the mother's body has an accurate picture of the baby's needs for food. However, it is not unknown for a well-meaning midwife, often at night, to give a baby a bottle of formula or Dextrose so a tired mother can get a better night's rest. This is fine if it is the mother's choice, but is not if it goes against her wishes. The best way to guard against it happening is to keep the baby with you at all times and to make your wishes known once you are on the postnatal ward. For babies born in families afflicted by allergies, just one bottle of formula milk could sensitize a baby so he or she might be prone to getting eczema or allergies in the future. For other babies, one bottle of formula milk would do no harm, although there is research to show that it could encourage the growth of different gut flora in a baby. If the baby does for some reason spend time in the nursery while you are asleep, a notice on the cot may prevent any possible confusion.

> *Would it be all right for me to breastfeed during the day and my partner to give the occasional bottle at night or at weekends to give me a break?*

Many women express breastmilk using a hand-held or battery-operated or electric pump (all available from the NCT) to get a break in this way. However, it is not something to be attempted during the very first weeks of breastfeeding. Since the hormonal balance is very delicate and the milk supply depends on the contact of the baby's mouth with the nipple as well as the breast being emptied. Once your milk supply is 'established', usually around four weeks after the birth, expressing some milk for an evening out can be a good way of getting some time alone with your partner or to yourself.

> *Every time I ask for help with breastfeeding, I am given different advice. Whose should I follow – my community midwife, my GP, my health visitor or the NCT breastfeeding counsellor?*

It is easy as a new parent to ask everyone you meet for advice about the different aspects of childcare and it is likely that you will get as many pieces of advice as the number of people you ask. On the whole, this does not matter, because you will eventually build up the confidence to rely on your commonsense and your knowledge of your baby. However, breastfeeding is an art, not a science, and every breastfeeding relationship is different, even that between the same mother and different babies (including twins and super-twins). It is therefore vital that when seeking support in the early days of breastfeeding you choose to listen to someone who has a lot of knowledge and practical experience of supporting breast-feeding mothers and who is prepared to give you the time to talk at length about your birth and your baby, so they are in a position to give you well-informed support.

Try to look objectively at the support available to you and decide who is most likely to meet the above criteria. For women who are the victims of conflicting advice, NCT breastfeeding counsellors are very good at listening to everything a woman has been told and helping her to sort out what might be the best course of action for her. They try as far as possible to avoid giving further advice, but will do their utmost to assist the woman by giving her accurate information and helping her achieve correct positioning of the baby. Problems such as apparently inadequate supply, sore and cracked nipples and mastitis are usually the result of incorrect positioning (see illustration on page 150).

I am expecting twins: can I still breastfeed?

Yes, you can. The Twins and Multiple Births Association – TAMBA – produces an excellent leaflet (see Bibliography and Useful Organizations). It is even more important for you to get enough rest and to eat regularly than if you were having a singleton and to get all the help you can with domestic chores.

Can I choose to breastfeed if my baby is premature?

Yes, you can. If babies are born so young that they cannot suck at the breast (sometimes the sucking reflex is not yet developed and/ or their mouths may be too small to latch on to the breast), they are tube-fed in the special care baby unit (SCBU) until they can. Their mothers establish and keep their milk supply going by expressing with an electric breast pump. The colostrum and early milk (different from the milk of a mother who has given birth at term) can be given to the baby by tube in addition to the special formula milk given to tiny babies. Many units are not happy to rely totally on the mother's milk, especially now that very little donated breastmilk is used. SCBU staff usually give mothers wanting to breastfeed a lot of support and encourage as much physical contact as is possible with the baby to stimulate the milk-producing hormones.

Keeping the breastmilk going during this time is very hard work, but many such mothers feel at a time when their baby is dependent on technology for survival, that it is the one thing only they can do for their baby. Certainly, breastmilk is even more important for premature and ill babies than it is for healthy ones. Sadly, with the advent of HIV, most hospitals have closed down their milk banks for tiny babies, to which many women donated their excess breastmilk: thus premature babies are dependent on their own mothers for any breastmilk they receive.

Establishing full breastfeeding once the baby is old enough is also very hard work, but women who succeed in doing so feel an enormous amount of satisfaction and are able to feel that at last their baby is really 'theirs'. NCT breastfeeding counsellors are trained to support mothers in this situation and there is a nationwide network of NCT pump agents who hire out electric breast pumps for use at home.

I didn't have enough milk for my first baby. Is there anything I can do because I would love to breastfeed my second child?

There are many women in your position who want to succeed at breastfeeding and it may be helpful to remember that if you want to, you can! Make sure you get the support of an NCT breastfeeding counsellor by contacting your local NCT branch or group (look in the telephone directory or telephone NCT Headquarters on 081-992 8637) and speak to her while you are still pregnant. You can talk about your previous breastfeeding experience and decide on strategies for success. Women usually have plenty of breastmilk: the problem may have been poor positioning or the baby not being allowed to feed for as long or as often as he or she needed. Once the baby is born, use the breastfeeding counsellor and well-informed midwives to help you get the positioning right; allow the baby to feed for as long and as frequently as he or she needs to; don't worry if your baby only feeds from one breast at each feed in the early days; get plenty of rest and eat regularly. It is more than likely that you will succeed.

19: The first few weeks

It is possible for the first month with a first baby to feel the longest of your life, but if you choose to use all the support available to you effectively, it can be made easier. If you are in any doubt about the health of your baby, do not hesitate to contact your GP or health visitor who are there to help you and usually understand that there is a lot for new parents to learn. If you find your GP's surgery is inconvenient or the attitude of the doctor(s) or staff makes you hesitate to contact them, even when seriously worried, you could choose to change to another practice. With the changes in the way that GPs are paid for immunization, you may be asked to attend a GP's clinic rather than a health visitor's clinic for routine checks on the baby. It is important to remember that the choice is yours: you may choose to go to the place which is easiest to get to; where the waiting times are shortest; where you feel most able to ask questions and to receive sympathetic listening.

86 per cent of the respondents to the *Good Housekeeping* Survey were satisfied with the care they received from community midwives at home; 71 per cent were satisfied with their advice; 61 per cent were satisfied with their health visitor's advice about the baby; 56 per cent with the health visitor's advice about themselves. 78 per cent of the women were satisfied with their six-week postnatal check, but there was great variation in the amount of time it took women to feel completely well following the birth. 38 per cent felt completely well less than six weeks after the birth; 28 per cent in six to eleven weeks; but it took 31 per cent three months or longer.

Do I need someone other than the community midwife to look after me at home?

You can choose for yourself whether this is what you want, but whether or not such help is available will depend on your circumstances. In the past, home helps were available to help new mothers, but nowadays most of their time is taken up with looking after the elderly and disabled at home. Community midwives can usually visit only once a day or so.

Most women at home with a new baby find it very helpful to have someone with them in the very early days. This is not only for practical help with the shopping, cleaning and preparation of meals, but also with moral support at a time when they are getting to know their baby's ways, learning to breastfeed and to care for their baby generally. These needs are increased for women who have had difficult births and assisted deliveries, it can take some time for such women to begin to feel as well as women who have had easier births. Women who have had Caesarean sections have to take extra care in recovery, avoiding heavy lifting, so the wounds in their abdomen and uterus can heal well.

Depending on their circumstances, some women choose to have their partner stay at home with them for a while or have their mother or mother-in-law or other friend or relative to stay. If this is not possible or desirable, women often find it helpful for their partner to come home early from work or to have relatives, friends and neighbours pop in with meals they have prepared and shopping, and to do necessary chores. Some women find telephone calls from people useful support, other women find they disrupt what peace they have.

76 per cent of the respondents to the *Good Housekeeping* Survey had someone to look after them at home for a week or longer; 28 per cent for less than a week; 6 per cent had no one.

How long should my partner have off work?

Since most new fathers in this country have to take paternity leave out of their annual holiday, it is important to use that time effectively. It is likely that your partner will want to spend some time at home with you, getting to know his new son or daughter, and you can decide between the two of you how long feels best. It might be worth keeping a few days in reserve, since life with a new baby in the early weeks is unpredictable and you may find it helpful for your partner to take the odd day or afternoon off work if you become very tired.

I never thought how much I'd love my baby. Is it all right to let her sleep in our bed?

Many parents derive enormous pleasure from having their babies sleep with them and it does save getting up in the night for feeds if you are breastfeeding! Some parents are anxious that they will roll over on the baby, but both men and women have been shown by research to avoid doing so instinctively (but even small amounts of drugs or alcohol might interfere with this mechanism). It is something which some people are extremely critical of, saying you will spoil your baby or never get it into its own bed, but you can choose to let it continue for as long or as short a time as suits you. However, it is not everyone's choice, and some parents prefer their baby to sleep in a cot in the same room or in a different room close by – whichever is chosen, babies are perfectly capable of making their needs known when they are hungry! You may find that you start with the baby sleeping in bed with you, then in a cot close to your bed, then further away or in a different room. (See Bibliography)

Can I stop my baby crying all the time, or do I just have to put up with it?

Some babies do cry more than others and many babies demand a great deal of attention. If the feeding is going well and the baby is thriving, it may just be that your baby is 'bored and lonely' and needs to be played with, cuddled and sung to. Such babies often enjoy going out for walks, for shopping expeditions and visits to other people: try to have a specific arrangement for every day, even if it is only to buy food at the supermarket, to give the baby and yourself a change of scene. Some babies respond to being held, in your arms or in a sling, or to lying on a lambskin (available from the NCT catalogue); or they like being tightly wrapped in a flannelette sheet, particularly at bed-time: this may remind them of life in the uterus! From the very beginning, babies are aware of what is going on around them and they like to be both stimulated and comforted. A range of different activities helps to break up the day into manageable periods of time, especially as very young babies have a short attention span. Babies like mobiles, the light of a window, the flickering of a television screen and being outdoors. Songs and rocking rhymes can soothe them. Many parents find they can help tired, fretful babies get to sleep more easily by turning on a womb music tape (see Useful Organizations), the washing machine or vacuum cleaner. Sometimes a walk outdoors in the buggy or pram or a drive in the car can help babies settle.

There is a school of thought which suggests that, after a difficult birth, babies are uncomfortable because a bone in their necks has become slightly displaced. Some parents have consulted cranial osteopaths and believe the treatment to have been useful. (See Useful Organizations).

It is also important to bear in mind that there may be nothing at all wrong with the baby. He or she may be responding to tension and anxiety in the home. These cannot always be avoided, but you can choose to look at what is going on and your own responses to the situation. A voluntary self-help group which offers information and support for parents with crying babies is CRY-SIS (see Useful Organizations).

My baby won't sleep, what can I do?

It is very easy to have unrealistic expectations of a baby's sleeping patterns. Young babies are growing at an enormous rate; have to take in an enormous amount of calories relative to their size to achieve this; and are gradually developing and getting used to a world almost totally new to them. In addition to this, the mechanism which enables most children and adults to sleep during the night and to be awake during the day is not fully developed until roughly five months. Some babies sleep more than others and babies' sleep patterns vary. Some parents are surprised to have it pointed out to them that it is unlikely their babies will need much sleep at night if they are sleeping for long periods during the day. As a short-term measure, try to sleep when the baby sleeps, so you do not get too exhausted.

If your baby is awake during the evenings and at night with colic, contact your health visitor or an NCT breastfeeding counsellor who may be able to help. If she cannot, you may just have to find ways of coping until the colic stops, as it usually does, at three months.

In the longer term, you can, however, reinforce any tendency of the baby to sleep more at night than during the day. When you give feeds at night, do it in the dark, don't change the nappy unless you have to and interact with your baby as little as possible. If the baby is given the message that all you are going to give is food, not fun, he or she is much more likely to go to sleep again quickly and grow accustomed to the principle that night-time is for sleeping and essential feeds, day-time is for social interaction. Even babies who don't want to go to bed until midnight at first, gradually go to bed earlier and earlier as they are awake more during the day and able to do and interact more. As soon as you are able to discern what appears to be a 'going to bed time' for the baby, even if it is very late and you and your partner are exhausted, you can initiate a bed-time ritual by giving the baby a bath, changing him or her into a clean babysuit or nightdress, wrapping him or her securely and giving a quiet, low-key, soothing feed in the dark before putting him or her to bed. It is up to you to decide whether you put your baby into the cot before he or she falls asleep. Some babies learn to settle on their own sooner than others. Some parents prefer to institute an early routine of the baby going off to sleep alone; others find this stressful and leave it until their baby is more mature. As the baby becomes ready to go to bed earlier, you can bring the bed-time ritual forward until it is at a time that fits in with your life. Having some kind of bed-time ritual can give children security, and becomes extremely useful later on if you use babysitters before your child or children are in bed: if the babysitter follows the ritual, children are more likely to go to bed at the usual time. Once children are able to add to the ritual, it is important you keep the ritual within bounds that you and your babysitters can tolerate!

Some families prefer to be spontaneous, responding to the moment; other families prefer a more or less regular timetable: you can choose which suits you and your lifestyle best.

> *Now my husband's back at work and my mum's gone home, how do I get in touch with other mothers?*

You can contact your local branch of the NCT or the Meet-A-Mum Association (MAMA) for your nearest postnatal group (see Useful Organizations) or your local clinic and also ask your health visitor if she knows other women in your area with babies the same sort of age as yours. The NCT and libraries have all sorts of information on local facilities and activities for mothers and babies such as swimming, gym, music and mother and toddler groups, many of which may be free of charge or very cheap.

> *We are continually being bombarded by advice from all quarters - what can we do?*

Most new parents are the victims of a never-ending stream of advice about how to care for their new baby. Some new parents choose to ignore it and work things out for themselves, others find what confidence they had being undermined and don't know which way to turn. Many women find the advice of a mother or mother-in-law particularly hard to ignore, because they may be in a better position than other people to check whether their advice is being followed. Unfortunately, many women of the generation who are now becoming grandmothers focus their attention on the frequency with which their daughters or daughters-in-law feed or pick up their babies, in case they get 'spoilt'. Each individual mother and father should do whatever feels most comfortable for them and their baby. Older women may feel threatened by someone doing things differently from the way they did them. You can point out that just as they chose how to care for their children, you are now choosing how to care for yours. Use what assertiveness you can muster and support each other.

I feel my health visitor is checking up on me when she comes. Do I have to see her?

It is your choice and it may be that you do not need her. When health visitors work with new families, the well-being of the baby is important, but they are also a valuable community resource. They can often answer any questions you do not want to bother your GP with and should know about local facilities for parents with young children as well as agencies for referral, particularly for families with children who have special needs. Sometimes, new mothers find the first few weeks with a new baby relatively easy, particularly if help is available from their partner or family, but that later, for a variety of reasons, things may become more difficult. That may be the time to ask the health visitor to call or to arrange an appointment at the clinic. It is usually possible to arrange for her to come at a definite time, if that is more convenient and you need time to talk at length.

One of my neighbours offered to help with shopping or ironing. I'd really like to say yes, but feel I can't because there's no way I can reciprocate. What should I do?

Say 'yes please' and accept all offers of help which come your way. Your neighbour may be remembering how busy she was with a new baby. You may be able to help her some time in the future – perhaps you could water her plants or feed her cat while she is away? Or perhaps you could help another new mother when your own child is older.

The breastfeeding is going really well and my baby is thriving. Do I need to go to the baby clinic every week?

The frequency with which you visit the baby clinic is your choice. It is often the case that first-time mothers need the reassurance of a health visitor weighing and examining their baby in order to believe that they are doing all right; but that second-timers or mothers with more children go much more rarely, partly because they are more confident and partly because they have less time! From the health visitor's point of view it is easier if new mothers come and see her at the clinic rather than having to visit each individually at home, so you may find her telephoning or visiting you to make sure everything is all right.

My in-laws would like to pay for a monthly nurse as a birth present and my husband thinks it's a really good idea so we could get plenty of sleep and go out alone together, but I am not sure. I don't want to offend anybody, what should I do?

Employing a monthly nurse is very common in certain social circles, particularly when the woman chooses to bottle feed, and many women find it useful to have someone to teach them how to look after a baby and get him or her into a manageable routine. They may ask the monthly nurse to get up in the night to feed the baby and to babysit if they are expected to go to social occasions without the baby. Some monthly nurses are very supportive of breastfeeding and do everything else for the baby, including washing its clothes, so the mother can concentrate on resting and establishing breastfeeding. However, this is not always the case, and not everyone wants someone living-in during the first month of being a family if it is a first baby. Choose what is right for you.

I'm physically disabled. Sometimes I feel I'm the only mum in the world who has my difficulties. How can I avoid being patronized?

You could use assertiveness skills to prevent this happening: there may be assertiveness training courses in your area. You could also contact other mothers with your disability to share experiences and ways of coping. This might help you feel less isolated and give you the confidence to communicate to other people your true capabilities and needs. You could find other disabled mothers by contacting your local hospital, organizations concerned with your disability and the NCT Parents with Disabilities Group (see Useful Organizations). Very often people are patronizing to the disabled because they are ignorant about the disability and unsure of how to react. Disabled mothers like you can teach the non-disabled what to do, so everybody feels more comfortable.

They want to put my baby in a clinical trial –
how do I know whether or not to agree to this?

The people organizing the trial should be able to give you some written information that you can read at home, at your leisure, with your partner. You might also ask your GP or health visitor or community midwife whether they know anything about the trial and to comment on the written information. You may want to consider the same sort of factors as a trial in which your own participation were proposed (see page 54).

If your baby has a particular condition, experimental treatment for which is the subject of the trial, you may or may not want your baby to be involved. Since in a randomized controlled trial, one of the main conditions is that participants are assigned to the different groups on a random basis, you cannot be sure that your baby would or would not have a particular treatment or the alternative form of treatment, if two different treatments are being compared.

Why do I feel so low, when everything is going
so well?

It may be that it is just the effect of disturbed nights, but it could be the case that you are suffering from postnatal depression. The symptoms of postnatal depression include insomnia; anxiety; constant tiredness; loss of libido; irritability; crying a lot; headaches; palpitations; panic attacks; feelings of guilt and failure as a wife and/or mother; obsessional thoughts; lack of affection for the baby; fear of loss of control; apathy; increase in appetite for food and drink; wanting to sleep endlessly; and lack of memory. Postnatal depression varies enormously in degree. It can range from a fully-fledged puerperal psychosis when a woman has to be hospitalized and receive drugs and other forms of treatment, to a vague feeling of being under the weather. In the range in between, women can suffer from either mild or severe degrees of depression which may require treatment with anti-depressants or psychotherapy. Postnatal depression can be difficult both to recognize and diagnose in its milder forms, particularly if a woman is 'coping', since sleep deprivation can make anyone feel dreadful.

You say that things are going well, so it is possible that you might have postnatal depression. You could talk to your GP or health visitor about it. For many women, having the illness recognized and taken seriously is help enough; others find it helpful to be prescribed anti-depressants for a time to lessen the symptoms and make life easier to cope with – your GP should be able to prescribe anti-depressants compatible with breastfeeding. Where the postnatal depression is caused by a hormonal imbalance, you could think about stopping the contraceptive pill and asking for progesterone treatment from your GP as advocated by Dr Katharina Dalton. You may also find it helpful to contact the Association for Postnatal Illness which produces excellent leaflets (useful for helping your partner and other members of the family to understand what you are going through) and can put you in touch with an ex-sufferer who can give you one-to-one support on a voluntary basis. The NCT can also help you contact ex-sufferers and produces a booklet called *Mothers talking about postnatal depression*. Many women suffering from postnatal depression find getting out of the house helpful and NCT postnatal groups can give you the chance to meet other women with new babies and build up a network of friends and mutual support. Many new mothers feel isolated even if they are not suffering from postnatal depression. (See Bibliography and Useful Organizations)

When is it normal to start making love again?

It can be six days, six weeks, six months or six years – it is a matter of personal choice. Any time is 'normal', provided you and your partner both feel happy about it. There is enormous variation: so you can choose what feels right for you. Many women's vaginas feel quite dry when making love again after a baby, so it is worth buying something like KY jelly or Vaseline as a lubricant. Some couples feel they should wait for the six-week postnatal check 'to make sure everything's all right', as if they needed a doctor to give them permission to go ahead, but if you feel fine and want to make love, you can choose to make love earlier. There is an argument for choosing to make love before your postnatal check-up to make sure everything does feel all right.

The first time you make love will feel different from before the birth, but each time you make love after that, the feelings should seem increasingly as they did before. It may help if you pamper yourself and give yourself time to become more relaxed. Relaxation and massage skills learned in antenatal classes may also be helpful. If you do find making love very uncomfortable, see your GP and ask for a referral if necessary: occasionally perineal repairs need re-doing and generally the sooner this is done the better, to save you further discomfort. It is not uncommon for physical discomfort to pass, but to be replaced by a reflex discomfort and tension which is perceived as physical discomfort, but is psychologically induced. Often in such cases, reassurance from a sympathetic GP or specialist can help deal with this particular fear-tension-pain syndrome. Sometimes sexual difficulties have a deeper psychological cause and it is then possible to consult a Relate counsellor, a psychosexual therapist or a hypnotherapist (see Useful Organizations). The NCT produces a leaflet called *Sex in Pregnancy and after Childbirth* and Sheila Kitzinger's *Woman's Experience of Sex* may also be helpful (see Bibliography).

My stitches still hurt, what can I do?

See your GP. He or she may diagnose an infection which could be treated with antibiotics or pessaries (remind him or her if you are breastfeeding) or it may just be that your perineum is taking a long time to heal. It often takes episiotomies a long time to heal completely, some time after the stitches have dissolved or been removed, so it may just be that you have to wait. Daily pelvic floor exercises can help as can gentle lovemaking. If the discomfort does not go, ask for a referral to an obstetric physiotherapist or your obstetrician.

Three months after the birth, I still 'leak' a bit sometimes when I cough or sneeze. Is there anything I can do about it?

If you have not already done so, try doing pelvic floor exercises on a regular basis, in groups of, say, ten, several times a day. If pelvic floor exercises make no difference, ask your GP for a referral either to the doctor who looked after you during your labour; the obstetric consultant responsible for your care; or to a genito-urinary specialist at the same or at a different hospital. You could discuss with your GP the best person to see, but whoever it is, make sure they have your obstetric notes so they know from them, as well as from you, whether your labour could have anything to do with what is after all urinary incontinence, albeit in a mild form.

Why am I still so fat? They said breastfeeding would make the weight fall off me and it did with my sister.

Women are all different in this respect, as in many others, and you could choose not to compare in this way. It takes time for the fat deposits built up during pregnancy for breastfeeding to go: it may be a few weeks after the birth, it may be longer and it may not happen until after a woman stops breastfeeding altogether. (Some women who do not breastfeed find the extra weight gained comes off very quickly, others find it takes a long time.)

Although it is unwise to diet while breastfeeding, you might choose to look at how much and what you are eating, since as in pregnancy, lactating women often find their metabolism enables them to use their normal food intake more efficiently so as to produce enough milk for the baby without needing much in the way of extra calories. It is important to eat regularly and often while breastfeeding, but there is no need for extra snacks of food high in sugar and fats, like cakes, biscuits and chocolate, since a normal intake of food can be divided into several small snacks rather than three large meals. Quality may be more important than quantity and cutting down your total intake of fats and sugar could also help. It is important to drink enough fluids while breastfeeding so you do not become constipated.

You might also choose to whittle away any extra inches by doing postnatal exercises which are an excellent way of getting your body back in trim. You could do these at home or ask your local NCT or health visitor if they know of any postnatal exercise classes: at some of them, babies are looked after, or join in the exercises! Going out for walks with the baby, perhaps with a friend and her baby, can be a pleasant form of taking exercise and getting away from the fridge and food cupboard! You could also go swimming while your partner or someone else looks after the baby.

How do I know my baby is the right temperature in bed?

This aspect of childcare has caused even more anxiety in parents than in the past as a result of the large amount of research into cot death (Sudden Infant Death Syndrome) which has shown that some of these deaths could be explained by the babies being overheated. There are several reasons for this happening. It is true that babies do not have fully-developed body temperature control: this is why hospital labour wards and postnatal wards are so hot. However, this imperfect temperature control works both ways: it is just as possible for a baby to become too hot as too cold. In the past in this country, babies were bundled up under piles of blankets in unheated bedrooms. Now more and more people have central heating and people without central heating keep their homes warmer than they used to, so babies sleep in much warmer environments. Rather than being in nighties, many babies sleep in babysuits (often with a vest underneath) which cover their feet and sometimes their hands, if they have a tendency to scratch, which also keep them warmer. There is also a fashion for baby duvets. All these things may lead to a baby being hotter than necessary. Even if the baby is not so hot as to be at risk, he or she may wake more frequently for thirst-quenching feeds.

Therefore, you can look at the baby him- or herself and the total environment. Remember, too, that if your baby gets too cold, he or she is likely to wake you up. You can listen to the weather forecast to see what the night temperature will be. If you feel it necessary to have heating on at night (particularly if you are getting up for feeds) keep it as background heat and put on a dressing-gown when you get up to feed the baby. You might choose to have an electric heater controlled by a simple time-switch synchronized with the central heating so it comes on when the central heating turns off. The recommended temperature for a baby's room is 65°F/17°C. Check that the baby's cot is not positioned over hot water pipes or too near a radiator – underfloor central heating may mean that your baby needs very few clothes in bed. By buying sheets and blankets rather than a duvet, you will have a flexible system for every temperature and season, if you have more babies born at different times of year. If, when you check the baby before going to bed, he or she feels too hot or too cold (you can check a baby's temperature by feeling the back of his or her neck) you can easily adjust the number of blankets. It is important to remember that folding a large blanket in quarters is equivalent to four blankets. If you do buy a duvet or have one given or lent to you, make sure the 'tog' value is no greater than 10 togs. Baby nests are not designed to be used for babies to sleep in, but only for them to be carried in when it is cold. The baby needs to be in only as many clothes as necessary for being fed in the night: in winter a babysuit and perhaps a vest; in a hot summer perhaps only a vest or a thin nightdress. When you have been out when it is cold, unwrap the baby when you come in, just as you take off your own coat, even if you risk waking him or her.

My cousin's baby had a cot death and I am really worried about our baby. Should I buy the kind of baby alarm that monitors the baby's breathing?

This is unnecessary unless there are medical reasons for monitoring the baby's breathing; too many parents are frightened into spending money on electronic gadgets for no good reason. The danger with commercially available machines is that they are not always well designed; and that parents may rely on them too heavily, instead of trusting their own judgement and keeping checks on their baby in the normal way.

If there is a medical reason for your baby needing such a monitor, it should be available through the special care baby unit of your local hospital who will train you in its use. It is important that parents of babies at risk have good support from their GP and/or hospital and receive proper training in how to resuscitate a baby.

It is natural that you should be anxious about your baby and need reassurance. It may help to discuss your reasons for anxiety with your GP and/or health visitor. This may also make you feel more comfortable about consulting them if you feel your baby is unwell. You could also think about having your baby near you at all times when asleep – both during the day and at night – so he or she is easier to check.

> *Which is the best side for my baby to sleep on?*
> *My health visitor says she should sleep on her*
> *side, but she will only settle on her back.*

Much conflicting advice is given about babies' sleeping positions. Many babies are happy with the position chosen by parents or health professionals, but others choose to assert their own preference and until they can roll over themselves (at about four and a half months), are dependent on their parents to help them into their chosen position! The side is thought by many to be the safest position if the baby possets up any of his or her feed, but even if a baby is on his or her back, he or she can turn their head sideways. In a Bristol study of cot death, there seemed to be an increased risk for babies lying on their tummies. This may have been due to the fact that babies lose less heat in this position and were already compromised by being kept too hot in bed.

> *The health visitor has said my baby is due for*
> *her first injection at two months. This seems*
> *very soon for such a tiny baby - can I put it off*
> *for a bit?*

It is your choice when to have your baby immunized, but the later you start the course of injections, the longer it will take to complete. Research has shown that the younger the age at which children are immunized, the higher the uptake. Many parents are finding themselves under increased pressure to immunize their babies now that GPs are paid for babies and children on their lists only if a certain proportion have been immunized. The Department of Health revised the child immunization programme in 1990 so that as many children as possible will be immunized. The aim of any national immunization programme is not only to protect individual children from dangerous diseases (in this case diphtheria, tetanus, whooping cough and polio), but also to eradicate the diseases from the community to protect children who cannot be immunized for medical reasons or who are unable to develop immunity from immunization.

The most controversial vaccine is that given for whooping cough, which has received much adverse publicity in recent years. However, provided whooping cough vaccine is given only to those children who have been shown not to be at risk from it (that is those who have had fits, who have a family history of epilepsy or who have had a severe reaction to a previous injection of the vaccine), the risks of the effects of the disease itself far outweigh the risks of adverse effects from the vaccine. About one in 100,000 children have febrile convulsions after administration of the whooping cough vaccine. Of these, most recover without any ill-effects, leaving only a few with brain damage. The risks of brain damage and death following an attack of whooping cough are higher.

We would like to have our son circumcised for social reasons, but the hospital doesn't seem to think it's a good idea. Is this so?

In countries and communities where male circumcision is not necessary for religious reasons, it is very much a matter of fashion. In the 1950s, when many of today's fathers were born, it was fairly fashionable in this country: but it is definitely out of fashion at the present time, and many members of the medical profession tend to discourage its practice. Some doctors feel it is a barbaric procedure and may see babies with problems following circumcision rather than those with no problems. It is extremely rare for anything to go wrong with this most ancient form of surgery, but if, for example, there is excess bleeding, the baby can be taken into hospital to have the wound stitched.

Many couples are in favour of circumcision for reasons of hygiene and aesthetics, but are dismayed when they receive a negative message from the medical profession. Studies have shown that babies experience pain during the operation and afterwards, but that it is possible to reduce the baby's discomfort by giving him a local anaesthetic in the form of a 'dorsal penile nerve block'.

If you have your son circumcised, you can have it done in an NHS hospital, or privately in hospital or at home. In either case, the operation should be done by someone experienced in the procedure. In Jewish families circumcision is traditionally performed on the eighth day after birth, but is postponed if the baby is premature or ill in any way, for example with jaundice. If you arrange a private circumcision for your son, you may contact a local Jewish synagogue (try the telephone directory) who will put you in touch with a *mohel*, usually a doctor, who is specially trained to do circumcisions. He will visit you at home, tell you what to expect, advise on aftercare and visit at home afterwards if necessary. The fee for a private circumcision varies in different parts of the UK. For families who are not orthodox Jews, some *mohelim* stitch the wound, which helps it heal more quickly and causes less discomfort to the baby afterwards.

I never thought the baby would take up so much time. How can I get organized?

Some people find that having children means they *never* get 'organized' again and they are resigned to living in a state of happy chaos. For other people, life needs to proceed more as normal, with some adjustments for babies and/or children. Babies do not see the point of rigid timetables and are adept at thwarting the most carefully-laid plans to get out of the house at a certain time or to do essential chores during the day. Most babies are incapable of beginning to fit into any routine until the age of about three months when many childcare books talk about 'settled babies': so do not expect too much too soon. Here are some ideas you can try:

1 Lower all domestic standards to a level of basic hygiene and good nutrition. If too many visitors are making you feel bad about your standards of cleanliness or cooking, ignore those feelings or have fewer visitors. How about visiting them instead?

2 As long as you are getting up in the night for feeds, etc, your next priority must be to get enough sleep and rest yourself, even if it means standards slipping further. If necessary, sleep when the baby does. Eat regular meals: a wholemeal bread sandwich and a piece of fruit can be as nutritious as a cooked meal. Convenience foods can be healthy, particularly if accompanied by wholemeal

bread, fresh fruit and salads. Don't forget to eat in the afternoon if there is a long gap between your mid-day and evening meals. If you are in good condition, you will cope better with everything.

3 If you need to get out of the house in the morning, get washed and dressed immediately after the baby's early morning feed. Babies are often in a good mood then and either go back to sleep or will sit in a bouncing chair or lie propped up on a pillow on the bathroom floor while you get ready. If you have a partner and he doesn't leave for work at the crack of dawn, ask him to look after the baby and make breakfast for you while you get ready.

4 Plan the week's meals in advance and, if you can, do one mega-shop a week with your shopping-list: this can save money and also avoid decision-making when you are tired at the end of a long day.

5 Try to take the baby out for a walk every day. As well as giving you both some fresh air, you can use the walk to buy fresh bread, collect child benefit, post letters, etc. Use your visit to the post office to pay bills by Giro, buy stamps, etc.

6 Keep your baby changing bag and handbag permanently packed and ready to go: two fewer things to think about when getting out of the house with the baby.

7 When going shopping for non-essential items, shopping centres are usually well provided with buses, car parks, baby changing rooms, etc. Go with a friend, take some sandwiches (make them the night before or buy them there) and make an expedition of it: your babies will enjoy the company and all the sights and sounds of the shops and other people.

8 The moment your baby starts showing any signs of a routine, reinforce it. A regular time for bathing and going to bed (gradually brought forward to a time which suits you) can eventually lead to evenings to do what you want to do.

9 Prepare your evening meal after breakfast so it is ready to cook at the end of the day when you may be feeling fraught.

10 Don't let messes accumulate: tidy up as you go. Tidy toys away each night so he or she can make a fresh mess tomorrow!

20: Making sense of the birth and giving feedback

My midwife was wonderful, can I write and thank her?

Your midwife would be delighted to hear from you, and you could choose to send a copy of your letter to her supervisor of midwives.

Everyone in any line of work appreciates praise, especially because in the nature of things they are more likely to hear from people who are dissatisfied with the service they have received. Midwives particularly value positive feedback, as they often feel under pressure due to low pay and status, staff shortages, hospital protocols and demands from users of the service.

In this country, midwives are trained to be practitioners in their own right and to regard childbirth as a natural process. However, their ability to work in this way has been eroded by the fact that over 99 per cent of births and most antenatal care now take place in hospital; whereas in 1968 18.6 per cent of births were at home. Hospitals are hierarchical institutions where the maternity services are, ultimately, under the direction of doctors. Doctors are usually trained to regard childbirth as normal only in retrospect and therefore tend to want to set up rules about routine medical interventions – to monitor the baby and speed up labour – in order 'to be on the safe side'.

Some midwives find they are unable to work freely with women experiencing normal pregnancies and births, building up women's confidence in their bodies by emphasizing the normality of the process and giving them the encouragement and support that only a good midwife can. Therefore all women who tell their friends, antenatal teachers, etc, about the wonderful midwifery care they have received, could also tell the person to whom it really matters – their midwife.

I feel I need to talk about my labour experience to someone. Who would be prepared to listen?

If appropriate, you could make an appointment to see the midwife/ midwives and/or doctor(s) who attended you in hospital or at home. If you prefer to speak to someone senior, you could talk to your consultant or the supervisor of midwives or another senior midwife. You could choose to talk to the midwife or GP who gave you antenatal care; or the midwife, obstetric physiotherapist or NCT antenatal teacher who gave you antenatal classes; or there might be a GP practice counsellor or psychiatric nurse or an obstetric counsellor attached to the hospital. Any of these people should be pleased to listen to you and help you make sense of your experience; it would also give them the, usually welcome, opportunity to learn something from your individual experience to help other women.

The birth was wonderful, how can we stop boring everyone with it?

Birth is such a miraculous experience that many parents feel the need to talk about it endlessly until it is resolved and assimilated and they can get on with the rest of their lives: this applies as much to parents who have positive as well as those who have negative experiences. You may find it helpful to share your experience with other new parents in your antenatal class, if you went to one, and/ or in a postnatal support group run by your local branch of the NCT. You could also write down your experience: it is extraordinary how often the mother and father have different perceptions of different parts of labour, and this could make fascinating future reading for your son or daughter! Antenatal teachers appreciate labour reports and many NCT branches print them in their local newsletters, so you could let a wider public benefit from your positive experience.

I want to make a complaint, but find it difficult to organize my thoughts. Is there someone who could help me?

You could get in touch with your local Community Health Council (look in your local telephone directory and see Bibliography) which may have someone with special knowledge of the maternity services. In any case they are experienced in supporting members of the public wishing to complain about the health services. Whether or not you have attended NCT antenatal classes you could contact an NCT antenatal teacher through your local NCT branch who would be prepared to listen to your story and help you get your thoughts in order. There are also other organizations who can help such as AIMS (see Useful Organizations).

It is important that you get a sympathetic hearing. There are people who will understand and listen. If at first you don't succeed, try again. It is very common for anyone wishing to complain to feel they are 'making a fuss about nothing'. Organizing your thoughts to put them into spoken words may be enough to resolve the experience or to feel enabled to put the complaint into writing. If not, you could ask the person who has listened to draft out a letter for you: you may end up choosing to send a completely different letter or not to send one at all, but this method might get you started, particularly if looking after a new baby is taking most of your time and energy.

Who should I complain to and will they take my complaint seriously?

If your complaint is about a hospital doctor or midwife or any aspect of hospital care, your complaint should be sent to the Unit General Manager at the hospital: he or she will then send copies of your letter to the personnel concerned, gather replies and reply to you accordingly. As a matter of courtesy, perhaps if you have built up a good relationship with them, you may choose to send disclosed copies to your consultant and/or supervisor of midwives. Unfortunately, it has been known for complaints not always to be dealt with efficiently when addressed directly to consultants, so even if you don't know the name of the Unit General Manager (though you could telephone and find out), it is best to send your complaint to him/her.

In all cases, whether or not you have sought their support, the Community Health Council (CHC) and your local branch of the NCT would appreciate receiving copies of your letter and any further correspondence, since they may be in a position to see if there have been several complaints about a particular problem area in the maternity services to which they could draw the attention of the appropriate district health authority with a view to achieving improvements.

In a serious case, you may choose to send a copy of your letter, or a separate letter, to the appropriate professional body: see the summary later in this chapter.

Provided your letter of complaint is sent to the right person, viz the Unit General Manager, etc, your complaint will be taken very seriously indeed. Some health professionals are aware that the letters of complaint they receive are the tip of an iceberg of dissatisfaction with the maternity services they provide. Many health professionals are prepared to acknowledge the grounds of complaint, apologize to the clients concerned and to try to find ways of preventing a recurrence. The attitude of the health professionals may be influenced by the tone of your letter: if you take time to describe the aspects of care you were satisfied with, they will be less likely to regard you as just a 'complainer'. Most people find criticism easier to take when it is constructive and when credit is given for what was done well. (See also Summary later in this chapter for time-limits, etc.)

> *Following an emergency Caesarean, I was in*
> *hospital for five days and received little help*
> *with breastfeeding and much conflicting advice.*
> *I should like to complain about the treatment I*
> *was given, but I don't want to get the*
> *overworked midwives into trouble.*

Many women and their babies suffer as you did from the understaffing of postnatal wards. If you felt able to, you could write to the Unit General Manager, telling him or her what happened and how you felt about it. However, you could also say that in your view the midwives tried their best against impossible odds and that there ought to be more staff on that particular postnatal ward. Such letters from the general public can be very useful for hospital administrators when trying to demonstrate to regional health authorities a case for more funding. If you were feeling energetic you could send a copy of your letter to your local MP who would be given first-hand evidence of the results of NHS underfunding. Another point you could make is that the local branch of the NCT and the Joint Breastfeeding Initiative (see Useful Organizations) could help the unit senior midwives find ways of dealing with the problem of conflicting advice about breastfeeding.

> *What is the point of complaining? What's done*
> *is done and can't be changed. Besides, it might*
> *change the way I'm treated if I go back again.*

The nature of the experience cannot be changed, but it is possible that your feelings about it might be. Also, unless individuals complain about their own cases, the same thing might happen again to another woman or to yourself in a subsequent birth.

The benefits of complaining are aptly put in ACHCEW's *NHS Complaints Procedures* (see Bibliography), page 3: 'It is the experience of CHCs that when a patient or relative complains they are usually seeking an explanation, an apology, a reassurance that the incident will not be repeated, and sometimes also compensation. Until all these needs have been met satisfactorily, it is unlikely that complainants will begin to forget and perhaps recover from their traumatic experience. It is important for service providers [that is health professionals] to understand why people complain, if they are going to be able to resolve problems satisfactorily and improve services to prevent recurrence'.

What would happen to them if they returned in the future is a common worry for women in your situation. On the whole, there is a tendency for people who complain to be treated better than they were before. If they are not, there is something very wrong with the particular system in question. If you do not complain, the same thing could happen again if you return. It may be that you have no choice and there is only one maternity unit in your area. But if there is a choice, have you thought about going somewhere else for your care in the future?

Is it better to get someone like a solicitor or my doctor to write a letter?

You may prefer to ask your doctor to write a letter, but it will carry no more weight than a letter from you. Your letter need not be full of medical jargon or obstetric details. It helps to make your letter as short and clear as possible, and to give as many hard facts, such as dates, times, names, etc, as you can remember. If there was something that was said or done that you do not understand, you might ask your doctor to explain it to you or include the query in your letter of complaint, asking for an explanation.

Asking a solicitor to write a letter would be appropriate if you have grounds for suing the district health authority (which carries responsibility for the hospitals within its area). There are grounds for suing only if there has been negligence (when compensation is payable) but not if there has been a true medical accident – that is an error made in good faith with normal efforts made to provide adequate care (when no compensation is payable). If you think you have grounds for suing, the sooner you get a solicitor involved the better, since medical negligence cases are notoriously long: it can sometimes take as long as five years to obtain compensation. It is said in legal circles that district health authorities tend not to take a claim for compensation seriously until a writ is issued. It is essential to instruct a solicitor experienced in medical negligence cases, since it is a very specialized area of the law. Your local

Community Health Council (look in your local telephone directory) may be able to support you as may the Association for Improvements in Maternity Services – AIMS (see Useful Organizations) who will tell you your choices for the best way to proceed; may have knowledge of other cases similar to yours and their outcome; and may be able to recommend a suitable solicitor. Another charitable organization called Action for Victims of Medical Accidents (see Useful Organizations) provides information and support both for the general public and for solicitors, one of its aims being to improve the standards of legal advice in medical negligence cases.

They ignored my birth plan, can I sue?

As stated in the answer to the previous question, you can sue and receive compensation only if you can prove there was negligence and you experienced a measurable loss of some kind for which damages may be calculated. If this is not the case, you may nevertheless wish to write a letter asking for an explanation of the hospital's failure to take account of your birth plan. You may then receive an explanation, an apology and an assurance that the hospital will try to prevent it happening again. You may find it helpful to talk to an NCT antenatal teacher, your local Community Health Council or AIMS (see Useful Organizations).

The Unit General Manager has suggested having a meeting to discuss my letter, but I am not sure I can handle it, what should I do?

Sometimes a meeting face to face with the health professionals involved, chaired by the Unit General Manager, can be very helpful as a way of clearing up points of detail or coming back on points which you may feel have not been adequately dealt with in the hospital's letter of reply. However, it can be an ordeal, particularly if the matters you have to complain about are of a painful nature.

It is your choice whether or not there should be such a meeting. You may choose to refuse a meeting and ask for a more detailed written report instead, or to look at your notes with your consultant or a registrar in a more informal way. Or you could choose to attend the meeting but to go accompanied by your partner, a friend, your NCT antenatal teacher and/or a member of your local Community Health Council (CHC). Members of CHCs are experienced in attending such meetings and getting the best out of them; and also at supporting members of the public in an informal, hand-holding way. You could meet with your CHC member beforehand and talk over what you would hope to achieve at the meeting: he/she is likely to know the Unit General Manager and may know the health professionals who will be present and may be able to guide you as to what to expect and how to handle the meeting. Once the meeting is over, you would have someone to talk it over with and to discuss whether you are satisfied with the outcome or whether you wish to take the matter further.

SUMMARY OF COMPLAINTS PROCEDURES IN NHS MATERNITY SERVICES

COMPLAINT	RELEVANT BODY	TIME LIMIT
Hospital care	Unit General Manager at hospital	1 year for official complaint procedure to apply
GP care	Local Family Health Service Authority	8 weeks
	Scotland: Primary Care Division of the Health Board	6 weeks
	N Ireland: Central Services Agency	
All doctors (serious matters)	The General Medical Council, 44 Hallam Street, London W1 (071-580 7642)	
Obstetricians	Royal College of Obstetricians and Gynaecologists, 27 Sussex Place, London NW1 4RG (071-262 5425)	
Midwives, nurses, health visitors (serious matters)	The United Kingdom Central Council, 25 Portland Place, London W1M 3AF (071-637 7181)	
Complaint not properly dealt with by hospital	Health Service Commissioner for England (The Ombudsman) Church House, Great Smith Street, London SW1P 3BW (071-212 7676)	

(See Bibliography for publications containing more details about complaints procedures.)

*I feel I gained so much from my NCT classes and
the experience of birth itself, how can I give
something back?*

It is marvellous that you should feel this way and there are all sorts
of ways in which you could contribute. The NCT would not exist
without the women and men who provide for those having babies
after them the continuing network of informal support from which
they themselves benefited. Your local branch of the NCT will be
delighted to hear from you.

Here are some ideas: You could join the NCT as a local or
national member if you have not done so already; you could run a
postnatal support group for new mothers and babies; you could
offer special support to pregnant women or new mothers if you
have had a particular experience; you could assist your local
branch of the NCT in its publicity and fundraising efforts, either
joining the committee or helping on an occasional basis with
whatever skills you have to offer; you could train as an antenatal
teacher or breastfeeding counsellor.

*I thought I was well prepared, but discovered I
had no idea and found talking to other mothers
a great help. How can I offer a listening ear to
other new mothers?*

Think about becoming a postnatal supporter for the NCT. These
women ring up mothers having new babies, often before the birth,
and offer them the chance to talk about what is happening to them.
They also run local groups, usually for mothers with babies of
about the same age, which meet on a weekly basis, giving all its
members an informal social event to enjoy and look forward to,
and a place where pleasures and worries can be shared.

*How can I help improve the maternity services
for other women?*

Think about representing the NCT on your local Community
Health Council (CHO) which represents consumer interests in the
local health services. There are often only a few full places, open to
election every three years, and these are competed for by representatives from different local bodies dealing with special interests
such as the disabled, the aged and ethnic minorities. However, the
CHC often has satellite groups working on specific issues such as
women's health and it is usually possible for an NCT representa-

tive to be co-opted. Membership of such a group would give you a wider knowledge of such issues as family planning, well woman clinics, cervical screening, etc. Whilst such representatives are not full voting members, they have access to all information held by the CHC, such as Department of Health circulars, and the support of the CHC. Co-opted members sometimes go on to be elected as full members.

District Health Authorities have a statutory duty to consult CHCs on all relevant issues. For example, following the NHS and Community Care Act 1990, the CHCs have been representing consumer interests in the drafting of the contracts for purchasing and providing maternity services; in many places this will have been the only form of consumer input.

The NCT also has representatives on Maternity Services Liaison Committees (MSLCs). Each District Health Authority (DHA) has been recommended by the government to set up an MSLC. Ideally an MSLC is a unique forum for all the different groups involved in the maternity services so that there are representatives of the obstetricians, hospital midwives, community midwives, paediatricians, health visitors, community health department and the consumer, that is the NCT and CHC. In practice, not every DHA has set up an MSLC and the nature of the forum and its willingness to have consumer representation is dependent on local conditions, including the individual MSLC chairperson. Sometimes MSLCs are set up as a result of requests by the local NCT branch; sometimes the chairperson is an NCT representative. The frequency of meeting and items on the agenda vary enormously from one MSLC to another, but they can consider such matters as the setting up of a Domino system; early discharge from hospital after the birth; whether women should carry their own notes; and individual complaints.

Other bodies where the NCT has representation include Family Health Service Authorities (which replace the old Family Practitioner Committees) and District Health Authorities.

Having children changed my life. Is it too late to train as a midwife at the ripe old age of 35?

Indeed it is not and there are now a number of colleges which accept women for direct-entry training, meaning they do not have to qualify as nurses first. Women who trained as nurses first may choose to train further as health visitors who also play a role in supporting mothers. (See Useful Organizations)

Glossary

As far as possible, only terms which are not explained in the text are defined here.

alphafetoprotein A protein crossing from the baby's into the mother's blood circulation. Levels in the mother's blood may be tested between 16 and 18 weeks. If they are abnormal they may indicate the need for further testing.

amniocentesis A test which involves the removal of a small amount of amniotic fluid from the uterus using a needle with the help of ultrasound. Cells are grown and investigated for abnormalities.

amniotic sac/membranes/fluid The sterile bag of fluid within the uterus in which the baby grows.

anaemia A low level of red blood cells (haemoglobin) in the blood. Since the haemoglobin carries oxygen round the human body, a deficiency leads to tiredness and can affect the condition of the baby.

assisted delivery When a mother needs help with giving birth to her baby. Usually refers to episiotomy, forceps, Ventouse and Caesarean section.

Braxton Hicks contractions Just as the baby kicks to develop its muscles and keep them strong, so the muscles composing the uterus contract for a minute or so every 20 minutes throughout pregnancy. These contractions are felt by many women towards the end of pregnancy as a strong tightening of the abdomen.

breech presentation The position of a baby who is head up before labour begins. (See illustration on page 114)

cephalic presentation The normal position for a baby before birth begins: head down. (See illustration on page 114)

cephalopelvic disproportion When the baby's head cannot pass through the woman's pelvis, either due to the size of the baby's head or the size or shape of the woman's pelvis, or because the position of the baby makes it impossible for the baby's head to pass through.

cerebro-spinal fluid The fluid which surrounds the brain and spinal cord. This can leak out if the membrane surrounding the spinal cord is accidentally punctured during the insertion of an epidural or a spinal block. The leak is called a 'dural tap' and can be followed by a severe headache unless the woman lies flat on her back for a few days. Some anaesthetists 'patch' a dural tap by injecting some of the mother's blood round the site of the puncture: this procedure can prevent the headache.

chorionic villus sampling/biopsy A procedure similar to amniocentesis whereby a sample of the placenta is taken, rather than amniotic fluid, and investigated for abnormalities. Results are obtained more quickly, because cells do not have to be grown.

colostrum The first milk produced by the breasts during pregnancy and for the first few days after birth. It is particularly rich in antibodies which protect the baby against infection.

Community Health Council A body set up in each district health authority to represent the interests of users of all local health services. Can help users with information and with making complaints.

consultant (doctor) The most senior hospital doctors who have teams of junior doctors working beneath them and who have considerable influence on the ways hospitals are run. They are often involved in research and teaching and tend to see complicated rather than normal 'cases'. Sometimes they are employed by a university rather than a health authority and have the title 'professor' rather than 'mister'. Consultants who are also physicians (a qualification requiring further study in their speciality) are called 'doctor'. If in doubt about what to call a consultant, look at his or her label or ask another member of staff!

contractions of the uterus during labour The periodic shortening and thickening of the muscles responsible for opening up the cervix and pushing out the baby.

counsellor Counsellors have highly developed listening skills which give their clients the opportunity to talk about their problems and use their own resources to find solutions. A counsellor should be non-judgmental.

cranial osteopathy A more gentle way of working than traditional 'structural' osteopathy. Osteopaths working cranially work by putting gentle pressure on different parts of the body, as well as occasionally performing 'corrections' of the joints.

cystic fibrosis A genetic disease affecting the mucus glands which causes chest problems and difficulty in absorbing food from the intestines. If both parents are carriers of the disease, the chances are that out of every four children they have, two will be carriers and one will have the disease. Carriers of the disease are recommended to have genetic counselling before starting a family.

Dextrose A sterile solution of sugar and water sometimes given to newborn babies in hospital. Healthy newborn babies should never be given Dextrose but should be put to the breast whenever they are hungry.

dilatation (often popularly called dilation) of cervix The opening of the neck of the uterus during labour. The cervix dilates or opens to about 10 cm so the baby can be born.

district health authority (DHA) The National Health Service is administered by about 195 DHAs in England and Wales. Individual hospitals obtain money from the DHAs and answer to them for the way in which the money is spent. DHAs at present obtain their budgets from fourteen regional health authorities (RHAs). The RHAs obtain their money in turn from the government's Department of Health. The Department of Health decides policies which are implemented down the line by the DHAs.

Doppler scanning A test sometimes given towards the end of pregnancy to assess the functioning of the placenta.

Down's syndrome Caused by an extra chromosome. It is more common in children born to mothers over the age of 35 (see page 203). There is now much more understanding of how to stimulate Down's syndrome children from an early age so that they are able to achieve their full potential. Good care for the medical problems that can accompany the syndrome has increased life expectancy for many sufferers to over 30 years.

endorphins The body's natural painkillers thought to be promoted in labour by the woman being in darkness and working with her body. It is thought that TENS stimulates the production of endorphins.

episiotomy A cut made using surgical scissors to enlarge the vaginal opening before delivery. It can be performed by a midwife or a doctor.

fallopian tube The tube that connects each ovary with the uterus and where conception takes place.

fetal distress When the baby in the uterus is short of oxygen. It can be diagnosed by changes in the baby's heart rate and sometimes from the baby having passed meconium into the amniotic fluid as well as fetal blood sampling.

fetal heart monitor A machine which collects information about a baby's heartbeat using ultrasound from a belt on the mother's abdomen or a clip fastened to the baby's head (fetal scalp electrode) and prints it out continuously on to a strip of paper which medical staff can read during labour and forms a part of the hospital's permanent records of the birth.

fetal scalp electrode See **fetal heart monitor** above.

fetus The medical word for a baby before he or she is born.

folates/folic acid A protein necessary for life and for the healthy development of a baby in small amounts, like vitamins and minerals.

forceps Medical instruments used to help a woman give birth to her baby. They are rather like a pair of salad servers which are inserted round the baby's head, fastened together and then pulled and sometimes turned during contractions to help the baby out. They come in various sizes, depending on the extent of help the baby needs, and can only be used by doctors. When the baby is quite high up in the vagina, many doctors prefer to perform a Caesarean section on the grounds that it is safer for the baby. Other obstetricians use Ventouse, possibly followed by forceps.

Gardosi cushion A cushion designed for use in labour, particularly in second stage – good if an epidural has not worn off.

General Practitioner Obstetrician (GPO) A GP who attends women in labour, providing cover for the midwives at home or in hospital in a GP unit. GPOs look after women antenatally.

geneticist A geneticist is a doctor specializing in medical conditions caused by abnormalities in the genes. Geneticists are often trained to explain to prospective parents the chances of their children inheriting a particular condition already in their family or families and to counsel them when making a decision. They also counsel parents whose babies are born with an abnormality as to the chances of future children being born with the condition.

gestation The average length of time needed for a baby to develop in the mother's body: this can be anything from about 38 to 42 weeks.

GIFT (gametes intra-fallopian transfer) A method of artificial fertilization whereby eggs and sperm are mixed outside the woman's body and up to four eggs are placed in one or both of the fallopian tubes for conception to take place in the usual way. GIFT has a lower success rate than IVF (see below).

haemoglobin The protein in red blood cells which carries oxygen around the body. A deficiency is known as anaemia and can adversely affect the health of the mother and her baby.

health visitor A community health worker trained originally as a nurse, and then receiving an extra year's training as a health visitor. Some health visitors also have midwifery training.

high risk (for a home birth) The definition of a woman being at high risk of complications at a home birth varies from one district health authority to another. Factors it can include are having a first baby; having had more than a certain number of children; being over a certain age, anything from over 30 to over 40 years of age; previous Caesarean section; previous post-partum haemorrhage; history of bleeding or threatened miscarriage in current pregnancy; and certain medical conditions.

human chorionic gonadotrophin (HCG) The hormone produced by the chorionic villi (the frond-like forerunners of the placenta which enable the embryo to embed itself in the side of the uterus) which can be measured in urine to diagnose pregnancy.

immunoglobulins (antibodies) These substances cross to the baby's system via the placenta before birth and in the colostrum and breastmilk after birth to confer on the baby the same immunities against disease as the mother has. Gradually the baby acquires the ability to develop its own immunities as his or her system is challenged either by diseases or by immunization.

'incompetent' cervix A condition where the muscles of the cervix are not strong enough to keep the neck of the uterus closed and where miscarriage usually occurs at about 20 weeks. In subsequent pregnancies a special stitch can be inserted to close the cervix at about 14 weeks: this is then removed at about 38 weeks so that labour can take place normally.

intra-uterine growth retardation (IUGR) When the baby appears not to be growing as it should. It is difficult to diagnose, even with ultrasound. If IUGR is suspected, there is an increasing tendency to deliver the baby by Caesarean section and look after him or her in a neonatal unit. More research is needed both on this practice and on the accurate assessment of fetal growth.

in vitro fertilization (IVF) A method of artificial fertilization whereby eggs and sperm are mixed and conception takes place outside the woman's body. After 48 hours, up to four healthy eggs are placed in the woman's uterus where it is hoped at least one will become embedded and grow.

junior medical staff At the bottom of the doctors' hierarchy in a hospital. They include junior house officers and senior house officers who are doing the practical part of their medical training. Some will go on to specialize and have more senior positions in hospitals; others will become GPs. They tend to be least experienced in August, and most experienced in July, the beginning and end of the academic year.

lactose An enzyme present in breastmilk, particularly the foremilk (the milk at the beginning of a feed) which in excess quantities can cause problems if a baby does not receive enough hindmilk (the milk at the end of a feed), the high fat content of which aids digestion of lactose.

meconium The waste products of pregnancy present in the baby's intestines during and after birth. If the baby passes meconium during labour, the amniotic fluid turns green and this can be, but is not always, a sign of fetal distress.

midwife Usually a nurse (most are women, but some are men) who undergoes further training in the care of women during pregnancy, labour and postnatally. In some institutions, direct-entry training is available whereby people train as midwives from the beginning and do not have to train as nurses first.

multigravida A woman who is having her second or subsequent baby.

neural tube defects These are defects of the brain or spinal cord caused by abnormal development of the embryo, that is the baby, in the first few weeks of life. The most common of these defects are anencephaly, where only part of the brain and skull have formed; hydrocephaly where there is too much cerebro-spinal fluid inside the brain – this can cause brain damage; and spina bifida where the spinal cord and/or vertebra may not have formed properly – in severe cases this causes mental handicap, paralysis and incontinence. Anencephaly is a condition incompatible with life, but the life expectancy and quality of life of children born with the other two defects will depend on the severity of the condition.

obstetric flying squad A special ambulance sent out by maternity units in case of emergency, for example if there is a problem with a woman having a planned home birth or if a woman suddenly goes into strong labour at home or elsewhere and cannot get to hospital. Depending on the assistance necessary, the ambulance can take one or two midwives and/or a doctor to look after the woman who may or may not need to be brought into hospital.

obstetrician A doctor specializing in pregnancy and childbirth. A gynaecologist specializes in women's medicine and may or may not have obstetric qualifications as well.

oestriol A hormone present in increased amounts during pregnancy which can be used to diagnose pregnancy and to assess whether the placenta is working well.

oxytocin A hormone which causes the uterus to contract during labour. It is also produced by the woman's body during orgasm and breastfeeding.

placenta The organ which grows during pregnancy with the developing baby and enables it to get food and oxygen from the mother's blood and get rid of carbon dioxide via the umbilical cord.

placenta praevia A placenta sited over the cervix. This condition usually necessitates delivery by Caesarean section.

posterior presentation When the baby at the beginning of labour faces towards the woman's front instead of her back. This may make labour slower and cause the woman to experience contractions as back pain.

postpartum haemorrhage The loss of more than 500 ml of blood by a woman after delivery.

pre-eclampsia (toxaemia) A condition which occurs towards the end of pregnancy and which, if left untreated, could cause fits (convulsions) in the mother and cut off the oxygen supply to her and her baby. Symptoms are increased blood pressure accompanied by swelling and protein in the urine. The only 'cure' is rest and relaxation or, if these do not lower blood pressure, induction of labour or delivery by Caesarean section.

presenting part That part of the baby pressing down on the cervix during labour and which can be felt by vaginal examination as the cervix dilates: usually the baby's head, but sometimes its bottom, if it is breech.

primigravida A woman having her first baby.

progesterone The hormone which maintains pregnancy. It is large amounts of progesterone produced by what is to become the placenta which make some women feel sick during the first three months of pregnancy; which makes many pregnant women 'bloom'; and the sudden withdrawal of which may cause the 'baby blues' a few days after birth and, it is believed by some doctors, postnatal depression.

prophylactic The giving of a drug or the administration of a treatment or procedure to prevent something adverse happening, for example the giving of Syntometrine to reduce the risk of postpartum haemorrhage or the performance of episiotomy to prevent tearing of the perineum.

prostaglandins Hormones which cause the cervix to become soft and ready to open before labour begins. It is thought that a 'sweep' (see page 82) given during a vaginal examination towards the end of pregnancy may stimulate the release of prostaglandins and cause labour to begin. Semen contains prostaglandins and synthetic prostaglandins are used in induction to soften the cervix and help get labour going.

protocol In a maternity unit, a written document specifying systems of care, such as the management of normal labour.

psychotherapist A qualified psychotherapist offers the same non-judgmental, advice-free, high quality, confidential listening as a counsellor, aiming to enable clients to achieve changes in themselves in order that they may lead happier and more satisfying lives.

registrar/senior registrar (doctors) A registrar is a qualified hospital doctor who is specializing in one area of medicine and is hoping eventually to become a consultant. Senior registrars are usually very skilled and experienced.

senior house officer/SHO (doctors) See **junior doctors.**

sickle cell anaemia Genetically caused inherited condition resulting in severe anaemia. It usually occurs in people of West African origin. It can be detected by both chorionic villus sampling and amniocentesis. Prospective parents who think they may be carriers of the gene may seek a special blood test and genetic counselling (see Useful Organizations).

small for dates (light for gestational age) A baby who is small for dates may be estimated to be smaller than the average baby at a certain time in pregnancy, but may be growing perfectly normally. There is therefore a distinction to be made between a baby who is small for dates and one whose growth is retarded. See also **intra-uterine growth retardation.**

Sonicaid A portable instrument for listening to the baby's heartbeat during pregnancy and labour. The baby's heartbeat is picked up using ultrasound and magnified so it can be heard. It works well in any position and can be used during a water birth: special jelly is put on the part which picks up the heartbeat (transducer) and then the instrument is protected by a condom.

special care baby unit (SCBU) Hospital department where intensive care is given to babies by specially trained doctors and nurses using sophisticated equipment. Not every hospital has one and not every SCBU is able to look after the illest babies who may need long-term ventilation.

stages of labour First: from the beginning of active labour until the cervix is fully open to 10 cm (full dilatation). Second: the time from full dilatation to the birth of the baby. Third: the time during which the placenta is delivered.

Syntocinon Synthetic oxytocin drug used to make the uterus contract more strongly during induction of labour or when spontaneous labour is thought to be progressing too slowly.

Syntometrine Mixture of two drugs – Syntocinon and ergometrine – used to speed up delivery of the placenta. It is usually injected into the muscle of the woman's thigh after delivery of the baby's first shoulder. The Syntocinon causes the uterus to contract down strongly so the placenta can detach itself or be pulled away from the wall of the uterus before the ergometrine tightly closes the neck of the uterus (cervix) about seven minutes after it has been administered. Sometimes only Syntocinon is given in the third stage.

Tay-sachs disease Genetically caused inherited condition where the absence of an enzyme essential for life causes children to deteriorate mentally and physically until they die at the age of three or four. Parents who are both carriers have a one in four chance of producing a child affected by the disease. It is more common among the Jewish community. It can be detected by both chorionic villus sampling and amniocentesis. Prospective parents who think they may be carriers of the Tay-Sachs gene may seek a special blood test and genetic counselling (see Useful Organizations).

thalassaemia Genetically caused inherited condition resulting in severe anaemia. It usually occurs in people of Mediterranean and eastern origin. It can be detected by both chorionic villus sampling and amniocentesis. Prospective parents who think they may be carriers of the gene may seek a special blood test and genetic counselling (see Useful Organizations).

toxaemia (pre-eclampsia) See **pre-eclampsia**.

trimester Obstetricians divide pregnancy into three trimesters of three months each: the first is months one to three; the second is months four to six; and the third is months seven to nine.

ultrasound scan Sound emitted at a frequency higher than the human ear can hear bounces off the different parts of the mother's and baby's bodies at different rates, enabling an image of the baby inside the mother's body to appear on a television screen. Ultrasound operators are trained to check that the baby is developing normally and are sometimes asked to measure the baby if there is some doubt about when the pregnancy began or the rate of growth of the baby. So far, there has been inadequate research on the effects of ultrasound on the developing baby, and some people treat the routine use of ultrasound with caution on the basis that it will be many years before any long-term effects of routine ultrasound can be assessed.

umbilical cord This is about 50 cm long and connects the baby to the placenta. Two umbilical arteries carry blood from the mother to the baby and one umbilical vein carries blood from the baby to the mother. The blood vessels are twisted together and surrounded by a slippery substance known as Wharton's jelly which protects the cord and stops it getting knotted as the baby moves around in the uterus.

Ventouse/vacuum extraction A method of helping a mother to deliver her baby. A cup is attached by a chain to a special vacuum apparatus. The cup is put on the baby's head, a vacuum created and then with one hand on the baby's head, the doctor pulls on the chain during a contraction to deliver the baby. The baby is left with a swelling on his or her head from the cup which subsides within a few hours of birth. If not much pulling is needed, a soft cup can be used which causes even less discomfort to the baby. The mother may need a small episiotomy or none at all, depending on the position of the baby.

Useful Organizations

All the following organizations, many of them voluntary, would appreciate a stamped addressed envelope (SAE) when you request information by post. For addresses and telephone numbers of organizations not listed here you can consult the Directory of British Associations which is kept by every public central reference library and many branch libraries.

The National Childbirth Trust Alexandra House, Oldham Terrace, London W3 6NH (Tel 081-992 8637) *Your nearest branch or group may be listed in your local telephone directory. Otherwise ring or write to headquarters for local antenatal teachers, breastfeeding counsellors, postnatal groups, feeding bra fitters, etc. Many families contact the NCT when moving to a different part of the country.*

The National Childbirth Trust (Maternity Sales) Limited Alexandra House, Oldham Terrace, London W3 6NH (Tel 081-992 6762) *Send a SAE for the current catalogue and price list of books, leaflets, feeding bras, nightwear, cat nets and many other goods available by mail order.*

Active Birth Movement 55 Dartmouth Park Road, London NW5 1SL (071-267 3006) *Antenatal classes and information on active birth, including water birth.*

ASBAH (Association for Spina Bifida and Hydrocephalus) Asbah House, 42 Park Road, Peterborough PE1 2UQ (Tel 0733 555988) *Information, advice and support for parents who give birth to a child with these conditions or who are deciding whether or not to have a termination if these conditions are diagnosed antenatally. Team of counsellors and disabled living advisers.*

ASH (Action on Smoking and Health) 5-11 Mortimer Street, London W1N 7RH (Tel 071-637 9843) *Information to help anyone wanting to cut down or give up smoking. See also* **QUIT.**

Association for Improvements in Maternity Services (AIMS) 40 Kingswood Avenue, London NW6 6LS (Tel 071-278 5628) *Offers information and support for anyone having problems in obtaining the maternity care they choose or wanting to make a formal complaint.*

Association for Postnatal Illness 7 Gowan Avenue, London SW6 6HR (Tel 071-731 4867) *Produces leaflets for sufferers and their families and offers one-to-one informal support for women with postnatal depression.*

Association of Sexual and Marital Therapists PO Box 62, Sheffield S10 3TS) *Offers a list of therapists working for acceptable organizations in your area.*

AVMA (Action for Victims of Medical Accidents) Bank Chambers, 1 London Road, Forest Hill, London SE23 3TP (Tel 081-291 2793) *Register of solicitors with expertize and experience in the field of medical litigation. Information and support for individuals thinking of suing for medical negligence.*

Birthworks Hill House, Folleigh Lane, Long Ashton, Bristol BS18 9JB (Tel 0272-394202) *Hire of portable birth pools and information about water birth.*

BLISS (Baby Life Support Systems) 17-21 Emerald Street, London WC1N 3QL (Tel 071-831 9393) *Offers help and advice for parents of babies needing special care.*

British Acupuncture Association and Register 34 Alderney Street, London SW1 4EU (Tel 071-834 1012) *Will send register of acupuncturists and handbook for £2.*

British Association for Counselling 37a Sheep Street, Rugby, Warwickshire CV21 3BX (Tel 0788 78328/9) *Register of counsellors and psychotherapists in the UK.*

British Association of Psychotherapists 121 Hendon Lane, London N3 3PR (Tel 081-346 1747) *Register of psychotherapists working with adults and children.*

British Chiropractic Association Premier House, 10 Greycoat Place, London SW1P 1SB (Tel 071-222 8866) *Will give the names and telephone numbers of local practitioners over the telephone or send a full register and other details for £1.*

The British Homoeopathic Association 27a Devonshire Street, London W1N 1RJ (Tel 071-935 2163) *Will send a list of homoeopaths who are also medically trained and pharmacists stocking homoeopathic remedies.*

British Hypnotherapy Association 1 Wythburn Place, London W1H 5WL (Tel 071-723 4443) *Will supply a list of qualified hypnotherapists and a leaflet answering questions for £2.*

British Institute for Brain-injured Children Knowle Hall, Knowle, Bridgewater, Somerset TA7 8PJ (Tel 0278 684060) *Offers assessment and treatment for brain damaged children.*

British Society of Clinical and Experimental Hypnosis Psychology Dept, Middlewood Hospital, Sheffield (Tel 0742 852222) *Register of psychologists, doctors and dentists also qualified in hypnosis.*

British Society of Medical and Dental Hypnosis 151 Otley Old Road, Leeds OS16 6HN (Tel 0532 613077) *Keeps a register of doctors and dentists also qualified in hypnosis.*

Caesarean support network in the NCT Lynn Mosley (Tel 0788 569458) *Will put you in touch with a local individual or group who can give information and informal support before and after Caesarean section.*

Caesarean Support Network 2 Hurst Park Drive, Huyton, Merseyside L36 1TF (Tel 051-480 1184) *Offers informal support for women before and after Caesarean section.*

Catholic Marriage Advisory Council Clitheroe House, 1 Blythe Mews, Blythe Road, London W14 0NW (071-371 1341) *Information on natural family planning and list of natural family planning teachers available to anyone, not just Catholics.*

Child PO Box 154, Hounslow, TW5 0EZ (Tel 081-571 4367) *Helps couples suffering from the problems of infertility. Offers fact sheets, 24-hour telephone answering service, quarterly newsletter, local groups and a medical advisor who will answer queries by letter.*

CLAPA (Cleft Lip and Palate Association) Dental Dept, The Hospital for Sick Children, Great Ormond Street, London WC1N 3JH (Tel 071-829 8614) *Information and support for parents of children with this problem. NCT breastfeeding counsellors can also give support for breastfeeding.*

College of Osteopaths Practitioners Association 1 Furzehill Road, Boreham Wood, Herts WD6 2DG (Tel 081-905 1937) *Register of qualified practitioners, many of whom are also qualified as naturopaths.*

The Compassionate Friends 6 Denmark Street, Bristol BS1 5DQ (Tel 0272-292778) *Offers informal support and friendship for parents whose children have died.*

Contact a Family 16-18 Strutton Ground, London SW1P 2HP (Tel 071-222 2695) *Information, advice and support for parents and children with all kinds of disability. Includes Genetic Interest Group which gives information and support to people with genetic concerns and can put them in touch with regional genetic centres for counselling.*

CRY-SIS BM Cry-sis, London WC1N 3XX (Tel 071-404 5011) *Leaflets and telephone support for parents with crying babies.*

Down's Syndrome Association 12-13 Clapham Common Southside, SW4 7AA (Tel 071-720 0008) *Information and support for parents.*

English Nursing Board Careers Advice Centre Woodseat House, 764a Chesterfield Road, Sheffield S8 0SE (Tel 0742 555012) *Offers details of direct-entry training for midwives.*

Foresight (Association for the Promotion of Preconceptual Care) The Old Vicarage, Church Lane, Witley, Godalming, Surrey GU8 5PN (Tel 042879 4500) *Information and postal hair analysis service.*

Foundation for the Study of Infant Deaths (Cot death research and support) 15 Belgrave Square, London SW1X 8PS (Tel 071-235 0965) and 24-hour Helpline: 071-235 1721 *Information, support and workshops for families. Promotes Care of the Next Infant (CONI) Project in every District Health Authority.*

General Council and Register of Osteopaths 56 London Street, Reading, Berkshire RG1 4SQ (Tel 0734 76585) *Will give information about local registered osteopaths over the telephone or you can send £2.50 for the full register. They do not have a separate listing of cranial osteopaths: you can ring local osteopaths to ask whether they work in this way.*

Gingerbread 35 Wellington Street, London WC2E 7BN (Tel 071-240 0953) *Organizes local self-help groups offering information and informal support for one-parent families.*

Health Visitors' Association 50 Southwark Street, London SE1 (Tel 071-378 7255) *Will send a list of institutions which offer training as a health visitor.*

Independent Midwives' Association 65 Mount Nod Road, London SW16 2LP) *Will put you in touch with an independent midwife in your area.*

International Federation of Aromatherapists 4 East Mearn Road, West Dulwich, London SE21 8HA *Register of qualified aromatherapists.*

Listeria Support Group Hewshott Lane, Liphook, Hants GU30 7SU (Tel 0428-723100)

MAMA (Meet a Mum Association) 5 Westbury Gardens, Luton, Bedfordshire OU2 7DW (Tel 0582-422253) *Informal support for mothers, including those with postnatal depression.*

Maternity Alliance 15 Britannia Street, London WC1X 9JP (Tel 071-837 1265) *Produces leaflets and other publications on different aspects of maternity care, including benefits.*

MENCAP (Royal Society for Mentally Handicapped Children and Adults) 123 Golden Lane, London EC1Y 0RT (Tel 071-454 0454) *Information, counselling and support for families with mentally handicapped children.*

Miscarriage Association 18 Stoneybrook Close, West Bretton, Wakefield, West Yorkshire WF4 4TP (Tel 0924-830515) *Offers information and support during and after miscarriage.*

Multiple Births Foundation c/o Dr Elizabeth Bryan, Queen Charlotte's Hospital, Goldhawk Road, London W6 0XG (Tel 081-748 4666) *Advice and professional support to families, both direct and through clinics. Includes Special Needs Group for the disabled and bereaved. Clinics also in Birmingham and York.*

National Association for the Childless 318 Summer Lane, Birmingham B19 3RL (Tel 021-359 4887) *Information, support and advice for couples with infertility problems. Fertility helpline.*

National Association of Parents of Sleepless Children PO Box 38, Prestwood, Gt Missenden, Buckinghamshire HP16 0SZ *Answers parents' enquiries by letter and produces leaflets.*

National Council for One-Parent Families 255 Kentish Town Road, London NW5 2LX (Tel 071-267 1361) *List of local self-help groups.*

National Institute of Medical Herbalists 9 Palace Gate, Exeter EX1 1JA (Tel 0392 426022) *Send SAE for register of qualified herbalists, some of whom are doctors.*

Nippers c/o Sam Segal, Perinatal Unit, St Mary's Hospital, Praed Street, London W2 *Information and practical help for parents of premature or sick new babies.*

OPUS (National Network for Parents under Stress) 106 Godstone Road, Whyteleafe, Surrey CR3 0EB (Tel 081-645 0469) *Telephone helpline and local contacts for parents in crisis.*

Parents with Disabilities Group c/o Postnatal Committee, NCT, Alexandra House, Oldham Terrace, London W3 6NH (Tel 081-992 8637) *Large contact register of parents with disabilities offering mutual informal support.*

PETS (Pre-eclamptic Toxaemia Society) 17 South Avenue, Hullbridge, Essex SS5 6HA (Tel 0702-232533 or 205088) *Information and advice about pre-eclampsia.*

Positively Women 333 Gray's Inn Road, London WC1X 8PX (Tel 071-837 9705) *Counselling and support for women who are HIV positive.*

Postnatal depression: Dr Katharina Dalton 100 Harley Street, London W1 (Tel 071-935 2146) *Will send details of progesterone therapy for postnatal depression, including timing and dosage of injections, to your GP and/or health visitor.*

QUIT 40-48 Hanson Street, London W1P 7DE (Tel 071-636 9103 and Quitline 071-323 0505) *Network of local groups helping people who want to give up smoking. Quitline offers counselling during usual office hours; recorded message at other times.*

Raymar PO Box 16, Fairview Estate, Henley-on-Thames, Oxon RG9 1LL (Tel 0491-578446) *Information on and hire of TENS machines.*

Relate - Marriage Guidance Herbert Gray College, Little Church Street, Rugby CV21 3AP (Tel 0788-73241) *Confidential counselling service for people with relationship problems of any kind. For local branch look in your telephone directory or ring national number.*

SATFA (Support after Termination for Fetal Abnormality) 29-30 Soho Square, London W1V 6JB (Tel 071-439 6124) *Information and support before and after termination.*

SANDS (Stillbirth and Neonatal Death Society) 28 Portland Place, London W1N 4DE (Tel 071-436 5881) *Information and support for parents losing babies in this way.*

Sickle Cell Society 54 Station Road, Harlesden, London NW10 4UA (Tel 081-961 7795/8346) *Information on sickle cell disease and trait. Free information pack available: please send large SAE.*

The Society of Homoeopaths 2 Artizan Road, Northampton NN1 4HU (Tel 0604 21400) *Will supply a list of qualified homoeopaths and leaflets on different aspects.*

The Society of Teachers of the Alexander Technique 266 Fulham Road, London SW10 9EL (Tel 071-351 0828) *Offers list of qualified teachers in your area.*

The Spastics Society 12 Park Crescent, London W1N 4EQ (Tel 071-636 5020) *Information and support for parents of children with cerebral palsy and related disabilities. Library and team of social workers.*

Splashdown Birth Pools 17 Wellington Terrace, Harrow on the Hill, Middlesex HA1 3ER (Tel 081-422 9308) *Pools to hire for water birth. Can be delivered anywhere in UK. Free information pack on water birth.*

Society to Support Home Confinement Lydgate, Lydgate Lane, Wolsingham, Bishop Auckland, Durham DL13 3HA (Tel 0388-528044) *Information and support for women having difficulty arranging a home birth.*

TAMBA (Twins and Multiple Births Association) 51 Thicknall Drive, Pedmore, Stourbridge, West Midlands DY9 0YH (Tel 0384-373642) *Information and informal support for parents of twins and super-twins. Supplies books and leaflets by mail order. Local groups sell secondhand clothes and equipment.*

Tisserand Aromatherapy Institute 10 Victoria Grove, Second Avenue, Hove East Sussex BN3 2LJ (Tel 0273 206640) *Register of qualified practitoners.*

VDU Workers' Rights Campaign City Centre, 32-35 Featherstone Street, London EC1Y 8QX (Tel 071-608 1388) *Information and advice*

Bibliography

The following publications will give you more information on the topics covered in most of the chapters. The list is not exhaustive since it has been carefully selected to include so far as possible only publications which we can wholeheartedly recommend. All books are in paperback. Those which are currently out of print are marked 'OP' and have been recommended only where there is no adequate alternative in print. Many of the books should be available from libraries. Those marked with an * are available by post from the NCT: write to NCT (Maternity Sales) Ltd, Alexandra House, Oldham Terrace, London W3 6HN for a catalogue and price list. Other books can be ordered from any bookseller.

General

* Glynnis Tucker for NCT: PREGNANCY AND PARENTHOOD 1991 Oxford University Press *Comprehensive guide to pregnancy, childbirth and early days of parenting, including what to expect from medical care.*

Janet Balaskas and Yehudi Gordon: ENCYCLOPAEDIA OF PREGNANCY AND BIRTH 1988 Macdonald Orbis *Lavishly illustrated comprehensive guide to active birth and parenthood, A-Z of medical procedures.*

* Murray Enkin, Marc Keirse and Iain Chalmers: A GUIDE TO EFFECTIVE CARE IN PREGNANCY AND CHILDBIRTH 1990 Oxford University Press *A summary of the results of a systematic review of clinical research studies into pregnancy and childbirth care. Written for health professionals, but useful for anyone wanting to know what research has to say on a specific point.*

Angela Phillips: YOUR BODY, YOUR BABY, YOUR LIFE 1989 Pandora *Balanced, non-moralizing, non-sexist, non-patronizing guide to pregnancy and birth.*

Anne Dickson: A WOMAN IN YOUR OWN RIGHT. ASSERTIVENESS AND YOU 1982 Quartet *How to be assertive at all times, not just when pregnant.*

Chapter 1: Becoming pregnant and preconceptual care

* NCT: RUBELLA 1984 Information sheet

Leeds NCT: LET'S HAVE HEALTHY BABIES 15p + SAE available from Anne Bond, 1 Park View, Adel, Leeds 16

Maternity Alliance: GETTING FIT FOR PREGNANCY SAE to Maternity Alliance, 15 Britannia Street, London WC1X 9JP (071-837 1265)

B Barnes and SG Bradey for Foresight: PLANNING FOR A HEALTHY BABY 1990 Ebury

Barbara Pickard: BE FIT AND HEALTHY BEFORE YOU START A BABY and ARE YOU FIT ENOUGH TO BECOME PREGNANT? 50p each + A4 size SAE to Dr B Pickard, Dept of Animal Physiology and Nutrition, The University, Leeds LS2 9JT

Katia and Jonathan Drake: NATURAL BIRTH CONTROL. A GUIDE TO CONTRACEPTION THROUGH FERTILITY AWARENESS 1984 Thorsons

J Michelson and S Gee: COMING LATE TO MOTHERHOOD 1984 Thorsons OP *Twenty women who became mothers for the first time in their thirties tell their stories.*

S Sharpe: FALLING FOR LOVE 1987 Virago *Teenage pregnancy.*

P Ashdown-Sharp: THE SINGLE WOMAN'S GUIDE TO PREGNANCY AND PARENTHOOD 1975 Penguin OP *Comprehensive, but benefits' information is out of date.*

* NCT: EXPERIENCES AND EMOTIONS OF DISABLED MOTHERS 1984 *Written from 24 indepth interviews with mothers with a wide range of disabilities, audio tape version available.*

* NCT: RESOURCE LIST FOR PARENTS WITH DISABILITIES free to disabled parents, 50p to organizations. Send SAE to NCT.

Mukti Jain Campion: THE BABY CHALLENGE 1990 Routledge *For any woman with a physical disability who is pregnant or contemplating pregnancy.*

Mukti Jain Campion: ISOBEL'S BABY Video Arrowhead productions 1989 *Follows a mother with multiple sclerosis through her pregnancy to motherhood.*

Lynda Birke, Susan Himmelweit and Gail Vines: TOMORROW'S CHILD. REPRODUCTIVE TECHNOLOGIES IN THE 90s 1990 Virago *A feminist view of treatments for infertility.*

Stephen Thomas: GENETIC RISK. A BOOK FOR PARENTS AND POTENTIAL PARENTS 1986 Penguin

Chapter 3: Choosing antenatal care and the place of birth

* NCT: GIVING BIRTH AT HOME Leaflet 1987

Association for Improvements in Maternity Services (AIMS): CHOOSING A HOME BIRTH available from AIMS, Goose Green Barn, Much Hoole, Preston, Lancs PR4 4TD, for £1.30, inc. p&p.

Vicki Junor and Marianne Monaco: THE HOME BIRTH HANDBOOK 1984 Souvenir

* Sheila Kitzinger: BIRTH AT HOME 1980 Oxford University Press *Practicalities plus the safety debate.*

Caroline Flint: SENSITIVE MIDWIFERY 1986 Heinemann *Written for midwives, but accessible to others and gives a picture of what care during pregnancy, birth and after can be.*

Beverley Lawrence Beech: WHO'S HAVING YOUR BABY? 1987 Camden Press

Marjorie Tew: SAFER CHILDBIRTH? 1990 Chapman and Hall *Shows in detail how the myth that birth is safer in hospital began and has been maintained.*

Chapter 4: Looking after yourself during pregnancy

* NCT: CARING FOR YOUR PELVIC FLOOR 1989 Leaflet

* NCT: SEX IN PREGNANCY AND AFTER CHILDBIRTH 1989 Leaflet

Janet Balaskas: NEW ACTIVE BIRTH 1989 Unwin *Includes exercises to prepare for childbirth. They are designed to keep a woman supple and many have specific benefits to combat the aches, pains and minor ailments of pregnancy.*

* Barbara Dale and Johanna Roeber: EXERCISES FOR CHILDBIRTH 1983 Sidgwick & Jackson *Easy to follow, well illustrated, not intimidating for those new to exercise.*

Sheila Kitzinger: WOMAN'S EXPERIENCE OF SEX 1985 Penguin *Good section on sex in pregnancy.*

Barbara Pickard: EATING WELL FOR A HEALTHY PREGNANCY 1984 Sheldon Press

Barbara Pickard: NAUSEA AND VOMITING IN EARLY PREGNANCY 1986 Pamphlet with suggested eating regime 50p + SAE from Dr Barbara Pickard, Lane End Farm, Denton, Ilkley, LS29 0HP

* Judy Priest: DRUGS IN PREGNANCY AND CHILDBIRTH 1990 Pandora *A clear, well researched guide for women to the effects of alcohol, tobacco, over the counter, social and prescribed drugs on conception, fetal development, pregnancy, labour and birth. Looks at risk-taking from the mother's as well as the baby's viewpoint in a balanced way, encouraging women to make informed choices.*

Active Birth Centre: YOGA FOR PREGNANCY AND BIRTH Audio cassette

D L Jones and J Sundin: PREGNANCY EXERCISE WORKOUT Video Potentialpointe Productions

Chapter 5: Testing for a healthy baby: antenatal screening

* NCT: CLINICAL TRIALS AND MEDICAL RESEARCH. HELPING YOU DECIDE 1988 Information Sheet

* NCT: CHORIONIC VILLUS SAMPLING 1988 Information Sheet

Chapter 6: Pregnancy, work and benefits

Lee Rodwell: WORKING THROUGH YOUR PREGNANCY 1987 Thorsons OP *Safety, rights, tactics and how to enjoy your pregnancy at work.*

Department of Social Security: BABIES AND BENEFITS available free from your local DSS office and, often, your local hospital. *Sets out benefits and how to claim them: make sure you obtain the most up-to-date edition.*

Maternity Alliance: MONEY FOR MOTHERS AND BABIES 1990 Leaflet available from Maternity Alliance, 15 Britannia Street, London WC1X 9JP (071-837 1265)

Chapter 8: When the unexpected happens

* NCT: BREASTFEEDING IF YOUR BABY NEEDS SPECIAL CARE 1983 Leaflet

* NCT: HOW TO EXPRESS AND STORE BREASTMILK 1983 Leaflet

* Twins and Multiple Births Association: SO YOU'RE EXPECTING TWINS. *Other leaflets also available from TAMBA (see Useful Organizations)*

Elizabeth Bryan: TWINS IN THE FAMILY 1984 Constable *Author paediatrician specializing in twins and multiple births who has produced a thorough book, also mentioning triplets and other multiple births.*

Audrey Sandbank: TWINS AND THE FAMILY 1988 Arrow

Barbara Glover and Christine Hodson: YOU AND YOUR PREMATURE BABY 1985 Sheldon

Redshaw, Rivers and Rosenblatt: BORN TOO EARLY: SPECIAL CARE FOR YOUR PRETERM BABY 1985 Oxford University Press

The following three books cover aspects appropriate to any special condition or disability.

D Mitchell (ed): YOUR CHILD IS DIFFERENT 1982 Unwin

B Furneaux: SPECIAL PARENTS 1988 Open University

D Kimpton: A SPECIAL CHILD IN THE FAMILY 1990 Sheldon

For a particular condition or disability, the relevant support group or other organization will be able to help you with specific books to read. Such organizations can be found in reference books such as DIRECTORY OF BRITISH ASSOCIATIONS (CBD Research) or HEALTH DIRECTORY (Bedford Square Press) which should be available in local reference libraries.

Mark Selikowitz: DOWN'S SYNDROME. THE FACTS 1990 Oxford University Press *A book for parents covering all aspects of development of the Down's syndrome child, from birth to adulthood.*

Chapter 9: When the baby dies
National Association for the Childless: Ectopic pregnancy leaflet.

* NCT: MISCARRIAGE 1983 Leaflet* NCT: MOTHERS WRITING ABOUT THE DEATH OF A BABY 1984 Booklet *Ten personal accounts of miscarriage, stillbirth and cot death.*

* Stillbirth and Neonatal Death Society (SANDS): SAYING GOODBYE TO YOUR BABY 1986 SANDS *Useful pamphlet for those who have suffered a loss (more for stillbirth and perinatal death than miscarriage) and those close to them. Good on emotional aspects as well as practical aspects such as funeral arrangements.*

SANDS: WHAT TO TELL YOUR OTHER CHILDREN Leaflet available from SANDS as above.

Hey, Itzin, Saunders and Speakman (eds): HIDDEN LOSS. MISCARRIAGE AND ECTOPIC PREGNANCY 1989 Women's Press *Feminist viewpoint of the way miscarriage is often dealt with in society.*

M Leroy: MISCARRIAGE Optima 1988 *In conjunction with the Miscarriage Association*

Ann Oakley, Ann McPherson and Helen Roberts: MISCARRIAGE 1990 Penguin *Thorough, sensitive, includes ectopic pregnancy and has many quotes from women's own experiences.*

Colin Murray Parkes: BEREAVEMENT. STUDIES OF GRIEF IN ADULT LIFE 1986 Penguin *Written for everyone working with the bereaved, but also useful for the bereaved and their friends and relatives wanting to understand the process of grief.*

Lily Pincus: DEATH AND THE FAMILY. THE IMPORTANCE OF MOURNING 1974 and 1976 Faber

Susan Hill: FAMILY 1989 Penguin *A beautiful and moving autobiography describing the birth and death of the author's daughter born very prematurely. Many issues to do with infertility and the loss of a baby are raised and expressed both with sensitivity and intelligence.*

Chapter 10: Self-help and natural therapies

* NCT: A GUIDE TO LABOUR FOR EXPECTANT PARENTS 1986 Leaflet *Brief guide designed to be taken into labour, reminding the woman and her labour partner about what happens in the different stages and how to cope and help.*

* NCT: THE PHYSIOLOGY OF BREATHING 1988 Information Sheet

Janet Balaskas: NEW ACTIVE BIRTH Unwin 1989 *Using your own resources for giving birth. Good, non-medical account of labour. Lots of exercises and ideas for active positions in labour.*

Janet Balaskas and Yehudi Gordon: WATER BIRTH 1990 Unwin *Everything you need to know about using water for birth as well as during pregnancy and after.*

* Grantly Dick-Read: CHILDBIRTH WITHOUT FEAR 1990 Harper and Row *The approach to natural childbirth which inspired the founding of the NCT in 1956.*

Ina May Gaskin: SPIRITUAL MIDWIFERY OP *Numerous accounts of labour, some complicated, nearly all dealt with in a home setting by midwives. Good for instilling confidence in the natural process of labour.*

Sheila Kitzinger: THE EXPERIENCE OF CHILDBIRTH 1987 Penguin

Sheila Kitzinger: GIVING BIRTH: HOW IT REALLY FEELS 1988 Viking *Thirty personal accounts of labour, illustrated with photographs.*

Frederick Leboyer: BIRTH WITHOUT VIOLENCE 1977 Fontana *Influential book looking at birth from the baby's point of view, promoting the practice of making the baby's arrival into this world as gentle and loving as possible.*

Michel Odent: BIRTH REBORN: WHAT BIRTH CAN AND SHOULD BE 1984 Souvenir *Non-interventionist birth as practised at the famous Pithiviers clinic. Odent's hands-off approach to childbirth.*

Chapter 11: Routine medical procedures

* NCT: EPISIOTOMY 1990 Information Sheet

* NCT: RUPTURE OF MEMBRANES IN LABOUR. A SURVEY OF WOMEN'S EXPERIENCES 1989 Booklet

Beverley Lawrence Beech: WHO'S HAVING YOUR BABY? 1987 Camden Press *Useful list of the statistics you should be looking for when asking local hospitals about routine medical procedures and intervention rates.*

* Sally Inch: BIRTHRIGHTS 1989 Greenprint *A critical review of hospital procedures, many of which have become routine in many hospitals.*

Chapter 12: Artificial pain relief

* NCT: THE USE OF PETHIDINE IN LABOUR 1989 Information Sheet

* Sheila Kitzinger for NCT: SOME WOMEN'S EXPERIENCES OF EPIDURALS 1987 Booklet

* Sally Inch: BIRTHRIGHTS 1989 Greenprint

Judy Priest: DRUGS IN PREGNANCY AND CHILDBIRTH 1990 Pandora

* Grantly Dick-Read: CHILDBIRTH WITHOUT FEAR 1990 Harper and Row *Tells how to prevent the fear-tension-pain syndrome.*

Chapter 13: Medical help for complications

* NCT: INDUCTION OF LABOUR 1990 Leaflet

* NCT: CAESAREAN BIRTH 1984 Leaflet

* NCT: BREASTFEEDING AFTER A CAESAREAN SECTION 1990 Leaflet

Colin Francome: CHANGING CHILDBIRTH – INTERVENTIONS IN ENGLAND AND WALES 1989 Maternity Alliance *Reasons for the increasing Caesarean section rate.*

Fran Reader and Wendy Savage: COPING WITH CAESAREANS AND OTHER DIFFICULT BIRTHS 1983 Macdonald

Diony Young: UNNECESSARY CAESAREANS AND WAYS TO AVOID THEM ICEA (USA) 1980

Cohen, Bergin and Garvey: SILENT KNIFE: CAESAREAN PREVENTION AND VAGINAL BIRTH AFTER CAESAREAN (USA) 1983

Chapter 16: The first few hours
Daphne and Charles Maurer: THE WORLD OF THE NEWBORN 1988 Penguin *Life from the baby's point of view, in the womb and in the world.*

Chapter 18: Breastfeeding and bottlefeeding
There are many NCT leaflets on specific aspects of breastfeeding:

THINKING ABOUT BREASTFEEDING? 1985; BREASTFEEDING - A GOOD START 1990; BREASTFEEDING - AVOIDING SOME OF THE PROBLEMS 1983; BREASTFEEDING - NOT ENOUGH MILK? 1985; BREASTFEEDING - TOO MUCH MILK? 1987; HOW TO EXPRESS AND STORE BREASTMILK 1983; BREASTFEEDING IF YOUR BABY NEEDS SPECIAL CARE 1983; BREASTFEEDING AFTER CAESAREAN SECTION 1990; BREAST-FEEDING - RETURNING TO WORK 1987; BREASTFEEDING A TODDLER 1983.

* Twins and Multiple Births Association (TAMBA): BREASTFEEDING TWINS

* Gabrielle Palmer: THE POLITICS OF BREASTFEEDING 1988 Pandora *Fascinating, well-written book which as well as being very sound on physiology of breastfeeding, puts it in a political, sociological and historical context.*

* Mary Renfrew, Chloe Fisher and Suzanne Arms: BESTFEEDING: GETTING BREASTFEEDING RIGHT FOR YOU 1990 *Clear, basic, authoritative guide with accurate information and good illustrations.*

* Royal College of Midwives: SUCCESSFUL BREASTFEEDING 1988 Booklet *The handbook for midwives: short, clear and authoritative. Useful if you are beset with conflicting advice.*

Chapter 19: The first few weeks
General
K Grieve (ed): BALANCING ACTS ON BEING A MOTHER 1989 Virago *Thirteen women, some well-known, several older mothers, give details of how they coped.*

Penelope Leach: BABY AND CHILD 1988 Michael Joseph *Comprehensive, easy to read, well-illustrated on care, development and play from nought to five years old.*

Brigid McConville: MAD TO BE A MOTHER 1988 Century *Being a mother in today's man-made world.*

Libby Purves: HOW NOT TO BE THE PERFECT MOTHER: THE CRAFTY MOTHER'S GUIDE TO A QUIET LIFE 1987 Fontana *Lighthearted approach, cheerful but realistic.*

Robin Skynner and John Cleese: FAMILIES AND HOW TO SURVIVE THEM 1983 Mandarin *Fascinating, amusing, easy to read account of how families work and children develop emotionally. Robin Skynner's positive viewpoint stems from an interest in what makes families emotionally healthy.*

D W Winnicott: THE CHILD, THE FAMILY AND THE OUTSIDE WORLD 1964 Penguin *Classic account by an eminent child psychiatrist of emotional development from baby to child of school age. Clearly, sensitively and sympathetically written, with awareness of the needs of both children and parents.*

Christina Hardyment: DREAM BABIES 1983 Oxford University Press *Fascinating account of professional childcare advice from the eighteenth century to the present day. Fosters a balanced view which can help you look objectively and critically at the advice given to you.*

Fitness and exercise

* NCT: CARING FOR YOUR PELVIC FLOOR 1989 Leaflet *Ways to help yourself before, during and after childbirth.*

* NCT: POSTNATAL INFECTION SURVEY 1988 Booklet

* Eileen Montgomery: REGAINING BLADDER CONTROL 1989 Clinical Press Booklet *Exercise, diet and advice.*

* Gillian Fletcher for NCT: GETTING INTO SHAPE AFTER CHILDBIRTH 1991 Ebury *Encourages you to look after yourself by avoiding stress and eating a good diet as well as exercising so you can enjoy motherhood.*

* Barbara Whiteford and Margie Polden: POSTNATAL EXERCISES: A SIX-MONTH FITNESS PROGRAMME FOR MOTHER AND BABY 1984 Century *Carefully graded programme includes exercises to do with your baby and shows average mothers and fathers in its illustrations.*

Sleep

Jo Douglas and Naomi Richman: MY CHILD WON'T SLEEP 1984 Penguin OP *Brief account of what to expect realistically from babies and children, how to foster good sleeping habits and how to solve sleep problems.*

Richard Ferber: SOLVE YOUR CHILD'S SLEEP PROBLEMS: A PRACTICAL AND COMPREHENSIVE GUIDE FOR PARENTS 1986 Dorling Kindersley *A longer book which explains sympathetically how things go wrong and the reasons for the various strategies recommended for solving problems. The chapter entitled, 'What your child associates with falling asleep', is especially good.*

Dilys Daws: THROUGH THE NIGHT: HELPING PARENTS AND SLEEPLESS INFANTS 1989 Free Association Books *Sensitive account of how family problems can become sleep problems and how applied psychoanalysis (ie short treatment!) from a sympathetic practitioner can help parents help themselves and their children.*

Deborah Jackson: THREE IN A BED. WHY YOU SHOULD SLEEP WITH YOUR BABY 1989 Bloomsbury *Enthusiastic account, supported from many scientific sources, of why this is best.*

Crying babies
P Gray: CRYING BABY - HOW TO COPE 1987 Wisebuy *Author is founder of Cry-sis.*

Sheila Kitzinger: THE CRYING BABY 1989 Dorling Kindersley

Cry-sis: IT WORKS FOR ME £1.50 from Cry-sis, c/o 121 Melbourne Road, Garden Village. Stocksbridge, Sheffield S30 5EF *A realistic and sympathetic guide to sleep problems, tantrums, clinginess and long-term crying.*

Postnatal depression
* NCT: MOTHERS TALKING ABOUT POSTNATAL DEPRESSION 1983 Leaflet *Overview of the subject and personal experiences showing the range of postnatal depression and its effects, and how one can help a sufferer.*

Katharina Dalton: DEPRESSION AFTER CHILDBIRTH 1989 Oxford University Press *How to recognize postnatal depression and how to treat it with hormone (progesterone) therapy.*

Vivienne Wellburn: POSTNATAL DEPRESSION 1980 Fontana *Some of the statistics are out of date (operative delivery rates have risen since 1980) but an excellent book which looks at all the factors which contribute to postnatal depression.*

Carol Dix: THE NEW MOTHER SYNDROME: COPING WITH POSTNATAL STRESS AND DEPRESSION 1986 Unwin *Becoming aware of postnatal depression, with descriptions of treatments and coping strategies. Too much emphasis on breastfeeding as a contributory factor: successful breastfeeding increases the self-esteem of many women with postnatal depression.*

Anne Marie Sapstead: BANISH POST BABIES BLUES: ADVICE, SUPPORT AND ENCOURAGEMENT FOR PREVENTING AND COPING WITH POSTNATAL DEPRESSION 1990

Cot death
Jacquelynn Luben: COT DEATHS: COPING WITH SUDDEN INFANT DEATH SYNDROME 1989 Bedford Square Press

Sarah Murphy: COPING WITH COT DEATH 1990 Sheldon Press *A sympathetic book written for parents.*

Chapter 20: Making sense of the birth and giving feedback
Association of Community Health Councils for England and Wales (ACHCEW): NATIONAL HEALTH SERVICE COMPLAINTS PROCEDURES available from ACHCEW, 30 Drayton Park, London N5 1PB (081-609 8405) £5 *A critical guide to complaints procedures in the NHS together with ideas for improvement.*

Beverley Lawrence Beech: WHO'S HAVING YOUR BABY? 1987 Camden Press *Includes a section on complaining.*

Birth Statistics

This appendix is not intended to be the last word on maternity statistics but is here to give you an idea of the national picture. The figures may help you to decide if you are choosing between hospitals. You can ask hospitals direct for their annual statistics (the administrators should be able to help you) or obtain them from your local Community Health Council. Some hospitals publish annual reports. Please note that government maternity statistics are very slow to be published: the ones given here are the latest available as at 1 November 1990.

Total live births in 1989: 687,700 (Source: Annual Abstract)

Average age of all women who gave birth in 1989: 27.4 years. This is six months older than the average age in 1979: the trend has been for the age to be rising slightly every year. The average age of women having their first babies was 26.9 years. (Source: Birth Statistics)

Births outside marriage in 1989: 27 per cent. This figure has been rising every year for some time. (Source: Birth Statistics)

Rate of multiple births in 1988 (England and Wales): 11.1 per 1,000 maternities. There were 7,452 sets of twins and 170 sets of triplets and higher order births. (Source: Birth Statistics)

Family size in 1988 (England and Wales): 1.8 children per family. This figure has remained the same since 1981. 49 per cent of the respondents to the *Good Housekeeping* Survey had only one child. (Source: Social Trends)

Ratio of boys to girls in 1988: (England and Wales): 104.8 boys were born for every 100 girls, that is a few more boys were born than girls, which is generally the case. (Source: Birth Statistics)

Place of birth in 1988: England and Wales: 97.8 per cent of women used NHS hospitals; 1.1 per cent private hospitals; 0.9 per cent of women had their babies at home and 0.1 per cent had their babies elsewhere. GP delivered births are not readily identifiable. *Scotland:* 99.4 per cent of women had their babies in hospital; 0.6 per cent at home. Of single births (ie not multiple births), 93.2 per cent were covered by obstetric consultants and 6.8 per cent by GPs. (Sources: Birth Statistics and Birth Counts)

Chances of having a Down's syndrome baby by age: at 25, 1 in 1,500; at 30, 1 in 800; at 35, 1 in 350; at 36, 1 in 300; at 37, 1 in 200; at 38, 1 in 170; at 39, 1 in 140; at 40, 1 in 100; at 45, 1 in 30. In 1988, 428 babies with Down's syndrome were born in England and Wales. (Source: Amniocentesis and CVS Trial, Patient Information Booklet)

Method of delivery (England)	1980	1985
Estimated episiotomy	52.2 per cent	36.6 per cent
Estimated induction	20.6 per cent	17.5 per cent
Estimated acceleration	10.8 per cent	12.1 per cent
Estimated spontaneous delivery	76.6 per cent	76.3 per cent
Estimated spontaneous breech delivery	1.2 per cent	0.9 per cent
Abnormal head presentation delivered without instruments	1 per cent	2.5 per cent
Total instrumental deliveries	13.3 per cent	10.7 per cent
Total forceps deliveries	11.4 per cent	9.1 per cent
Low forceps deliveries	6.2 per cent	5.3 per cent
Ventouse/vacuum deliveries	0.7 per cent	0.7 per cent
Breech assisted deliveries	1.3 per cent	0.9 per cent
Total Caesarean sections	9 per cent	10.5 per cent
Elective Caesareans	4 per cent	4.9 per cent

Between 1980 and 1985 there was a fall in instrumental deliveries and a rise in deliveries by Caesarean section: it is important to look at these two figures together when looking at an individual hospital's statistics and at the figures as a whole. When hospital figures show a dramatic change from one year to the next, it may be possible for reasons to be given, such as a change in hospital policy. (Source: HIPE)

Perinatal death rate, that is stillbirths and babies who died within six days of birth in 1988: Rate per 1,000 live births: England 8.7; Wales 8.3; Scotland 8.9; N Ireland 9.3 (Source: Annual Abstract)

Sudden infant death syndrome in 1988 (England and Wales), that is babies who died within one year of birth: 2.35 per 1,000 live births, the number of babies who died being 1,629. (Source: DH3, Hansard)

Breastfeeding in 1985: Women who breastfed initially: England and Wales, 65 per cent; Scotland, 48 per cent. Women who breastfed for four months or more: England and Wales, 26 per cent; Scotland, 22 per cent. (Source: OPCS)

Postnatal infection in 1987: 3,000 women who had babies in 1987 replied to an NCT survey on rupture of the membranes in labour which also contained questions on postnatal infection. The basis for this survey was quite different from the surveys giving rise to national statistics, which are derived from health authority figures, but unfortunately national postnatal infection rates are not available from the government. The postnatal infection rates shown by the NCT survey were as follows:

Overall
infection rate 18.0%
  home births 4.2%
  hospital births 18.6%

Sites of infection
pelvis/uterus 5.9%
stitches in perineum 10.2%
Caesarean incision 30.2%

Infection rates by type of delivery
normal 13.5%
Ventouse 31.1%
forceps 30.1%
Caesarean section 46.3%

Index

Bold page numbers indicate Glossary entries.